Belgrade
THE BRADT CITY GUIDE

Laurence Mitchell

Bradt Travel Guides Ltd, UK
The Globe Pequot Press Inc, USA

First published December 2005

Bradt Travel Guides Ltd
23 High Street, Chalfont St Peter, Bucks SL9 9QE, England; www.bradtguides.com
Published in the USA by The Globe Pequot Press Inc, 246 Goose Lane, PO Box 480,
Guilford, Connecticut 06437-0480

Text copyright © 2005 Laurence Mitchell
Maps copyright © 2005 Bradt Travel Guides Ltd
Illustrations © 2005 Individual photographers and artists

A catalogue record for this book is available from the British Library

ISBN-10: 1 84162 145 5   ISBN-13: 978 1 84162 145 6

Front cover View of the Saborna Church from the Sava docks (Dragan Bosnic/NTOS)
Text photographs Laurence Mitchell
Maps Matt Honour   *Illustrations* Carole Vincer, Dave Colton

Typeset from the author's disc by Wakewing
Printed and bound in Spain by Grafo SA, Bilbao

Authors

AUTHOR

After graduating with a degree in environmental science Laurence Mitchell went on to sandwich long periods of travel abroad between various jobs that included English teaching in Sudan and surveying historic farm buildings in Norfolk. He retrained as a geography teacher in the late 1980s and worked at this for a dozen or so years before giving it up for the uncertain rewards of travel writing and photography. He is the author of *Serbia: The Bradt Travel Guide*, published in 2005. His photographic website may be seen at www.laurencemitchell.com.

CONTRIBUTORS

I am grateful to Paul Stott for his piece on Red Star Belgrade FC.

Contents

Contents

Contents

Acknowledgements

I would like to thank the following for the help they gave me in the research and writing of this guide. Firstly, thanks go to Branko Rabotić for his boundless enthusiasm and erudition concerning all matters Serbian. I am grateful to Ivan and Ivana Dukčević Budja for the hospitality they extended in the city and for painstakingly conveying their insider knowledge of Belgrade to me. Similarly, I owe gratitude to Milorad Ivanović and his colleagues at Blic for their warm friendship, encouragement and interest in the project and for their willingness to share their native Belgrader's perspective. Milica Čubrilo of the Tourist Organisation of Serbia also offered useful suggestions.

In the UK I would like to thank Paul Stott for his written contribution and Sandie Reed for her regular emails encouraging my efforts. It goes without saying that I am grateful to Hilary Bradt and Tricia Hayne for entrusting me with this project and for giving me the opportunity to travel to Serbia once more. Finally, I owe heartfelt thanks to my wife Jackie for joining me in Belgrade to assist with essential café and restaurant research, and also for tolerating my long absences when I was bent over a laptop late at night.

Pocket an expert!
More city guides from Bradt

Comprehensive coverage of a range of European cities, complemented by full-colour street maps.

Bratislava Lucy Mallows

This Slovak capital boasting stunningly restored baroque and rococo buildings begs to be explored on foot with the author's walking tour of the highlights. Full details of the practicalities of visiting are provided, including accommodation, eating out, transportation and excursions into the surrounding country.

Budapest Adrian Phillips & Jo Scotchmer

This guide offers a fascinating insight into one of the world's great romantic capitals. A wide range of options are covered – including the caves and Roman ruins of Buda, the vibrant shops and restaurants of Pest, and the city's best walks and thermal spas.

Dubrovnik Piers Letcher

Piers Letcher brings his in-depth knowledge of Croatia to this historic walled town, fast becoming a popular short-break destination. Here is everything for that idyllic break, from nightlife and the best local restaurants to island retreats and nearby national parks.

Ljubljana Robin & Jenny McKelvie

Slovenia's capital blends Austro-Hungarian and Italian influences, offering a lively nightlife buzz and classic cultural attractions. Travellers are provided with a range of places to stay, from new luxury hotels to family-run guesthouses that retain their typical Slovenian charm.

Available from all good bookshops, or by post, phone or internet direct from:

Bradt Travel Guides Ltd

Tel: +44 (0)1753 893444 www.bradtguides.com

Introduction

Like the country it is capital of, Belgrade has something of an image problem. For the uninitiated, the city may conjure up visions of bombings and recalcitrant autocrats; undoubtedly, the widespread demonisation that took place during the tenure of the old regime managed to tarnish the image of the city. As a result, Belgrade has had some way to go to work its way back into people's affections. With Belgrade opening up to the rest of the world once more, following the return to democracy after the downfall of the Milošević regime, the city has not so much needed to reinvent itself, rather it has needed to remarket what it already has.

So what does Belgrade have to offer? It is certainly not the 'new Prague' that everyone seems to be so desperately searching for, and its name is rarely uttered in the same sentence as 'Tallinn', 'Krakow' or 'Budapest' either. Belgrade is very much its own city and nothing like any of these. While it may not be a quaint genteel town of fine Baroque architecture, the city does have its own undeniable charm. It is, without doubt, a vibrant cosmopolitan city whose greatest assets are its atmosphere and its people. Belgrade is not so much a jewel, more a diamond in the rough.

The atmosphere of the city is quite unique, and those expecting to find a bomb-damaged, war-ravaged city on its uppers may be disappointed – despite the extensive damage done by the NATO bombing of 1999, little physical evidence remains of this today. Similarly, the mood on the streets is upbeat. Whatever the weather or the time of year the city's streets are normally thronged with people of all ages out enjoying themselves. Some, if they can afford it, may go out clubbing into the early hours but the majority are in search of simpler pleasures: talking with friends at a pavement café; taking part in the evening *korso*; window shopping with an ice cream in hand. It might be 18.00 or midnight when they do this: natives of Belgrade do not pay too much attention to the time of day – or night – or the day of the week. With a weekend that seems to begin on Tuesday and end on Monday, every night is Saturday night.

I mentioned people – Belgraders are a pretty special bunch. Having had to withstand more than their fair share of deprivations and hardships over the past 600 years, their shared history has helped to shape the character of the city's natives. It is a character that is resilient, resourceful and generous, but perhaps a little cynical; a character that is capable of hard work and hedonism in equal measure, and one that comes with a sardonic sense of humour that is as dry and intoxicating as vintage *šljivovica*.

How to use this book

Map references (eg: [1 D2]) relate to the colour maps at the end of this guide.

Hotels are subdivided by area and then listed by price category. **Restaurants**, **cafés** and **bars** are subdivided by area and then listed alphabetically. **Clubs** and **floating restaurants** are simply listed alphabetically.

Opening times are given where known for restaurants, cafés, bars and museums.

Chapter 9 gives four walking tours: two in the Old Town, one in the city centre and one in Zemun. Sights are cross-referenced to *Chapter 10*, which gives full details of museums, churches, historic monuments and parks.

> ### FEEDBACK REQUEST
> It doesn't matter how often I visit Belgrade: every time I go there, there is something new to entice the visitor. If you would like to share your comments about places I have mentioned in the guide, or tell me about something new that you have discovered, please do drop me a line at bradtserbia@btopenworld.com or c/o Bradt Travel Guides, 23 High Street, Chalfont St Peter, Bucks SL9 9QE.

BELGRADE AT A GLANCE

Location Southeast Europe, at the confluence of the Sava and Danube rivers. Longitude 20°28'E, latitude 44°49'N

Population Approximately 1.6 million according to the 2002 census, although the total population is now perhaps approaching two million

Language Serbian

Religion Mostly Serbian Orthodox with small minorities of Roman Catholics, Protestants and Muslims

Time CET (GMT+1 hour)

International telephone code +381

Currency Serbian dinar; €1 = 83din (July 2005)

Electricity 220V AC, frequency 50Hz. Round, two-pin plugs

Public holidays 1–2 January (New Year), 7–8 January (Orthodox Christmas), 15 February (Statehood Day), 1–2 May (Labour days), Orthodox Easter is variable. (2006: Good Friday, 21 April – Easter Monday, 24 April; 2007: Good Friday, 6 April – Easter Monday, 9 April)

Feast day Belgrade's *slava* is on Ascension Day (*Spasovdan*), which falls on a Thursday, 40 days after Easter

Climate A moderate continental climate with warm summers and cold winters. The hottest month is July; the coldest is January.

Contents

INTRODUCTION TO THE CITY

Serbia's capital does not really live up to its name – *Beograd* (the 'White City'). While pessimists might tell you that it ought to be called the Grey City – there is certainly plenty of concrete about in New Belgrade – a better appellation might be 'Green City'. The fact is: Belgrade has more park space than almost any other European city, the exception being Glasgow, another much-maligned metropolis. True, the city can look gloomy under a leaden winter sky but this stereotypical Eastern-Bloc greyness is deceptive because, although the monolithic high-rises of New Belgrade might do their best to dispirit the first-time visitor, it quickly becomes apparent that the city is a far more attractive place than it might initially appear.

For a start, there is the Belgrade Fortress perched high above the town, overlooking the confluence of the Sava and Danube rivers. The fortress is impressive enough but it is Kalemegdan Park, the ample green space of the parkland and gardens that surround it, which holds most year-round appeal for Belgrade's citizens. Nudging the park to the south and east is Stari Grad, the Old City, with its cathedral, secessionist buildings and a few, and now sadly rare, Ottoman remnants. Running through the elegant streets that lead down to the city's more prosaic commercial centre is pedestrianised Kneza Mihaila – a constant stream of humanity, particularly in the evening when Belgrade's younger citizens take their place in the Balkan equivalent of the *korso*, the southeast European evening promenade.

The view from Kalemegdan Park gives a clue to the way Belgrade's history has unfolded by virtue of its geographical position. Belgrade's singular geography has been both a blessing and a curse; its strategic vantage point at the confluence of two great rivers, and its position as a sort of crossroads between northern and southern Europe, has led to it being attacked, sacked, plundered and bombed numerous times during its long history. The city lies at a political and cultural tectonic boundary, at a point where, historically, civilisations have collided, and where cultures and religions have clashed for over a millennium with furious upheavals: Christianity and Islam; the Catholic and Orthodox schism; the westward-looking Croats and eastward-facing Serbs; communism and free markets. Even today, Belgraders who live in Novi Beograd or Zemun joke about some of their fellow citizens being 'Turks', as if the city is still divided by some invisible cultural fault line.

Celts, Avars, Hungarians, Romans, Byzantines, Goths and Turks have all taken turns in building and destroying the city over the centuries; the stones of both Belgrade and Zemun are much-used palimpsests. Other nations and pacts in more recent years have inflicted untold damage too: Belgrade has the dubious distinction of the only European city to have been bombed on five separate occasions in the same century: during World War I (twice), followed by Nazi bombers in 1941, Allied bombers in 1944 and NATO bombers in 1999. Somehow, Belgrade always manages to rebuild and resurface like a concrete phoenix, only too aware that, lying as it does on a geopolitical, religious and cultural fault line, inconveniences such as war, invasion and air raids inevitably go with the territory. So far, the 21st century has been quiet – very good news: Belgrade has had quite enough 'history' for the time being.

HISTORY

The first evidence of settlement in the Belgrade region comes from Zemun, across the Danube from Old Belgrade. At Zemun, formerly a separate town but now effectively a suburb of the city, archaeological evidence has been found to suggest that the banks of the Danube were first settled here about 7,000 years ago. The Celts were the first to colonise the opposite bank, on a bluff overlooking the confluence of the Danube and Sava rivers, founding the settlement of Singidunum in the 3rd century BC. Next to come were the Romans, who arrived in the 1st century AD and remained for the best part of the next 400 years.

Roman and Byzantine rule

The Romans made their mark on the region in typical fashion, building roads and constructing garrisons for their troops. They conquered Singidunum, which had been built on a hill overlooking the confluence of the Sava and Danube rivers, a settlement that occupied the site of present-day Upper Town at Kalemegdan. Similarly, they developed the fortress at Taurunum at modern-day Zemun and built a bridge over the Sava to connect the two. Singidunum became an important crossroads for the Byzantine Empire, linking the Roman provinces of Moesia, Dacia,

Pannonia and Dalmatia, while a military road – a *Via Militaris* – passed through from west to east, from Sirmium (now Sremska Mitrovica) through Singidunum to Viminacium (Kostolac) and on to Byzantium. One consequence of this expansive and disciplined road building was the provision of the route for present-day Kneza Mihaila, Belgrade's first and, still very important, thoroughfare.

Three centuries later, with the emergence of a rival empire to the east, the Roman Emperor Theodosius was forced to divide the territory into two halves, so that in AD395, the eastern half – that which roughly corresponds to modern-day Serbia, Montenegro, Macedonia, Bulgaria and Greece – found themselves under the influence of Byzantium. As a result of this political, cultural and religious division, Singidunum found itself as a border town on the very edge of the eastern empire, a hazardous location in geopolitical terms that would have some bearing on its later misfortunes.

During the course of the next few centuries the city was attacked by Slavs, Huns, Goths and Avars, all of whom took turns at occupying the city but, by the 10th century, the largest population in the city was that of the Slavs. By this stage, the Slavic name *Beograd* has already been recorded, having been mentioned for the first time in a dispatch from Pope John VIII to Prince Boris I Mikhail in Bulgaria in 878.

Large groups of Crusaders started to arrive en route to the Holy Land during the late 11th century and over the next few turbulent centuries Belgrade passed through Byzantine, Hungarian and Bulgarian hands. Following the Serbs' flight from their southern territories after the defeat at the Battle of Kosovo in 1389, the first attempted Turkish siege of the city took place in 1391 just before Despot Stefan Lazarević made Belgrade the seat of his throne in 1403. Despot Stefan began reconstruction of the city in the same year, going on to describe this activity in *The Belgrade Charter*: 'I found the most beautiful place of all times, the great city of Belgrade, which had been destroyed and deserted, I have rebuilt it and dedicated it to the Mother of God.'

Ottoman rule and Serbian uprisings

A large-scale Serb migration north to Hungary and west to the Adriatic began soon after the defeat at the Battle on the Marica River in 1371 and continued with the loss at the Battle of Kosovo in 1389. An unstable period followed, with a shrinking nation that was ruled jointly by Prince Lazar's son, Despot Stefan Lazarević, and by his cousin, Đurađ Branković, who moved the state capital to the newly built fortified town of Smederevo on the Danube. The final fall came in 1459, when Smederevo fell into Turkish hands. This brought a northern migration on a much larger scale.

Although there had been many attempts by the Turks, Belgrade itself did not finally succumb until 1521, when it was finally besieged and burnt down by Sultan Suleiman the Magnificent. The city remained in Turkish hands until 1717 when it was conquered by the Austrian prince, Eugene of Savoy. This was only a temporary state of affairs however, as a Turkish–Austrian treaty two decades later in 1739 returned

History

Belgrade to Ottoman control. With the exception of a brief interval from 1789 to 1791, when the city was captured by the Austrian field marshal Gideon Ernest Laudon, it would remain under Turkish control until the uprisings of the early 19th century.

By the turn of the 19th century, the Ottoman leadership was corrupt, profligate and in decline, and the Janissaries, who originally had been selected and trained by the Turks, had become an unruly elite that were a law unto themselves. As the years of Turkish domination progressed, small-scale resistance to Ottoman rule, especially to that of the hated Janissaries and the *spajis* – Turkish cavalry units of similarly rapacious character – started to emerge. This came in the form of rebel bands known as *hajduks*. These had started to form in the 15th century but became far more numerous and troublesome during the later years of Turkish domination. It was the actions of the *hajduks* that inspired the first larger-scale rebellion against the Turks in the **First National Uprising** of 1804.

This, the first of two national revolts, was headed by a pig-farmer called Đorđe Petrović, better known as Karađorđe ('Black George'), who hailed from the Šumadija region to the south of Belgrade. The rebellion started early in 1804, when Janissaries executed up to 150 *kneze* (local leaders) in an operation they termed 'The Cutting Down of the Chiefs'. This action was viewed as a pre-emptive strike against those who were plotting against them but all it really achieved was to precipitate a widespread rebellion. Karađorđe was elected leader and the rebels soon managed to liberate most of the Belgrade *pashalik* (district) from Janissary control. At first, the Serbs were joined by many from the Muslim population, who suffered as much from the excesses of the *dahis* – the Janissary commanders – as anyone else, but this relationship turned sour when it became clear that the Serbs were rebelling not just against Janissary tyranny but against all aspects of Turkish rule. Under Karađorđe, the Serbs demanded complete autonomy, which alarmed the Turkish rulers to the extent that they set up an Ottoman army to fight them. The Ottoman army was beaten soundly at Ivankovac in August 1805 and, after two years of fighting, Belgrade was liberated on 8 January 1807. Karađorđe, with his army of about 25,000 rebels, found the city in ruins but it was soon rebuilt to become the capital of the territories that made up newly liberated Serbia. The fledgling Serbian government held its first assembly in 1807, and by 1811 the first ministries had been set up.

By the end of 1806, the Russians too had joined the fight on the Serbian side. However, a short time afterwards, the Russians and Turks signed another peace treaty together, which specified that Serbia would return to Ottoman rule on the condition that amnesty be given to all participants in the insurrection. This was rejected outright by the Serbs. Karađorđe, along with thousands of others, fled north across the Danube to safety in the Habsburg provinces. Meanwhile, the Turks took their revenge: hundreds of villages were sacked, and thousands of Serbs, particularly women and children, were taken into slavery. In 1813, the city of Belgrade, which had enjoyed just a few years of freedom, was conquered once again by the Turks.

In 1814, one of Karađorđe's former commanders attempted to start up a fresh rebellion but this was soon quelled. However, in the wake of the brutal reprisals that followed, new plans were hatched for another, far more ambitious, uprising. **The Second National Uprising** of 1815 was led by Miloš Obrenović, a veteran of the first campaign, who, after the failure of the first rebellion, rather than fleeing north with Karađorđe, had tried to make a deal with the Turks instead. In contrast to Karađorđe, Obrenović possessed diplomatic skills as well as military ones and by mid-July 1815, Obrenović's rebels had succeeded in liberating most of the Belgrade *pashalik*. He had negotiated for the Belgrade *pashalik* to become autonomous to the extent that the Turks would remain only in the towns and forts of the province, and that it would be only Serbian chiefs who had the right to collect taxes from now on. As he sought these concessions he cleverly managed to undermine the power of the Turks in other ways, such as in encouraging Serbs from the south to move to Belgrade, which resulted in many Turks being obliged to sell their houses and land at prices far below their real worth.

Karađorđe returned to Serbia in 1817, but Obrenović, suspicious of the former commander's motives, had him murdered by his agents. This action prompted the beginning of a dynastic feud that would last for almost 100 years. Miloš Obrenović turned out to be as avaricious as the Turks when it came to tax collecting, and his increasingly oppressive rule prompted seven uprisings against him between 1815 and 1830, when the edict of Sultan Mahmud II granted Serbia self-rule and Serbian state independence was re-established for the first time in nearly four centuries. From now on it was agreed that the Turks would leave the countryside and would remain in only six garrisons throughout the country.

Despite the uprisings, it was a progressive and prosperous time for Belgrade. Many new buildings were constructed during this period: Princess Ljubica's *konak*, the cathedral and the king's palace complex at Topčider. Great scholars and educators also emerged during this period; like Dositej Obradović, who became minister of education and opened the Great School, the country's first institution of higher education, and Vuk Karadžić who collected epic poems, developed the Cyrillic alphabet for modern Serbia and single-handedly reformed the Serbian language. Influenced by these innovators, Belgrade soon became a centre for literary activity: in 1831 the first printing press was opened, and in 1837 the first bookshop. Soon after, newspapers would be printed in the city for the first time. It was a rapid advance from Ottoman stagnation and, from the 1830s onwards, Serbia started to develop an identity that was more akin to central European society than to that of a peripheral province of a flagging empire. In 1841, Belgrade became the capital of the principality of Serbia. An incident between Turkish soldiers and Serbian apprentices in June 1862 led to a brief bombardment of the city from the Belgrade Fortress but by now the Turks' days were numbered. Ottoman soldiers left Belgrade for the last time on 18 April 1867. The Principality of Serbia received full international recognition at the Congress of Berlin in 1878 and the Kingdom of Serbia was proclaimed four years later.

The early 20th century

Serbia in the latter part of the 19th century was ruled by a dynasty descended from Miloš Obrenović, with the exception of Prince Alexander Karađorđević who reigned from 1842 to 1858 and was the son of Karađorđe. A military coup d'etat in May 1903 brought Karađorđe's grandson to the throne with the title of King Petar I. Petar had received a European education and had been influenced by liberal ideas, especially those of John Stuart Mill. He introduced a democratic constitution and initiated a period of parliamentary government that encouraged political freedom.

This new-found political freedom was interrupted by the outbreak of liberation wars in the region in 1912 and 1913, in which the whole of the Balkans underwent rapid change as new Balkan states were created in the vacuum left by the Turks. By 1914, Turkish domination in the region had finally ended for good but now there were fresh problems of national sovereignty to deal with. Bosnia-Herzegovina had been part of the Ottoman Empire but was governed by Austria since its annexation in 1908. Discontent here caused a number of pan-Slavic movements to agitate for union with Serbia, something that greatly worried the Austrians. The assassination of the Austrian prince, Archduke Franz Ferdinand in Sarajevo on 28 June 1914 gave the Austrians the excuse they needed to attack Serbia, first politically, then militarily. On 28 July 1914, Belgrade was shelled by boats of the Austro-Hungarian navy: World War I had begun. In the autumn of the following year, Belgrade was attacked once more and approximately 25,000 shells were fired on the city by the Austro-

Hungarian and German artillery. By the end of the war Serbia had lost over one million of its total population. Belgrade itself was economically devastated: it had lost half of its population and most of its industry. As war ended and Europe reshaped itself, Serbia became unified with its neighbours as a component in a greater South Slav nation. On 1 December 1918, the Kingdom of Serbs, Croats and Slovenes came into existence with Belgrade as its capital, which united the territories of these three republics along with Bosnia-Herzegovina and Macedonia. This short-lived federation would become the blueprint for the future Yugoslavia.

The Yugoslav state of the inter-war years 1918–39

The post-World War I state had come into existence, under Western supervision, as a monarchy headed by King Petar I. When Petar died in 1921, his son Prince Aleksandar I Karađorđević took over the reins of power. Inevitably, having a Serbian monarch in power soon led to accusations of Serbian dominance. When the constituent states of the new kingdom met to draw up a constitution in 1921, the Croats, led by Stjepan Radić, refused to vote on any of the proposals and returned to Zagreb. As a result, a centralist constitution favoured by the Serbs was drawn up: the Croat withdrawal had merely exacerbated matters and made the new constitution more Belgrade-centred than it might have been had the Croats participated. Radić was assassinated in 1928 by a Serbian member of the National Assembly. In January 1929 Aleksandar (now King Aleksandar after the death of his father King Petar I in 1921), perturbed by the attempts to promulgate a workable constitution, banned all political parties, dissolved parliament and imposed a Royal Dictatorship, renaming the country Yugoslavia. This did not solve any of the existing problems, however, as it failed to bring any Croats into positions of power. A new constitution was proclaimed in 1932, ending the king's personal rule. King Aleksandar I was assassinated on a visit to France in 1934 by a member of VMRO, an extreme nationalist organisation in Bulgaria with close links to the Croatian Ustaša. Aleksandar's son, Prince Petar, was just ten years old at the time of his father's death and so authority passed instead to the three members of the Regency, one of whom was the assassinated king's cousin, Prince Pavle.

World War II

At the breakout of World War II, Yugoslavia found itself surrounded by hostile countries. Hitler was pressuring Yugoslavia to join the Axis powers so, after a period of neutrality, the regent, Prince Pavle, decided to align the country with the Nazis. This prompted rebellion from many quarters, with massive protests in Belgrade two days later on 27 March 1941. On the same day, a group of air-force officers arrested Prince Pavle and proclaimed Petar as king, even though he was not legally old enough to become monarch. The reaction from Berlin was to bomb Belgrade, which the Nazis carried out with great ferocity on 6 April 1941. This was followed by a land invasion of both German and Italian forces. Petar, now King Petar II, fled with his government to exile in London. Belgrade was occupied just a few days later on 12 April and Yugoslavia capitulated on 17 April.

The country was divided up between the Axis powers. Germany took most of Slovenia, Italy annexed Montenegro and the Adriatic coast, while Bulgaria occupied much of Macedonia. Meanwhile, Croatia and Bosnia-Herzegovina combined to become a Nazi puppet state, called the Independent State of Croatia (NDH), with the head of the Ustaša fascists, Ante Pavelić, a natural choice as its leader. Serbia was occupied by German troops, apart from its northern territories in Vojvodina, which were annexed by Axis Hungarians and Croats, and parts of eastern and southern Serbia by Bulgaria. Kosovo and Metohija were mostly annexed by Albania, which at that time was governed as part of the fascist Italian Empire.

The lust for genocide displayed by the Ustaša, and the presence of a ruthless German occupation force, prompted Serbian resistance on a large scale. Two very different resistance groups emerged. One of these was the Chetniks, supported by King Petar's government in exile in London, who were devoutly royalist and anti-communist, and headed by Colonel Dragoljub Mihailović. The other resistance group – the Partisans – was pro-communist and led by Josip Broz Tito, who had previously worked in Moscow for the Third International and had been elected as chairman of the Yugoslav Communist Party in 1939. Despite early co-operation by both resistance groups, they soon became involved in a bitter three-way struggle with each other and with the Nazis. Towards the end of the war, Belgrade once more became a target for bombers, this time the Allied forces: during the spring and early autumn of 1944 the Allies bombed Belgrade 11 times, causing heavy loss

History

JOSIP BROZ TITO

Tito was born Josip Broz in 1892 in Kumrovec, Croatia. As a soldier in the Austro-Hungarian army he was imprisoned in Russia before escaping to join the soon-to-be victorious Red Army. Tito returned to Yugoslavia to become a member of the Yugoslavian Communist Party. From 1941 to 1945 he was the Chief Commander of the National Liberation Army (Partisans) who became entrenched in a bitter, three-way war with the Nazis and Royalist Chetniks.

After victory in 1945, Tito became both prime minister and minister of foreign affairs of the new communist republic. Following a serious rift with Stalin in 1948, he decided that Yugoslavia should follow its own path and developed the idea of a non-aligned version of socialism. Tito became president of Yugoslavia on 13 January 1953 and in 1961, along with Gamal Abdel Nasser and Jawarhalal Nehru, co-founded the Non-aligned Movement. On 7 April 1963 he was named 'President for life', which he remained until his death in May 1980.

Tito died in Ljubljana, Slovenia on 4 May 1980. His funeral was a solemn occasion that drew world leaders of every political persuasion. His grave is at the mausoleum in south Belgrade called 'The House of Flowers' (Kuča cveća).

of life. Shortly after this, following a heroic struggle with enormous loss of life, Tito's National Liberation Army, along with Soviet Red Army units, entered Belgrade on 20 October 1944. By early spring of the following year they were in full control of all Yugoslav territory.

Tito's Yugoslavia

Tito reached an agreement with King Petar's government in exile in which he was given temporary authority as a leader. By the end of 1945, elections were held throughout the country. The Communist Party, which was still technically illegal, stood as the People's Front and won, with some degree of manipulation, 90% of the vote for the Federal Council. Such a landslide victory resulted in the royalist members of Tito's provisional government resigning. King Petar remained in exile in London, while Mihailović, the commander of the royalist forces, was executed along with many other troublesome opponents.

Although Tito was no stranger to autocracy, he soon turned his back on Stalin's hardline brand of communism and went it alone with his own vision of socialism. He instigated a federal system, which gave each of the constituent republics individual autonomy for its internal affairs. In 1961, the First Conference of Non-aligned Countries was hosted by Belgrade. With continued reforms, and a determinedly non-aligned approach, Tito steered Yugoslavia into becoming a relatively free and prosperous state, which reached its zenith in the 1960s and 1970s.

Tito's death and its aftermath 1980–91

When Tito died in May 1980, many commentators predicted imminent economic collapse. Tito had achieved much on the strength of his personal charisma and his skill in dealing with problems of nationalism. Before his death, Tito had laid down conditions for a power-sharing leadership that would guarantee the survival of the federation and avoid the emergence of any dictator-like figures. The new constitution that he introduced in 1974, in which presidential authority was to change yearly from one republic to the next, was meant to ensure this but it could also be seen as the cornerstone for the future disintegration of the federation.

The predictions came true: within five years Yugoslavia had accumulated a massive foreign debt, had 60% inflation and was suffering from high unemployment throughout the republic. Membership of the Communist Party started to decline and many critics were arguing for modernisation and liberalisation of the economy. The Party, without Tito at the helm, was starting to become something of a behemoth that could respond to criticism only by clamping down on such dissidents.

The break-up of Yugoslavia 1991–2000

By 1991, the tensions between the six republics had grown to crisis point. Slovenia was the first to withdraw from the federation, after fighting a brief war of independence. This was followed by Croatia, which still had a sizeable Serbian minority in the Krajina and Slavonia regions of the country. The Serbian population had already been radicalised by state television propaganda and the branding of the Croat leader, Tuđman, as little more than a born-again Ustaše. Serb nationalists further manipulated these fears by publicising false reports of the planned slaughter of ethnic Serbs. When Tuđman declared independence in July 1991, the Serbian dominated JNA responded by leading an all-out attack on Croatia. Not surprisingly, this led to reprisals on the remaining Serb population. A United Nations protection force was enlisted to protect Serbian interests in 1992 but by now the Serbs in Croatia were leaving in droves, sometimes because they were burned out of their homes, often because of a well-founded fear of the consequences if they remained. By 1995, over 200,000 Serbs had left Croatian soil to become refugees in Serbia.

A parallel crisis developed in Bosnia-Herzegovina. With a mixed population of Catholic Croats, Orthodox Serbs and Muslim Bosniaks, Bosnia-Herzegovina had its own special problems. The Croats and Muslims wanted to secede from the federation (although not necessarily together), while the Bosnian Serbs wanted to remain tied to Belgrade. Bosnia's independence was recognised internationally in 1992, much to the chagrin of the Belgrade government who feared for the future of Serbs in Bosnia. Fighting raged between all three factions – Serbs, Croatians and Bosnian Muslims – from April 1992 until the signing of the Dayton Peace Accord in November 1995.

With Macedonia newly independent as well, it left just two of the former republics – Serbia and Montenegro – to constitute what was by now a severely eroded Yugoslavia. Belgrade was still unwilling to let go of the idea of federation and announced, in April 1992, the establishment of the new Federal Republic of Yugoslavia, a creation made up of just these two remaining countries, which from now on would each have their own president and legislature.

In 1998, Kosovo erupted into violence. This was, after all, the region from where everyone had always expected trouble to emerge. The Kosovo Liberation Army (KLA), supported by many of the ethnic majority Albanians, came out in open rebellion against Serbian rule. President Milošević sent in Serbian troops to quell the uprising but soon international pressure was demanding that he withdraw. After the failure of peace talks in early 1999, NATO launched air strikes against Serbia on 24 March of that year. Although all of Serbia was targeted, Belgrade suffered particularly badly because the city served as the political, military and propaganda headquarters of the Milošević regime. The bombing lasted for 78 days in all. On 3 June 1999, Milošević accepted a peace plan brought by EU and Russian envoys that required withdrawal of all forces from Kosovo and the entry of an international peacekeeping force under UN mandate. Serb forces started to leave the province a week later, and NATO halted the bombardment of Serbian territory on 9 June. Russian peacekeepers entered Kosovo for the first time on 11 June and, a day later, NATO troops crossed the border.

The downfall of Slobodan Milošević

Slobodan Milošević had already been active in Serbian politics for some considerable time, having been president since 1989. There had been protests against him in 1996 because of his rejection of opposition victories in municipal elections. Now, following the humiliation of NATO bombing, and having already suffered from years of economic sanctions, many Serbs were becoming increasingly disenchanted with Milošević as leader. In April 2000, more than 100,000 Serbs assembled in central Belgrade to listen to opposition leaders call for early general elections: an act of defiance that prompted Milošević to set presidential, parliamentary and local elections for September of that year. Opposition candidate Vojislav Koštunica won by 48.22% to 40.23%, but a second round was called as neither candidate had an absolute majority. Koštunica's supporters accused the federal election commission of fraud and rejected the result. This rejection set in motion a campaign of strikes and civil disobedience that finally forced Milošević to relinquish power. On 6 October, he conceded defeat and Koštunica was sworn in as Yugoslav president the following day.

The post-Milošević period

In January 2001, three months after Milošević's involuntary step-down from power, the Yugoslav parliament overwhelmingly approved a reform government headed by Zoran Đinđić, head of the Democratic Party. However, a rift soon started to develop between Đinđić, an enthusiastic reformer, and the new president Vojislav Koštunica, a conservative who had been in favour of Milošević going on trial in Belgrade, rather than The Hague as Đinđić had wanted. In August 2001, Koštunica's Democratic Party of Serbia pulled out of the government in protest over alleged corruption charges and, in June of the following year, all 45 deputies belonging to Koštunica's party walked out of parliament in protest at the prime minister's decision to replace 21 of the party's members for absenteeism.

In February 2003, under pressure from the UN, the constitutional charter for the two remaining Yugoslav republics changed the country's name from Yugoslavia to Serbia and Montenegro. Under this new constitution the office of President of the Federal Republic of Yugoslavia held by Vojislav Koštunica ceased to exist and Svetozar Marović was sworn in as president of Serbia and Montenegro.

In the following month, in March 2003, Prime Minister Đinđić was assassinated in Belgrade while stepping out of his car. Đinđić had made enemies in some quarters for his unpopular reforms and pro-Western stance, as well as for his threats of clamping down on organised crime. A number of figures associated with the 'Zemun clan', an organised crime network, were accused of this and other murders. Some were arrested and put on trial, while others were charged *in absentia*. Among these were Milorad Ulemek, aka 'Legija', a former supporter of Milošević and 'Red Berets' paramilitary fighter, who would later give himself up to be put on trial for allegedly masterminding the assassination.

In the aftermath of the assassination the government imposed a 42-day State of Emergency and a crackdown on organised crime designated 'Operation Sword'. Twelve thousand people were arrested as a result, not just as suspects in the assassination but also in connection with other murders, kidnappings and drug-related crimes.

To replace Đinđić, Zoran Zivković was appointed as the new Serbian prime minister on 18 March 2003. Serbian parliament speaker, Nataša Mićić, stepped in as acting president but attempts to elect a new president were declared invalid because voter turnout failed to reach the required 50%. A third attempt on 16 November 2003 failed yet again, largely due to a boycott by opposition parties.

Parliamentary elections took place in December 2003, in which the Democratic Party of Serbia (DSS) emerged as the largest of the democratic parties and Koštunica was elected prime minister in March 2004 to head a minority government. The election of the new president took place in June 2004. Because of repeated low turnouts of the past the 50% minimum was abolished – after three previous attempts it was essential that one be elected this time. In the first round, on 13 June, the largest share of the vote went to Tomislav Nikolić for the Radical Party and Boris Tadić for the Democratic Party, with the government's DSS candidate, Dragan Maršićanin, only coming in at fourth place. The biggest surprise perhaps was Bogoljub Karić, Serbia's wealthiest businessman, who won nearly 20% of the vote and came in at third place. All the early polls suggested that it would be the Radical candidate who would win but in the end it was Boris Tadić, the former minister for defence, who received the support of both the government and Bogoljub Karić to win with 53.2% of the vote. He was sworn in as president in July 2004. Since his election Tadić has impressed many with his progressive outlook and willingness to acknowledge the wrongs of the past. His representation of Serbia at the July 2005 Srebrenica memorial ceremony in Bosnia-Herzegovina was welcomed by many abroad as a positive step forwards, although this same act was criticised at home by those who wanted the same compassion to be shown towards the many Serb victims who also died at Srebrenica.

A Belgrade timeline

c7000BC	The first Neolithic settlements are established in the region
AD91	Romans found Singidunum around the military camp of Flavius's IV legion
AD441	Huns destroy Singidunum
AD450	Singidunum falls under the rule of Sarmatians
AD504	Goths capture the settlement
AD510	Singidunum falls under the control of the Byzantine Empire
AD535	Byzantine emperor, Justinian I, rebuilds Singidunum
AD584	Avars burn and destroy the town
AD878	First written record of the name 'Beograd' being used
AD896	Hungarians attack Belgrade
AD971	Byzantine Empire re-conquers Belgrade
1096–1189	Crusaders pass through Belgrade on the way to the Holy Land
1127	Hungarian King Stefan II destroys Belgrade and uses the stone to build Zemun
1154	Byzantines under Emperor Manuel I destroy Zemun and rebuild Belgrade

Contexts

1182	Hungarians attack and ransack Belgrade
1185	Byzantine Empire regains Belgrade
1230	Belgrade becomes a possession of Bulgaria
1232	Belgrade becomes part of Hungary
1284	Serbian King Dragutin is given Belgrade by the Hungarian Crown; for the first time, the city falls under Serbian rule
1316	Dragutin's brother Milutin takes control of Belgrade
1319	Hungarians take over Belgrade once more
1403	Belgrade becomes the capital of medieval Serbia under Despot Stefan Lazarević
1427	Hungarians take over Belgrade; Đurađ Branković moves capital to Smederevo
1440	Turks unsuccessfully attack Belgrade
1456	Another unsuccessful Turkish siege on city by Sultan Mahmud II
1521	Turks under leadership of Sultan Suleiman the Magnificent take over Belgrade
1688	Maximillian of Bavaria conquers Belgrade
1690	Belgrade falls under Turkish rule once more
1717	City captured by Prince Eugene of Savoy
1723–36	The Belgrade Fortress is constructed
1739	A peace treaty between Austria and Turkey gives Belgrade back to the Turks

History

1806	Karađorđe liberates Belgrade, returning it to Serbian control
1815	Second Serbian Uprising begins under leadership of Miloš Obrenović
1841	Belgrade becomes the capital of the Princedom of Serbia
1882	Belgrade becomes capital of the Serbian Kingdom
1903	Assassination of King Aleksandar Obrenović; Petar Karađorđević takes the throne
1914	Austrians bombard Belgrade
1915	German and Austrian troops capture Belgrade
1918	Serb and Allied forces liberate the city; Belgrade becomes the capital of the newly created Kingdom of the Serbs, Croats and Slovenes
1929	King Aleksandar Karađorđević dissolves National Assembly
1941	Nazi bombing on 6 April; Germans occupy the city on 12 April
1944	Allies bomb Nazi-held Belgrade; on 20 October, Belgrade is liberated by Tito's Partisans with help of the Soviet Red Army
1945	Yugoslav Monarchy abolished. The Federal People's Republic of Yugoslavia is established under the communist leadership of Josip Broz Tito
1968	Student protests against Tito's rule
1992	Federal Republic of Yugoslavia proclaimed; UN Security Council impose sanctions
1993	The world's highest-ever recorded inflation hits the city

Contexts

1999	Belgrade and much of Serbia is bombed by NATO for a period of nearly three months
2000	Widespread protests remove Slobodan Milošević from power
2003	Prime Minister Zoran Ðinđić is assassinated

POLITICS

On 4 February 2003 the Federal Republic of Yugoslavia agreed to change its name to that of Serbia and Montenegro, a loose federation of the two remaining Yugoslav republics, Serbia and Montenegro, along with the two nominally autonomous states of Vojvodina and Kosovo and Metohija. Kosovo, of course, is currently under United Nations administration.

Following Milošević's removal from power the country was governed temporarily by the Democratic Opposition of Serbia, an alliance of various political parties that excluded the centre-right Democratic Party of Serbia (not to be confused with the Democratic Party of which Zoran Ðinđić was former president). By 2004, however, the Democratic Party of Serbia had gathered enough support to form another government in coalition with G17 Plus, a party with neo-liberal economic views, and the Serbian Renewal Party.

The current prime minister is Vojislav Koštunica of the Democratic Party of Serbia, while the president is Boris Tadić, leader of the liberal, centrist Democratic Party. Tadić's Democratic Party currently sits in opposition with just 37 out of 250 seats on the Serbian National Assembly. The party with the largest representation in both the Parliament of Serbia and Montenegro and the National Assembly of Serbia is the nationalist Serbian Radical Party, which has a total of 82 seats but is also part of the opposition. Officially, the Serbian Radical Party leader is Vojislav Šešelj, who has been in The Hague since 2003 awaiting trial for alleged war crimes, but the party is currently led by its deputy president, Tomislav Nikolić, who was defeated in the Serbian presidential elections by Boris Tadić in June 2004.

The current mayor of Belgrade is Nenad Bogdanović, of the Democratic Party, who was elected in October 2004 for a four-year term.

ECONOMY

Serbia's economy is slowly recovering after years of sanctions, war and inner turmoil. The serious problems started around 1991 when secession by Croatia, Slovenia and Macedonia meant that Serbia had to radically rethink its economic framework, which previously had been centrally planned with the focus of power in the capital. With secession came the loss of much of its manufacturing base that had favoured Croatia and Slovenia; the revenue from package tourism, too – enormously important to the pre-war Yugoslav economy – had come mostly from the Adriatic region of Croatia but, with the advent of war, tourism ceased to be a reality anywhere in the region for many years. Fortunately, the Vojvodina region continued to be the most productive agricultural region in the whole of the Balkans, and raw materials were still being unearthed from the coal mines in the southeast and the mineral mines of Kosovo.

Nevertheless, the unhappy break-up of the Yugoslav federation meant that Serbia's economy soon became deficient in terms of raw materials, manufacturing base and a market for its goods. Successive wars and sanctions compounded the problem until a point was reached in the mid 1990s when inflation reached the world's highest-ever figure – a staggering 600,000% – that eclipsed even that of pre-war Germany. Serbia, shunned by most of the world, had reached a point where some of its people were living in conditions of almost Third World-style poverty. Many of those that could leave – the young and well educated – did so, which left a skills shortage that further inflamed the situation. Finally, when popular protest finally brought the regime of Slobodan Milošević to its knees in late 2000, the widespread protest was fuelled as much by dissatisfaction with the dire shape of the economy as it was by political and ideological rejections of Milošević's plans for a greater Serbia.

The coalition government that followed Milošević inherited an economy shattered by war and nearly a decade of sanctions. The Serbian government has since taken several bold economic decisions: stabilising the dinar, streamlining the tax system and reforming the banking sector. In 2001, Serbia, then still the FRY, became eligible for interest-free loans from the World Bank and a credit of US$540 million was authorised to contribute towards political, economic and social reforms. In 2003, the European Union granted €242 million in aid to Serbia and Montenegro, €229 million of which was destined for Serbia. With corruption and organised crime steadily on the wane, foreign investment slowly increasing and what looks to be a far more stable government in power, the current mood is one of quiet optimism.

Economy

PEOPLE

Belgraders are on the whole astonishingly friendly people who are delighted to welcome foreign visitors to the city they love. Many speak English – particularly the young – and communication is rarely a serious problem. Because of the general lack of visitors, certainly in comparison with other east European capitals, Belgrade's citizens are more than pleased to show you the city from their perspective and share its secrets with you. Despite the recent memory of economic sanctions, NATO bombings and the pariah status of the country during the Milošević era, open resentment towards foreigners from western Europe and the United States is very rare indeed.

CULTURAL ETIQUETTE

Discussion of politics in Serbia should be approached with caution. Opinion is frequently divided and sometimes it is best just to have an open mind and listen, offering opinions only when they are asked for. Serbians are only too aware of the problems facing their country and do not take warmly to foreigners who claim that they know all the answers. The same might be said of conversations about Belgrade's football teams too.

When paying the bill in a restaurant it is customary for the host to pay the whole bill. This is done regardless of the host's financial standing, and in most circumstances foreign visitors are automatically considered to be guests. Often the bill is paid surreptitiously to avoid protest. The idea of breaking a bill down so individuals can pay for their own share of food and drink is unheard of. Similarly, if you are invited to have something to eat or drink, even if it is just a cup of coffee, it is always best to accept graciously. To refuse may cause offence as it could give the impression that you are behaving in a haughty manner.

Eating and drinking is a serious business in Belgrade, as is the conversation and toasting that punctuates a meal. When sharing a toast with someone it is imperative that you look into their eyes as you do this. To avoid eye contact is considered disrespectful or, at best, weak.

Despite meagre incomes, most Belgraders make an effort to dress smartly and stylishly. Although smart-casual dress is generally acceptable, top-notch restaurants have a dress code just like anywhere else and may turn you away if you are in shorts and sandals. Generally, though, dress conventions are fairly relaxed. Dress should be conservative and respectful when visiting churches and monasteries: no shorts, short skirts or flip-flops.

GAY BELGRADE

Homosexuality is tolerated, officially at least, but open displays of same-sex affection are frowned upon and could well provoke a hostile reaction. The gay scene in Belgrade is extremely discreet, to say the least – so discreet that there is hardly any visible 'scene' at all. This is hardly surprising: as elsewhere in the Balkans, the general attitude is fairly unenlightened, with many viewing homosexuality as distinctly un-Serbian and a form of aberrant behaviour that is imported from the

West. Such social pressures oblige most gays and lesbians in Serbia to lead a double life. A gay and lesbian pride march in 2001 ended in bloodshed when crowds of skinheads, nationalists and members of *Obraz*, an orthodox religious group, attacked lesbians and gay men taking part in the march. The police were criticised for appearing to stand by and let it happen. The attack was subsequently condemned by Amnesty International as a human rights violation. Similarly, another march planned in 2003 had to be called off for fear of attacks.

INTERACTING WITH LOCAL PEOPLE

The majority of Belgrade's younger generation speak and understand English to some extent – some with quite remarkable fluency – but a few words of Serbian go a long way and will always be well received. Older people may speak German or French rather than English, as well as Russian, which was the second language taught in most schools during the Tito era.

If you are invited to someone's home for a meal it is a nice gesture to take flowers, chocolates or perhaps a bottle of wine. If you are staying with a Serbian host, any offers of cash will probably be swept aside, but small gifts of a non-monetary nature will be gladly accepted. Suitable gifts might be books, foreign magazines or clothing items like T-shirts with foreign logos. Business cards, family photographs and postcards of home are always appreciated. Most professional Serbs have their own business cards and like to exchange them on first meeting.

Nicotine and caffeine are the twin fuels of Serbian youth culture, with alcohol sitting firmly in third place. In Serbia, tobacco smoking is less of a habit and more a way of life, as is the frequent consumption of strong coffee. There is little point in complaining if you notice people lighting up under the gaze of no-smoking signs. Such complaints are generally met with quiet bemusement and you will just have to grin and bear it.

GIVING SOMETHING BACK – LOCAL CHARITIES

Although to my knowledge there is no organisation that works specifically in Belgrade, several charities work in Serbia to alleviate the suffering of refugees and displaced people. Serbia's Roma community, given the straitened circumstances in which they often find themselves, are frequently targeted as being an especially deserving cause. The Roman Catholic charity **CAFOD** (*Romero Close, London SW9 9TV, United Kingdom;* ℄ *+44 20 7733 7900;* f *+44 20 7274 9630;* e *cafod@cafod.org.uk*) does much good work in this field: helping to educate Roma children, providing a counselling service for refugees, and assisting Roma families in getting access to clean water, medical treatment and the basic necessities of life.

Save the Children UK is also active in Serbia, most notably in working with local Roma non-government organisations to improve educational achievement for Roma children. They can be contacted by writing to them at FREEPOST NAT7383, Witney, OX29 7BR, United Kingdom, or via their website at www.savethechildren.org.uk.

Those who would prefer to help Serbian wildlife might be interested in the activities of the **League for the Ornithological Action of Serbia and Montenegro** (LOASM), whose goal is that of protecting birds, their habitats and sites through the involvement of people, and is dedicated to educating the people of Serbia and Montenegro in the importance and enjoyment of birds. For information, write to: Liga za ornitolosku akciju Srbije i Crne Gore 51 Njegoseva St, 11000 Belgrade; or directly to the LOASM chairman, Dragan Simić, at e goingbirding@yahoo.com.

A simple and direct way of 'giving something back' would be to purchase your souvenirs from **Artefakt**, the showroom of the **Women's Textile Workshops Network** at Trg Nikole Pašića 8 (see *Shopping*, page 166), which sells handicrafts made by disadvantaged women from all over the former Yugoslavia. The goods are of high quality and all proceeds go to the artisans who make the goods on display.

RELIGION

The majority religion is Orthodox Christianity. Although Belgrade has churches for Catholics and Protestants, these are not very numerous in the city. Belgrade used to have a sizeable and prosperous Jewish community but many of those who survived World War II migrated to Israel. Today, it numbers just a few hundred. Considering that Belgrade was under Ottoman rule for so long it may come as a surprise that, of the 30 mosques that used to stand in the city, only one remains, the Bayrakli Mosque (1690). This was fire-damaged during riots in 2004 but has since been repaired and still serves a small Muslim community.

The 1991 census records that 87% of Belgrade's citizens consider themselves to be Orthodox, 2% Catholic or Muslim, just 0.2% Protestant, Jews 0.03%, 6% belong to unspecified religions and 3% consider themselves to be atheist.

BUSINESS

Many entrepreneurs in Belgrade are keen to develop business links overseas, especially with western Europe. By and large, doing business in Serbia is little different from anywhere else in eastern Europe. Serbian entrepreneurs like to take their time, and to impress: business in Serbia is often conducted over a large shared meal or, more likely, after it; inevitably, the host will pick up the bill.

The Serbian Chamber of Commerce and Industry has lots of useful advice for businesses wishing to invest in Serbia at www.pkj.co.yu/en, while information on facts and figures, regional data, and rules and regulations that affect businesses in Serbia are available at www.invest-in-serbia.com.

Foreign banks that have branches in Belgrade include:

HVB Rajićeva 27–29; ꙮ 3204 500
Micro Finance Bank Gospodar Jevremona 9; ꙮ 3025 625
National Bank of Greece Kralja Petra 22–24; ꙮ 3281 498
Raiffeisenbank Resavska 22; ꙮ 3202 121
Sociéte Generale Vladimira Popovića 6; ꙮ 3111 515

CULTURE AND FESTIVALS

Belgrade is a city soaked with culture and, apart from the numerous museums and galleries that can be visited at any time of year, there are plenty of special annual cultural events, especially outside the winter months, that embrace every aspect of the arts. All of the arts are well represented, with theatre, cinema, visual arts and music all being celebrated in annual events. There is also a number of events that cater especially to children and young adults.

January–February
FEST – International Film Festival (*www.fest.org.yu*) is held from the last Friday in February through the first week in March and is a showcase for the latest releases in world cinema.

March
International Music Youth Competition (*www.music-competition.co.yu*) is an annual event for singers, instrumentalists, composers and ensembles under the age of 30, held in the second half of March for ten–15 days.
Festival of Documentaries and Short Films (*www.kratkimetar.org.yu*) is a competitive film festival of documentaries, animated and experimental film and video. It is held in the last week of March and lasts for four–five days.
In Vino International Wine Festival (*www.invino.co.yu*) at the Sava Centre
Spring exhibition of ULUS at Cvijeta Zuzorić Art Pavilion in March–April (with another autumn exhibition taking place in November).

April
Guitar Art Festival (*www.gaf.co.yu*) features a range of soloists and guitar ensembles and is held at the Cultural Centre of Belgrade and Foundation of Ilija M

Contexts

Kolarac. Check the website for exact dates: in 2005 this was held in February rather than April.

The **Belgrade Marathon** takes place in the second half of the month.

May

International Festival of New Music 'Ring, Ring' (*www.rex.b92.net/ringring*) takes place over a period of two weeks at Rex Cultural Centre and Dom Omladine highlighting jazz, folk and avant-garde music.

International Platform of Composers (IPCS) in the second half of May at the SKC.

June

International Theatrical Belgrade Adventure (TIBA) is a children's drama festival held at various Belgrade theatres in June for ten days.

Choirs among Frescoes is a series of events that feature sacred choral music held at the Fresco Gallery in June–July.

Kalemegdan Twilights is a series of performances of popular classical music held from June–July in Kalemegdan Park, on the plateau in front of the Belgrade City Institute for the Protection of Cultural Monuments.

July

Pantomime Festival is held at 'Pinokio' puppet theatre at the beginning of the month.

ECHO Festival (*www.echofest.com*) is a large-scale pop, dance and rock music festival centred on Lido beach at Veliko Ratno island in the middle of the confluence of the Danube and Sava rivers. It usually takes place in the middle of the month to follow Novi Sad's similar, but even larger, EXIT festival.

BELEF (*www.belef.org*) is Belgrade's summer festival of theatre, contemporary dance, visual arts and music held every year at various venues around the city in July and August. Outdoor venues such as Kalemegdan Park and the Sava and Danube riverbanks are utilised for performances as well as theatres and larger venues such as Dom Omladine and the Sava Centre.

August

Belgrade Beer Festival (*www.belgradebeerfest.com*) is held at Kalemegdan Lower Town near the end of August. As well as a wide range of beers to sample there is a music stage where live performances by Serbian and international bands can be seen throughout the night. Other cultural events such as beer-drinking competitions also take place.

September

BITEF Belgrade International Theatre Festival (*www.bitef.co.yu*) is an international festival of drama that takes place at several of Belgrade's theatres and also at the Sava Centre over a period of about 15 days.

October–December

BEMUS Belgrade Music Festival (*www.bemus.co.yu*) is an international musical event of ensembles and soloists from around the world. This takes place in the first half of the month; the main emphasis is on classical and contemporary music but there is some 'world' music too. BEMUS is staged at the Sava Centre, the Foundation of Ilija M Kolarac and other theatres across the city.

Joy of Europe or **International Meeting of Children of Europe** (*www.joyofeurope.org.yu*) is an international children's event, held in the first week of October, which promotes socialising and shared artistic creativity between children from all over Europe. It takes place at the Children's Cultural Centre of Belgrade, at Ada Ciganlija, the Sava Centre and various galleries around the city.

October Salon (*www.oktobarskisalon.org*) promotes the most recent significant achievements in the field of fine and applied arts and design. Held at Cvijeta Zuzorić art pavilion in Kalemegdan Park and at various ULUS (Association of Fine Artists of Serbia) galleries such as Zvono, Artget and the Faculty of Fine Arts.

Belgrade Book Fair (*www.sajam.co.yu*) is an international event of book publishing and booksellers held at Sajam fairground from the end of October to the beginning of November.

GEOGRAPHY AND CLIMATE

Belgrade's position is located in southeast Europe, at the northern end of the Balkan Peninsula at 20°28'E longitude and 44°49'N latitude. The city lies at the confluence of the Sava and Danube rivers. The Sava flows from Bosnia-Herzegovina to the west while the Danube arrives from the countries of the northwest to pass through northern Serbia on its journey to the Black Sea. Immediately to the north of Belgrade is the province of Vojvodina, a flat agricultural plain that was formerly the Pannonian Sea; to the south are the rolling hills of the Šumadija ('Wooded Country'), the Serbian heartland.

Belgrade's climate is moderately continental with quite cold winters with snow, and temperatures regularly down to −5°C or so. Summers are warm, even hot, with the highest temperatures occurring in July and August and an annual temperature of 21.7°C. Belgrade receives an average of 139 days of precipitation per annum (including 27 days of snow) and an average rainfall of around 700mm. The wettest months are May and June although not significantly so. A characteristic wind from the southeast called the *košava* (not to be confused with *Kosovo*) sometimes blows in the autumn and winter bringing fair and dry weather.

NATURAL HISTORY

Belgrade has far more wildlife than you might imagine. Birds in particular are well represented and the city's parks and riverside areas provide an ideal habitat for a wide variety of species. So far, 127 species have been recorded within the immediate urban area, with an additional 50 or so more species finding suitable habitat within the wider Belgrade area.

More spectacular breeding residents include: white-tailed eagle (*Haliaeetus albicilla*), peregrine and saker falcons (*Falco peregrinus*, *F. cherrug*), and various owls and woodpeckers. Breeding migrants include a number of herons – little bittern (*Ixobrychus minutes*), night heron (*Nycticorax nycticorax*), little egret (*Egretta garzetta*) and purple heron (*Ardea pupurea*) – as well as black and white storks, (*Ciconia ciconia* and *C. nigra*). Numerous waders and cranes pass through on migration in spring and autumn and a large number of water birds – divers, grebes, swans, geese and ducks – are also present during the winter months.

In winter, the best birding spots are Veliko Ratno Ostrvo (Great War Island) at the confluence of the Danube and Sava rivers, which is reachable by ferry (and in summer by a pontoon bridge from Zemun), and Ada Ciganlija, both of which have large concentrations of wildfowl and water birds. In spring and summer, the trees of Kalemegdan Park are full of songbirds and woodpeckers.

More information may be found at www.birdtours.co.uk/tripreports/serbia/serb1/birdwatch-belgrade.htm.

Black stork

Planning

THE CITY – A PRACTICAL OVERVIEW

Belgrade is a large, sprawling city that stretches across the confluence of two of eastern Europe's greatest rivers, the Danube and the Sava. On the west bank of the Sava lies New Belgrade (Novi Beograd), which leads almost seamlessly into Zemun, formerly a separate town but now a borough of the city. In the east, the city sprawls across to suburbs like Zvezdara and Karaburma before eventually reaching open country. Similarly, the south of the city leads through leafy suburbs like Kneževac and Resnik to reach the undulating greensward of the Šumadija, Serbia's central heartland.

The wide extent of the city is hardly an issue to the casual visitor as most of what there is to see is tightly contained in a small area of the Old Town (Stari Grad), the historic area immediately south of Kalemegdan Park that overlooks the Danube and Sava's confluence. This is not to say there is nothing to see elsewhere – you should certainly visit Zemun, St Sava's Church and some of the sights and museums in the city centre – but the chances are that you will probably spend at least 75% of your time in and around the Old Town.

WHEN TO VISIT (AND WHY)

Belgrade has a climate similar to the rest of southeast Europe, although it rarely gets as hot as Athens during the summer months or as cold as Bucharest in winter.

Winter is not a good time to visit unless you have a particular reason for going then: it will be cold and wet, perhaps snowing, and many of the city's less expensive hotels have inadequate heating. In contrast, the summer months are rarely oppressively hot, although it can become quite sticky in Belgrade during the dog days of August.

Generally speaking, the best time to visit is anytime between late spring and early autumn. Depending on personal interests, it is a good idea to try and make your

BELGRADE'S MODERN-DAY GATES

The modern city, like its medieval counterpart of old, can be said to have 'gates' leading into it. The contemporary western gate is actually the city's tallest building – the 'Genex' building in Blok 33 of New Belgrade, otherwise known as Zapadna kapija Beograda (Belgrade West Gate). This building, which has mixed residential and commercial use, is quite unmistakeable with its twin towers joined by a corridor across the top. Its eastern counterpart is found in the Konjarnik suburb. The East Gate (Istočna kapija Beograda) is composed of three sloping residential blocks that almost abut with one another to form a steep pyramid. This, too, can be seen from most high points in Belgrade as well as welcoming visitors arriving in the city by way of the southern highway.

visit coincide with particular events that are taking place in the city: the Belgrade Music Festival – BEMUS (Classical) that is hosted by the capital in October, or BITEF, the international theatre festival that takes place in September. Alternatively, you may wish to time your visit to coincide with religious and cultural celebrations like Orthodox Easter, which can be an enjoyable time to visit. Overall, May, June and September are probably the most perfect months, although May and June are also marginally the wettest. Hotel accommodation and public transport can be at a premium at certain times of year like Easter, or during the Belgrade Book Fair in October, but as a rule this presents few problems.

SUGGESTED ITINERARIES
One day

If you are in the city for just one day, then most of your time should be spent in and around Stari Grad, the Old Town. You might wish to spend the morning visiting St Sava's Church just south of the city centre at Vračar before heading north to Trg Republike. If time permits, and it is not a Monday, you can then visit the National Museum before lunching at restaurants nearby. After lunch, a leisurely stroll along Kneza Mihaila will give you ample opportunity to window shop and to experience the bustling but easygoing atmosphere of modern-day Belgrade. You should ensure that you see the Orthodox Cathedral and perhaps have a drink at the '?' (Znak pitanje) café across the street. Princess Ljubica's mansion, a house museum in Turkish–Balkan style, lies just around the corner, which is well worth visiting if you want to get an idea of aristocratic Serbian life at the beginning of the 19th century. You should ensure that you visit Kalemegdan Park in the hour or two before sunset, which will be busy, especially in summer, with strollers enjoying the expansive views over the confluence of the Sava and Danube rivers. This is where native Belgraders go to relax and to take the air and it is a thoroughly enjoyable experience to go and join in with them.

Dinner should be in one of the restaurants along Skadarska, a sloping cobbled street a five-minute walk east of Trg Republike. Here, you can eat Serbian national food served by waiters in national dress to the accompaniment of Roma musicians. It is slightly self-conscious and the closest that the city gets to being touristy (ie: not very) but is great fun nevertheless. If you still have any energy left after all of this, and are not too stuffed from your meal, you could then investigate Belgrade's club scene. Many lie close by in the area near the top end of Kneza Mihaila and Kalemegdan Park. A more relaxing alternative would be to have another stroll along Kneza Mihaila (the *korso* lasts until the early hours) before having a nightcap at one of the street cafés here or perhaps at one of the trendier café-bars along nearby Obilićev venac.

Two or three days

With two or more days you should endeavour to do all of the above; extra time will allow you to spread it all out a little more. On the second day, you might wish to visit New Belgrade – at least the Danube shore there – paying a visit to the

Gallery of Modern Art before an evening stroll along the Danube walkway and dinner in one of the fish restaurants along the New Belgrade or Zemun shore. There are plenty of *splavovi* (floating rafts) along here that serve as both restaurants and nightclubs and the area is lively until the early hours – follow your ears to find a place that has music to your own taste. Another possibility is to visit Zemun in the daytime. If you go nowhere else in Serbia then this, at least, will give you a better idea of what a smaller, more traditional Serbian town is like. As well as the National Museum you should endeavour to visit the Ethnographic and Military museums as well – both are excellent – although it probably makes more sense to enjoy one thoroughly rather than try to rush through several. For a slightly different night-time scene on a second or third day you might wish to investigate the smart cafés along Strahinjića bana, Belgrade's so-called 'Silicon Valley'.

Three days or more

A lengthier stay will allow you to get out to more far-flung parts of the city, to visit the 'House of Flowers' at Topčider Park and perhaps look in on some of the more specialist but equally interesting museums that the city has to offer – the Museum of Nikola Tesla, the house of Vuk Karadžić or the Fresco Gallery. By now you might feel in need of a break from the city and in mind to take a day trip somewhere. Smederevo, with its magnificent medieval riverside castle, is within easy reach, as is Pančevo; even Novi Sad, Serbia's second city, can be reached in two hours by bus or train, although it is probably best to stay over there to fully appreciate the different atmosphere that the city has to offer. If your visit includes a weekend, guided trips are run by the Belgrade Tourist Office on Sundays to visit the nearby archaeological site of Vinča and, in summer, steam-train excursions to Sremski Karlovci are organised that leave in the morning and return to Belgrade in the evening. Similar excursions also run to Smederevo in the summer months.

TOUR OPERATORS

For the time being, there is a limited choice of operators that organise breaks to Belgrade. This is likely to change in the near future as the city becomes more recognised as a cultural destination and a *bona fide* weekend getaway.

UK

Regent Holidays 15 John St, Bristol BS1 2HR; ✆ 0117 921 1711; f 0117 925 4866; e regent@regent-holidays.co.uk; www.regent-holidays.co.uk. Regent organise three-day city breaks to Belgrade throughout the year, leaving on Mondays, Wednesdays, Fridays and Sundays. Costs depend on the class of hotel chosen and are between £290 and £495 per person for flights (British Airways), hotel and breakfast. Private car transfers from airport to hotel cost £26 each way.

USA

Kutrubes Travel 328 Tremont St, Boston, MA 02116; ✆ +1 800 878 8566, +1617 426 5668; f +1 617 426 3196; e adventures@kutrubestravel.com; www.kutrubestravel.com.

Kutrubes organise ten-day tours to Serbia, beginning and ending in Belgrade, for US$1,394 per person dbl occupancy, based on a group of six travellers; for a group of four, it is US$1,522 per person; for two, US$1,899. This price includes tour service, bed and breakfast and transfers but excludes airfares from the United States. They can also arrange individualised custom tours.

RED TAPE
Passports and visas

Since 2003 most foreign visitors no longer require a visa for a short stay in the country. Passport holders of the following countries may stay in Serbia for a period up to 90 days without the requirement of a visa: Andorra, Argentina, Armenia, Australia, Austria, Azerbaijan, Belgium, Bolivia, Canada, Chile, China (for purposes of business only), Costa Rica, Croatia, Cuba, Cyprus, Czech Republic, Denmark, Ecuador, Egypt (diplomatic passports only), Estonia, Finland, France, Georgia (for business purposes), Germany, Greece, Guinea, Iceland, Ireland, Israel, Italy, Kyrgyzstan (for business), Latvia, Liechtenstein, Lithuania, Luxembourg, Malta, Mexico (180 days), Monaco, Mongolia (for business), Netherlands, New Zealand, North Korea (for business), Norway, Peru, Poland, Portugal, Russian Federation (for business), San Marino, Seychelles, Singapore, Slovakia, Slovenia, South Korea, Spain, Sweden, Switzerland, Tajikistan (for business), Tunisia, Turkmenistan (for business), United Kingdom, United States of America and Vatican City.

The following are granted 30 days' visa-free stay in Serbia: Albania, Belarus, Bosnia-Herzegovina, Bulgaria, Hungary, Macedonia (60 days), Romania and Turkey (for diplomatic, special and official passports only).

For those requiring a visa, an application should be made at one of Serbia's foreign embassies where the applicant will be required to produce a valid passport, a letter of introduction (this can be organised through a Serbian tourist agency or a business contact), a return ticket, proof of funds and evidence of medical cover for the duration of the stay.

Funds in excess of €2,000 should be declared on arrival in the country as, in theory at least, failure to do this could result in confiscation on leaving Serbia.

Embassies of Serbia and Montenegro abroad

UK 28 Belgrave Sq, London SW1X 8QB; ☏ +44 (0)20 7235 9049; f +44 (0)20 7235 7092; e londre@jugisek.demom.co.uk; www.yugoslavembassy.org.uk

USA 2134 Kalorama Rd, NW Washington, DC 20008; ☏ +1 (1) 202 332 0333; f +1 (1) 202 332 3933, 332 5974; e info@yuembusa.org; www.yuembusa.org

Albania Skender Beg Building 8/3-II, Tirana; ☏ +35542 23 042, 232 091; f +35542 32 089; e ambatira@icc-al.org

Australia 4 Bulwarra Cl, O'Malley, ACT 2606, Canberra; ☏ +61(0)2 6290 2630, 6290 2948; f +61(0)2 6290 2631; e yuembau@ozemail.com.au

Austria R Rennweg 3, 1030 Wien; ☏ +431 713 2595, 713 2596, 712 1205; f +431 713 2597; e ambasada@scg-diplomat.at; www.scg-diplomat.at

Belgium Av Emile de Mot 11, 1000 Bruxelles; ☎ +322 647 5781, 647 2652, 647 2651, 649 6545, 649 8349; f +322 647 2941; e ambaserbiemontenegro@skynet.be

Bosnia-Herzegovina Obala Marka Dizdara 3a, 71000 Sarajevo; ☎ +38733 260 090, 260 080; f +38733 221 469; e yugoamba@bih.net.ba

Bulgaria Veliko Trnovo 3, 1504 Sofia; ☎ +3592 946 1635, 946 1633, 946 1636; f +3592 946 1059; e ambasada-scg-sofija@infotl.bg

Canada 17 Blackburn Av, Ottowa, Ontario KIN 8A2; ☎ +1 (0)613 233 6289, 233 6280, 565 9263; f +1 (0)613 233 7850; e diplomat@yuemb.ca; www.yuemb.ca

Croatia Pantovcak 245, Zagreb; ☎ +3851 457 9067, 457 9068, 457 3330, 457 3334; f +3851 457 3338; e ambasada@ambasada-srj.hr

France 54 Rue de la Faisanderie, 75116 Paris; ☎ +33(0)1 40 72 24 24, 40 72 24 10; f +33(0)1 40 72 24 11, 40 72 24 23; e ambasadapariz@wanadoo.fr

Germany Taubert Strasse 18, D-1 4193 Berlin; ☎ +49 (0)30 895 7700, 895 770222; f +49 (0)30 825 2206; e info@botschaft-smg.de

Hungary Dozsa Gyorgy ut 92/b, H-1068 Budapest VI; ☎ +361 322 9838, 342 8512, 352 8847, 322 1436, 322 1437; f +361 322 1438, 352 8846; e ambjubp@mail.datanet.hu

Israel 10 Bodenheimer St, 62008 Tel Aviv; ☎ +972 (0)3 604 5535; f +972 (0)3 604 9456

Italy Via dei Monti Parioli 20, 00197 Roma; ☎ +3906 320 0796, 320 0890, 320 0805, 320 0959; f +3906 320 0868; e amb.jug@flashnet.it

Japan 4724 Kitashinagawa, Shinagawa-ku, Tokyo; ☎ +81 (0)3 3447 3571, 3447 3572; f +81 (0)3 3447 3573; e embassy@embassy-serbia-montenegro.jp

Macedonia St Pitu Guli 8, Skopje; ☎ +3892 3129 298, 3131 299, 3128 422, 3129 305; f

+3892 3129 427, 3131 428; e yuamb@unet.com.mk

Netherlands Groot Hertoginnelaan 30, 2517 EG The Hague; ☏ +70 363 2397, 363 2393, 363 6800; f +70 360 2421; e yuambanl@bart.nl; http://users.bart.nl/~yuambanl

Romania Calea Dorobantilor Nr34, Bucarest; ☏ +4021 211 9871, 211 9872, 211 9873; f +4021 210 0175; e ambiug@ines.ro

Russian Federation Mosfiljmovskaja 46, R-119285 Moscow; ☏ +7 (8)095 147 4106, 147 9008, 147 4105, 147 4108; f +7 (8)095 937 9615, 147 4104; e ambasada@co.ru

Slovenia Slomskova 1, 1000 Ljubljana; ☏ +3861 438 0111, 438 0110; f +386 434 2688, 434 2689; e ambasada.scg.ljubljana@siol.net

South Africa 163 Marais St, Brooklyn 0181, PO Box 13026 Hatfield 0028, Pretoria; ☏ +2712 460 5626, 460 6103, 346 4139, 246 6191; f +2712 460 6003; e info@sgembassy.org.za; www.sgembassy.org.za

Spain Calle de Velasquez 162, E-28002 Madrid; ☏ +3491 563 5045, 563 5046, 564 2250, 562 6040; f +3491 563 0440; e Madrid@embajada-yugoslavia.es; www.embajada-yugoslavia.es

Switzerland Seminarstrasse 5, CH-3006 Bern; ☏ +4131 352 6353, 352 6354, 352 6355; f +4131 351 4474; e info@yuamb.ch; www.yuamb.ch

Turkey Paris Caddesi 47, PK28 Kavaklidere, TR-Ankara; ☏ +90312 426 0236, 426 2432; f +90312 427 8345; e yugoslav@tr.net

Registration with police

Foreigners visiting Serbia are obliged to be registered with the police. This is normally done automatically by hotels on checking in, although if you are staying privately or with friends you are supposed to visit a police station in order to do it yourself. You will be registered anew each time you change hotels and given a registration card when you check out. This requirement is likely to change in the near future. There was talk of compulsory registration with the police being relaxed in 2004 but at the time of writing no-one seemed very certain about this and hotels were still providing the documentation.

Customs

Foreigners are not restricted in the number of personal belongings they can bring into Serbia. Inspections, if they occur at all, are usually relaxed and fairly perfunctory. One litre of wine, $^3/_4$ litre of liquor, $^1/_4$ litre of perfume and 250 cigarettes, 50 cigars or 250 grams of tobacco are the permitted duty-free limits for importation. Although tobacco-smuggling is big business in Serbia, the restriction on alcohol importation has a somewhat 'coals to Newcastle' ring about it. It is recommended that you declare valuable items such as laptops or video cameras to ensure that you can re-export them without fuss but it is highly unlikely that you will run into trouble if you do not. Foreign nationals are allowed to take in or out up to 120,000din in Serbian currency although it is hard to imagine why you would want to do this given how difficult it is to change dinars out of the country. Foreign currency up to €2,000 may be taken out of the country. If you arrive with substantially more than this amount it is probably best to declare it on entry just to be on the safe side.

Any questions regarding customs can be answered by contacting the Federal

Custom Service at Bulevar AVNOJ-a 155, 11070 Novi Beograd; ✆ +381 11 694 823, 3115 472; www.fcs.yu.

GETTING THERE AND AWAY
By air
Several airlines serve Belgrade's Surčin Airport (international code: BEG) directly. These include the national carrier JAT Airways, British Airways, Air France, Alitalia, Austrian Airlines, ČSA Czech Airlines, KLM, Lufthansa, Malev, Olympic Airways, Swiss and Turkish Airlines. Terminal 2 deals with the airport's international traffic, while domestic flights use Terminal 1. For international flights, Belgrade Airport charges all adult passengers a departure tax of 1,000din, although this is usually included in the ticket price with JAT services.

From the UK
There are direct flights with JAT from Heathrow every day of the week that arrive in Belgrade late afternoon. JAT also offers a combined service with British Midland that links other British cities and Dublin with Belgrade by way of Heathrow. British Airways flies to Belgrade five times a week with flights that leave Heathrow in the morning to conveniently arrive in Belgrade about midday. The return flight leaves early afternoon to arrive at Heathrow by mid afternoon.

The best return prices from London are around £165 for BA, and £150 for JAT, including tax, although it may be difficult to get this price during busy holiday periods or at short notice. BA flights can be booked online at the website address below. JAT has two websites that give information on flight times and prices but which do not permit online booking.

British Airways ⟍ 0870 850 9850 (reservations); 0870 55 111 55 (flight arrival and departure information) lines are open 06.00–21.45 daily. Online booking and timetables at: www.britishairways.com

JAT London office: 7 Dering St, London W1S 1AE. Reservation and ticketing ⟍ 020 7629 2007; f 020 7493 8092; e sales@jatlondon.com; www.jat.com; www.jatlondon.com. *Open Mon–Fri 09.30–17.30.*

Indirect flights are also available at similar prices with some European carriers like Alitalia, Czech Airways and Swissair. Online flight bookers such as Cheapflights.com and Expedia.com should come up with some of these options when a search for 'Belgrade' is carried out.

From Europe

JAT has direct flights that connect Belgrade with Amsterdam, Athens, Banja Luka, Berlin, Brussels, Copenhagen, Düsseldorf, Frankfurt, Göteborg, Hamburg, Hanover, Istanbul, Kiev, Larnaca, Ljubljana, London, Malta, Munich, Moscow, Paris, Prague, Sarajevo, Skopje, Sofia, St Petersburg, Stockholm, Trieste, Vienna, Warsaw and Zurich. The best-connected of these are Paris with 15 flights a week, Skopje with 13 and Zurich with 22 weekly connections. There are also limited services to the Middle

East with Beirut, Cairo, Damascus, Tel Aviv, Tripoli and Tunis all being served by JAT.

Air France, Alitalia, Lufthansa and Swissair all have services to Belgrade from their respective capitals.

From the US
There is no longer a direct flight to Belgrade from New York with JAT although this service may be resumed at sometime in the future. Instead it is necessary to

BUDGET FLIGHT/LAND COMBINATIONS FROM THE UK
Budget flights to Eastern Europe continue to fly closer and closer to Belgrade but, for the time being at least, do not quite reach it. To save money, it is possible to combine a cheap budget airline flight with a train or bus journey through to Belgrade. For example, by taking a cut-price Ryanair (*www.ryanair.com*) flight to Trieste in Italy, or Graz or Klagenfürt in Austria, and then continuing the journey through Slovenia and Croatia, or Hungary, by train or bus. Another option is to fly with easyJet (*www.easyjet.com*) or SkyEurope (*www.skyeurope.com*) to Budapest or Ljubljana, which are even closer to the Serbian capital. It is unlikely that great savings will be made by doing this, especially if sleepers need to be booked, but it is a good way of seeing more of the region.

connect a transatlantic flight in one of the European hubs like London, Paris or Amsterdam. Air fares from the east coast of the United States to Belgrade start at about US$1,000 return in low season, more in summer. A search of US websites like www.expedia.com or www.farebeater.com will give a good idea of what is available.

By boat

Sadly, no international public river transport currently plies the Danube or Sava waterways, although some international cruises visit Belgrade as they transit Serbia en route to the Black Sea.

By train

To travel all the way to Belgrade by train from Britain requires time, money and planning. It is actually cheaper to fly, but the following may appeal to rail buffs. The first stage is to take the 12.09 Eurostar from London Waterloo to Paris Gare du Nord, arriving at 15.59. This costs from £59 return (one-way fares are actually more expensive!). At Paris Gare du Nord you then walk to the nearby Gare de l'Est and travel overnight on the 'Orient Express' (the real one, not the tourist train), which leaves Paris at 17.47 and arrives in Vienna at 08.30. This section of the journey costs from £120 single, £240 return for a bed in a six-berth couchette, the cheapest option. From Vienna you take the 'Avala' straight through to Belgrade, which leaves Vienna at 10.03 and arrives in Belgrade at 20.21, costing approximately £42 one-way,

£84 return, in second class. To book this, you can use a number of UK agencies like Deutsch Bahn's UK office (☏ 0870 243 5363) or Rail Europe (☏ 0870 5848 848).

A better bet is to travel by rail to Belgrade from somewhere rather nearer, perhaps in combination with a low-budget flight. Belgrade can be reached directly by train from all of the surrounding countries, as well as some beyond. From Zagreb the fare is about € 14, and the journey takes six hours. From Venice via Zagreb the overnight journey to Belgrade costs € 104, including a € 13 couchette supplement. It is possible to save € 30 by buying a ticket from Venice–Zagreb and then getting off when the train arrives in Zagreb in the early morning to buy a fresh ticket through to Belgrade. There is plenty of time to do this as the train remains in Zagreb station for almost an hour as the carriages are split between those that will go on to Budapest and those that continue to Belgrade, but it does mean that you must forsake an early morning lie-in in your couchette. The overnight express leaves Venice about 21.00, reaches the Slovenian border about midnight, the Croatian border about 04.00, and arrives in Zagreb just after 05.00. It finally reaches Belgrade about 12.30. Direct services are also available from Ljubljana: an overnight service leaves Ljubljana about 21.00 and arrives in Belgrade early the next morning.

Rail connections are also good with Budapest to the north, and go via Novi Sad, Subotica and the Hungarian border at Horgoš, although the journey is not really long enough to be convenient for an overnighter. Direct routes also exist to and from Greece, Romania, Turkey, Macedonia and Bulgaria, although the railway route between Sarajevo and Belgrade is rather circuitous and it is generally better to travel between Bosnia-Herzegovina and Serbia by bus. From Montenegro, there is a convenient overnight service between Bar and Belgrade by way of the Montenegrin capital, Podgorica. This journey can also be done during the daytime to make the most of the stunning scenery along the way.

By bus

There are direct bus routes to Serbia from all over western and northern Europe. For the longer journeys, given the cost and the time involved, flying is probably a more attractive option. **Eurolines**, which in Serbia are operated by the **Lasta** bus company (*www.lasta.co.yu*), run services between Serbia and Austria, Benelux, Bosnia-Herzegovina (and Republika Srbska), Croatia, Czech Republic, Denmark, France, Germany, Greece, Hungary, Macedonia, Slovakia, Slovenia, Sweden and Switzerland. Another company, **Srbija Tours International** (*Lička 3, Belgrade;* ✆ *3619 576, 3611 576, 3614 545;* f *3618 227;* e *office@srbija-tours.com*) operates services to various destinations in Germany.

From the UK

The Eurolines service from London to Belgrade requires a change at Strasbourg or Brussels. They leave on Friday nights throughout the year, travelling by P&O ferry to Brussels where there is a five-hour wait for the connecting service to Belgrade via Luxembourg, Germany, Austria, Slovak Republic and Hungary. Between late June and the end of October there is a service which leaves London Victoria early on Wednesday, Friday and Sunday mornings for Strasbourg where there is a change of coaches; this service arrives in Belgrade in the afternoon of the second day. Both services take between 33 and 37 hours in all and cost £109 one-way, £179 return with a £10 reduction for youth and senior concessions.

Eurolines booking ☎ 08705 143219 from 08.00–20.00 Monday–Friday or online at www.eurolines.co.uk.

Some sample fare and frequencies for other European services of Lasta–Eurolines are given below.

From Germany
Munich–Belgrade: 8 times a week, €55 one-way, €75 return
Berlin–Belgrade: 6 times a week, €95 one-way, €170 return
Frankfurt–Belgrade: 3 times a week, €90 one-way, €150 return

From France
Paris–Belgrade: twice weekly, €97 one-way, €130 return
Lyon–Belgrade: twice weekly, €92 one-way, €168 return
Marseille–Belgrade: twice weekly, €107 one-way, €184 return

From Austria
Salzburg–Belgrade: twice weekly, €40 one-way, €65 return

From Benelux

Amsterdam–Belgrade: twice weekly, €118 one-way, €193 return
Brussels–Belgrade: twice weekly, €102 one-way, €174 return

From Bosnia-Herzegovina

Banja Luka–Belgrade: 7 daily, 17 Bosnian marks one-way

From Slovenia and Croatia

Ljubljana–Belgrade: daily, €31 one-way, €44 return
Zagreb–Belgrade: daily, €22 one-way, €38 return
Dubrovnik–Belgrade: 6 times a week, €26 one-way, €45 return
Split–Belgrade: 6 times a week, €27 one-way, €45 return

From Scandinavia

Malmö–Belgrade: once a week, €114 one-way, €174 return
Göteborg–Belgrade: once a week, €120 one-way, €190 return
Copenhagen–Belgrade: once a week, €113 one-way, €199 return

By car

If you are driving to Belgrade from one of the surrounding countries there is a large number of entrance points to Serbia that you could use. From Hungary there are crossing points at Bački Beg, Bezdan, Kelebija, Subotica and Horgoš, and from

Romania at Srpska Crnja, Zrenjanin, Vatin, Vršac, Kaluđerovo, Bela Crkva, Đerdap and Kladovo. From Bulgaria, crossings exist at Mokrinje, Negotin, Vrška Čuka, Zaječar, Gradina, Dimitrovgrad, Strezimirovci, Ribarci and Bosilegrad; and from Macedonia at Prohor Pčinjski, Bujanovac, Preševo, Đeneral Janković, Globočica and Uroševac. Croatian border crossings are at Batrovci, Bačka Palanka, Bogojevo, Odaci, Bezdan, Sombor and Šid, while land crossings across to Bosnia-Herzegovina are at Sremska Rača, Sremska Mitrovica, Badovinci, Trbušnica, Loznica, Mali Zvornik, Ljubovija, Bajina Bašta, Kotroman, Đajetina, Uvac and Priboj. All of the crossings listed are open around the clock. Insurance policies from countries that have signed the vehicle insurance convention are fully valid, but citizens of other countries must purchase an insurance policy when they enter Serbia. Green Card cover can be issued for drivers of the following countries:

Great Britain, Germany, France, Czech Republic, Norway, Turkey, Denmark, Romania, Croatia, Hungary, Bulgaria, Macedonia, Bosnia-Herzegovina, Slovakia, Moldova, Cyprus, Albania, Andorra, Greece, Spain, Austria, Iceland, Sweden, Belgium, Ireland, Switzerland, Finland, Italy, Netherlands, Luxembourg, Portugal and Tunisia. Drivers who have insurance policies issued in countries other than these will be required to purchase a short-term insurance policy of about €80 per month for a passenger car.

On entering Serbia, drivers with foreign registration plates have to pay motorway road tolls at a higher premium, although they may be paid in euro as well as Serbian dinars. The toll charges to Belgrade coming from the Hungarian border to the north are in the order of €10. In the case of breakdown or emergency, the roadside service of the **Automobile and Motorists Association of Serbia and Montenegro – AMS SCG** (formerly known as *Auto-moto savez Jugoslavije*, or *AMSJ*) – is available for assistance and the towing or transport of damaged vehicles (✆ 987). If a vehicle with foreign licence plates is abandoned, it should be reported to the local AMS SCG unit so that a certificate may be released. Similarly, if a foreign tourist enters Serbia driving a vehicle with damaged bodywork, they should receive a certificate from the officials at the border crossing that clearly evaluates the extent of the damage. In the case of a traffic accident, the Traffic Police (*Saobraćajna policija*) should be summoned (✆ 92), who will then issue an accident report.

HEALTH

Health insurance is recommended even though, on the whole, Belgrade is a perfectly healthy place to be. If you are planning an extended stay in the country and plan to visit remote rural areas as well as the capital it is wise to visit your doctor or a reputable travel clinic at least four weeks before travel. There is no legal obligation but it is wise to be routinely up to date with tetanus and diphtheria, which is now given as a combined vaccine that lasts for ten years. Although bottled water is widely available, tap water is perfectly safe to drink in Belgrade.

Up-to-date health information can be found at:

UK

MASTA (Medical Advisory Service for Travellers Abroad) Keppel St, London WC1 7HT; ☎ 09068 224100. This is a premium-line number, charged at 60p per minute.

NHS travel website www.fitfortravel.scot.nhs.uk. Provides up-to-date country advice on immunisation.

USA

Centers for Disease Control 1600 Clifton Road, Atlanta, GA 30333; ☎ 888 232 3228 (toll-free 24-hour service) or 800 311 3435; f 877 FYI TRP; www.cdc.gov/travel

SAFETY

Belgrade is a remarkably safe city and feels very safe indeed when compared with more crime-ridden capitals like London, Paris or New York. In fact, it is the sort of city where anyone – young or old, male or female – can more or less walk around safely at any time of day or night. The Western (mostly British) disease of aggressive binge drinking does not seem to exist here; instead, the streets at night are calm and civilised, with well-behaved young people crowding the pavements or drinking coffee at outdoor tables. If this all sounds a little too good to be true, the statistics bear it out: robbery and violent crime *are* rare, which is not to say that visitors should be complacent as opportunist thieves exist everywhere, and perhaps should be expected in a country that has suffered continual economic hardship for such a long period.

There are less savoury elements, of course, but you are unlikely to come across them unless you go out of your way to find them. It goes without saying that you should exercise more caution if visiting some of the rougher areas of the city, like the more run-down *bloks* of Novi Beograd or the impoverished Roma settlements near the river bridges. As in any city, you should avoid seemingly deserted streets and parks late at night. If there is any change from the current, relatively stable political situation, British FCO advice (*www.fco.gov.uk*) should be consulted and its counsel taken seriously.

Women

Women undergo no particular risks in visiting Belgrade – the majority of Serbian men are courteous in the extreme. Sexual harassment is not unknown but it is by no means commonplace. Some young Serbian women dress in a way that might seem quite provocative to North Americans and Western Europeans but relatively conservative dress is required when visiting churches or other religious institutions – no shorts, skimpy tops or short skirts.

WHAT TO TAKE

You can have the luxury of packing lightly when visiting Belgrade – if you do not have a particular item with you then the chances are that you will be able to buy it quite readily in the city at a fraction of its cost at home. Commonsense is required of course – personal medication should always be brought with you, and spectacle-wearers will probably not need reminding that they should bring a spare pair, and their own prescription sunglasses, essential in the summer glare. A plug adaptor (two-prong, round-pin) will enable you to use your own electrical devices whilst in the country, and, in considering such devices, a shortwave radio or an i-Pod is probably the most useful in terms of its size-to-satisfaction ratio. American 110-volt electrical devices will require an adapter to use the 220-volt European current.

Photographers need not worry too much about bringing adequate film stock along unless they require professional-quality slide film, which can be quite hard to find. Although there are now many foreign bank-friendly ATMs in the city, it is best to back up plastic with an emergency supply of cash – euro preferably, but dollars or sterling will suffice.

Insect repellent is a good idea as mosquitoes can be quite a nuisance in summer in the city. Kalemegdan Park can be particularly bad around dusk on a warm summer's night and the application of a repellent with a high 'deet' component is a wise precaution.

As for clothing, be prepared for cold in winter, early spring and late autumn, and anticipate the possibility of rain, even in the summer months, by bringing along a waterproof jacket or an umbrella.

ELECTRICITY

The current is 220 volts AC, 50Hz, with round, two-pin plugs. Both British and North American visitors will need to use a plug adaptor, readily available at airport shops.

MONEY

The official monetary unit is the dinar, usually abbreviated as din. At the time of writing there were approximately 124 dinar to the pound sterling, 83 to the euro, and 70 to the US dollar. In recent years, the Serbian dinar has become a reasonably stable currency and thankfully the days of hyperinflation are a thing of the past. Inflation is still high enough, however, for hotels to quote their rates in euro even though it is technically illegal to pay for your room using this currency.

The Serbian dinar is divided into 100 para, although these are almost never used. Banknotes come in denominations of 10, 20, 50, 100, 200, 1,000 and 5,000din; coins are 50para (rare), and 1, 2, 5, 10 and 20din. Current Serbian currency shows a nation still in transition: older coins and banknotes say 'Yugoslavia', whereas those from 2003 onwards are denoted 'Serbia' even though their designs are similar to the older notes.

Budgeting

Belgrade is a relatively inexpensive city and considerably cheaper than neighbouring capitals like Zagreb or Budapest. Even with the slightly higher prices that you might expect of a capital city, Belgrade remains a bargain: food, drink and transport are all very good value, and consumer items like clothing and CDs can be purchased at a fraction of their cost in western Europe. Prices are increasing in the city, however, in line with the country's current inflation figure of around 11%.

For some idea of costs: a meal with wine, depending on the exclusiveness of the establishment, will cost anything between 400 and 1,500din; an espresso coffee,

40–70din; a beer, 65–100din. A short taxi journey in the city should not cost much more than 150din or €2. Most museum entrance fees are low: 50–100din. Accommodation is not quite such good value, although this too is rarely prohibitively expensive. Allow €25–30 per night for a double room in a budget hotel; €40–60 for a mid-range and €100–150 for a four-star establishment.

Tipping

In cafés and run-of-the-mill restaurants, it is customary to round up the total rather than adding a percentage. In smarter establishments, 10% would be considered more than adequate. Although it is not necessary to tip taxi drivers rounding up the fare is considered normal and, naturally, any gratuity offered will be gladly accepted.

Money

Practicalities

CHANGING MONEY AND CREDIT CARDS
Changing money

Exchange rates vary very little between banks and exchange offices (*menjačnica*) and so it is not really worthwhile shopping around. As well as the usual manned outlets, there are also money exchange machines that accept euro, dollars or pounds sterling; you are required to feed your notes into the machine, which will then, hopefully, provide the correct equivalent in Serbian dinars.

Foreign exchange of cash can be performed at banks and post offices throughout the city, as well as at numerous small exchange offices where the transaction is usually much quicker. Euro usually get the best rate. Travellers' cheques are a little harder to change: branches of Raiffeisenbank or Komercijalna banka are probably the best bet but beware of high commission charges. For Eurocheques, branches of ProCredit Bank are probably the best bet. Neither personal nor travellers' cheques can normally be exchanged for goods in shops, so credit cards make far more sense.

Banks are generally open from 08.00 to 19.00 on weekdays and from 08.00 to 15.00 on Saturdays. Some banks and post offices are also open on Sundays.

Credit cards

It is usually far easier to withdraw cash from one of the city's numerous ATM machines. The most widely accepted credit cards are Visa, closely followed by

MasterCard, and cash can be withdrawn from ATMs bearing these symbols. Maestro and Electron debit cards may also be used where the symbol is displayed. American Express and Diners Club are not so well accepted, although they may be used in payment for goods in some shops, top hotels and car-rental agencies. Currently, there are no Diners Club or American Express-linked ATMs anywhere in Belgrade. It is worth remembering that, even for the payment of goods with MasterCard, you will need to know your PIN code.

Electronic banking is moving swiftly forwards but it is inevitable that there may be occasional hiccups. To be on the safe side, it is probably wise to carry more than one type of card if at all possible; say, two different credit cards – Visa and MasterCard – as well as a debit card.

Emergency help numbers for credit cards: Visa (011) 3011 550; MasterCard (011) 3010 160; Diners Club (011) 3440 622; American Express cardholders may be able to receive help from the emergency service of Komercijalna Banka (011) 3080 115.

For those arriving by plane, there is an ATM at the arrivals hall (downstairs) of Belgrade's Surčin Airport, which will accept Visa, Visa Electron, Visa Plus, MasterCard, Maestro and Cirrus cards.

Money transfer

The best way to arrange a fast transfer of funds from abroad is to make use of the services of Western Union Serbia (*www.wu.co.yu*). Whatever the currency your money is sent in, you will receive it in euro. All Serbian banks are members of

SWIFT, and so another alternative for money transfer is to open a bank account in Belgrade then arrange for a transfer. A SWIFT transfer will take between two and seven business days to come through.

Taking money out of the country

Foreign nationals may take a maximum of 120,000din in or out of the country in 1,000din banknotes or smaller. If you are travelling beyond Belgrade it is important to remember that the Serbian dinar is not used in either Montenegro or Kosovo, where the euro is the official currency. It is hard to exchange Serbian dinars at a reasonable rate in either of these places, and virtually impossible beyond, although dinars may be exchanged in some of the banks in Szeged, just across the Hungarian border. If flying in, there is little point in trying to obtain dinars in advance of your visit as cash can easily be exchanged at the airport for Serbian currency.

MEDIA
Newspapers

Serbia's biggest-selling daily newspaper is *Večernje Novosti*, closely followed by *Glas Javnosti* and *Blic*. The oldest and probably most prestigious is the 100-year-old *Politika*. Of the various news weeklies, *Vreme* is probably the most highly thought of, although its future remains in jeopardy because of low circulation figures.

All of the above newspapers are in Serbian only, although *Blic* does have an English-language digest on the web at www.blic.co.yu. It is usually possible to find day-old copies of some of the international press like *The Times* or the *New York Herald*, and possibly French, Italian and German newspapers, too, in the bookshops and postcard booths along Kneza Mihaila. The **Plato** newsagents [3 E5] next door to the Giros fast-food take-away on Vase Čarapića is a particularly good place to look.

Television

Serbia's state television network, RTS, was considered so powerful during the Milošević years that its headquarters became a legitimate target for NATO bombers in the 'war of propaganda'. Today, RTS has a much smaller share of the media, with independent channels like RTV Pink and BKTV equally, if not more, popular.

Another independent television station is TV B92, which grew out of the radio station, B2-92, a rebel voice that was very critical of the old regime. Although it does not have anything like the market share of Pink TV, which has 30%, or BKTV with about half this, B92 wields a disproportionate amount of influence thanks to its perceived integrity and the international respect it earned for its anti-Milošević stance during the late 1990s.

Radio

As well as two stations on state-run RTS Radio, other prominent broadcasters include **Radio Index** and **Radio B2-92**, which has live news radio on Real Audio and MP3.

Media

English-language broadcasting can be heard on the **BBC World Service**, which can be received on short wave at 6195 and 9410 kHz mornings and evenings; 12095 kHz throughout the daytime. **Voice of America** can be received on 9760 and 6040 kHz.

Internet news and information sources
ANEM www.anem.org.yu
BETA www.beta.co.yu
B92 www.b92.net
Belgrade Media Centre www.mediacenter.org.yu

COMMUNICATIONS
Telephones
Phone calls can be made from any post office, where you are directed to a booth and pay for a call when you have finished. The code for dialling abroad is 99; you then dial the country code then the city and the recipient's number. To phone Belgrade from abroad, you must first dial the international access code (which is usually 00), then 381 for Serbia; then you dial the city code 11 and the number. The telephone centre in the Main Post Office is open 07.00–midnight Monday to Friday and 07.00–22.00 at weekends; at the Central Post Office, calls can be made from 07.00–22.00 daily.

A simpler solution may be to buy a Halo card for 200, 300 or 500din from a booth and use it at one of the plentiful red Halo street phones; 300din gets you about 8–10 minutes to the UK. Unless you have an unlimited supply of cash do not be tempted to dial abroad from your hotel room as the tariffs charged are almost always inordinately steep.

Mobile phones

Mobile phones in Serbia all begin with 06 (063 for Mobtel, 064 for Telekom Srbija). The Serbian mobile-phone network is currently being developed and undergoing privatisation, which should see an improvement from what is currently a slightly ragged service.

063 Mobtel Bulevar umetnosti 16; ✆ 063 98 63; f 063 311 311 or 063 97 97; www.mobtel.co.yu
064 Telekom Srbija Makedonska 2; ✆ 064 789; www.064.co.yu

Useful telephone numbers

Serbian online telephone book www.telekom.yu
Important phone numbers Police 92, Fire department 93, Ambulance 94

Post

Belgrade's **Main Post Office** is located on Tavoska 2, near Sveti Marko Church, while the more conveniently located **Central Post Office** [3 E5] is at Zmaj Jovina 17. Other branches are at: Slobodana Penezića Krcuna 2, Šumadijski trg 2a, and at

Glavna 8 in Zemun. They are all open 08.00–20.00 weekdays, 08.00–15.00 Saturdays, with some branches also opening on Sundays.

The cost of sending a postcard to elsewhere in Europe is 35din. Letters cost 35din for those weighing less than 35g, 41din for up to 45g and then the tariff increases with 10g increments. Post from Serbia to the United Kingdom takes between a week and ten days. All of the major express courier companies like DHL and FedEx have offices in Belgrade.

The basic ZIP code for Belgrade is 11000.

Express mail couriers

DHL Omladinskih brigada 86; ✆ 3181 844
FedEx Express Autoput 22; ✆ 3149 075
RGV Express Belgrade Airport; ✆ 601 555, ext 2409
TNT Cvijićeva 60; ✆ 769 232
UPS Belgrade Airport; ✆ 601 555, ext 2112

Internet

Internet cafés come and go in the city; some of those published in city listings no longer operate. Below is a list of those that were all open for business on last inspection. The usual charge is in the order of 60–80din per hour.

Cybershark Tržni centre, Trg Republike, on the first floor of the Tržni centre opposite Trg Republike [4 G6] Open 24 hours. 80din per hour.

Maverik Makedonska 22; ☎ 3222 446 [4 G7] Inside the Dom Omladine Centre, on the first floor above the Living Room café.

McDonald's Terazije. Conveniently situated and free (!) but not always working.

Nethole Nušićeva 3 [4 F8] This place is a 'hole' in the sense that it is down in a basement. Various computing and copying services are available. 80din per hour.

Plato Akademski plato 1; ☎ 3030 633 [3 E5] The most popular with visitors to the city, this is found at the back of the Plato bookshop, underneath the café of the same name. 50din per half-hour.

Wi-Fi is available at a few locations in Belgrade if you have a laptop that comes complete with Wi-Fi technology.

Hot Spot Café Studentski trg 21 [1 D4]
Hotel Moskva Balkanska 1
Lava Bar Kneza Miloša 77
Municipality of New Belgrade (lobby) Bulevar Mihaila Pupina 167

EMBASSIES

Albania Bulevar mira 25A; ☎ 3065 350; f 665 439; e albembassy_belgrade@hotmail.com
Australia Čika Ljubina 13; ☎ 624 655; f 624 029, 628 189, 3281 941 (Visas Department); e austemba@eunet.yu; www.australia.org.yu
Austria Kneza Sime Markovića 2; ☎ 3031 956, 3031 964, 635 955; f 635 606; e OB@bmaa.gv.at

Belgium Krunska 18; ☎ 3230 016, 3230 017, 3230 018; f 3244 394;
e embassy@belgium.org.yu

Bosnia-Herzegovina Milana Tankosića 8; ☎ 3291 277, 3291 993, 3291 995, 3291 997;
f 766 507; e ambasadabih@yubc.net

Bulgaria Birčaninova 26; ☎ 3613 980; f 3611 136; e bulgamb@Eunet.com

Canada Kneza Miloša 7; ☎ 3063 000; f 3063 042 (Consular section: ☎ 3063 039; f 3063
040); e bgrad@dfait-maeci.gc.ca; www.canada.org.yu

Croatia Kneza Miloša 62; ☎ 3610 535, 3610 153; f 3610 032 (Consular section: Mirka
Tomica 11; ☎ 3613 592, 3670 076; f 3670 078); e croambg@eunet.yu

Czech Republic Bulevar Kralja Aleksandra 22; ☎ 3230 133, 3230 134; f 3236 448;
e belgrade@embassy.mzv.cz

Denmark Neznanog Junaka 9a; ☎ 3670 443; f 660 759

Finland Birčaninova 29; ☎ 3065 400; f 3065 375; e finembas@eunet.yu

France Pariska 11; ☎ 3023 500; f 3023 510 (Consular section: ☎ 3023 561; f 3023 560);
e ambafr_1@eunet.yu; www.france.org.yu

Germany Kneza Miloša 74–76; ☎ 3064 300; f 3064 303; e germemba@tehnicom.net
(Consular section: Bircaninova 19A; ☎ 3615 282, 3615 290, 3615 323; f 3612 607;
e germcons@tehnicom.net)

Greece Francuska 33; ☎ 3226 523; f 3344 746 (Consular section: Strahinjica Bana 76;
☎ 3341 507; f 3344 746); e office@greekemb.co.yu; www.greekemb.co.yu

Hungary Krunska 72; ☎ 4440 472, 4447 479, 4447 039, 4443 739; f 3441 876;
e hunemblg@eunet.yu

Israel Bulevar Mira 47; ✆ 3672 400, 3672 401, 3672 402, 3672 403; **f** 3670 304
Italy Birčaninova 11; ✆ 3066 100; **f** 3249 413; **e** italbelg@eunet.yu; www.italy.org.yu
Netherlands Simina 29; ✆ 3282 332, 3281 147, 3281 148, 3282 127; **f** 628 986;
e info@nlembassy.org.yu; www.nlembassy.org.yu
Norway Užička 43; ✆ 3670 404, 3670 405; **f** 3690 158; **e** emb.belgrade@mfa.no
Poland Kneza Miloša 38; ✆ 3615 287, 3615 297; **f** 3616 939; **e** ambrpfrj@Eunet.yu
Portugal Vladimira Gaćinovića 4; ✆ 662 895, 662 894, 662 897; **f** 662 892;
e embporbg@yubc.net
Romania Kneza Miloša 70; ✆ 3618 327; **f** 3618 339 (Consular section: ✆ 3618 359)
Russian Federation Deligradska 32; ✆ 657 533, 658 251, 646 068; **f** 657 845 (Consular
section: ✆ 3610 192, 3613 964); **e** ambarusk@eunet.yu
Slovak Republic Bulevar Umetnosti 18, Novi Beograd; ✆ 3010 000; **f** 3010 020, 3010 021;
e skembg@eunet.yu
Spain Prote Mateje 45; ✆ 3440 231; **f** 3444 203; **e** embajada@sezampro.yu or
embespyu@mail.mae.es; www.spanija.org.yu
Switzerland Birčaninova 27; ✆ 3065 820, 3065 825 (Consular section: ✆ 3065 815); **f** 657
253
Sweden Pariska 7; ✆ 3031 600; **f** 3031 601 (Consular section, ✆ 627 047; **f** 3031 602);
e swedeemb@eunet.yu
Turkey Krunska 1; ✆ 3235 431, 3235 432; **f** 3235 433; **e** turem@eunet.yu
UK Resavska 46, ✆ 645 055, 3060 900, 3615 660, 642 293, **f** 659 651 (Consular section,
✆ 3061 070); **e** ukembbg@eunet.yu; www.britemb.org.yu]

Embassies

USA Kneza Miloša 50; ☎ 3619 344, 361 3041, 361 3909, 361 3928; f 361 5489; www.usemb-belgrade.rpo.at

HOSPITALS/PHARMACIES
State-run clinics

Clinical Centre of Serbia (Klinički Centar) Pasterova 2; ☎ 3617 777
Emergency Centre (Urgentni Centar) Pasterova 2; ☎ 3618 444
KBC Zemun Bežanijska kosa bb, Zemun; ☎ 667 122, 660 666
KBC Zvezdara Dimitrija Tucovića 161; ☎ 3406 333

Private clinics

Bel Medic Viktora Igoa 1; ☎ 3065 888. Open 24 hours, with ambulance for emergencies.
Dr Ristić policlinic Narodnih heroja 38, Novi Beograd; ☎ 2693 287
Medicom Braničevska 8/I; ☎ 3443 781
Petković Clinic Maglajska 19; ☎ 667 078
Senjak Koste Glavnića 9; ☎ 3692 724

Dentists

AB Poželka 77/V; ☎ 3544 299
Beldent Brankova 23; ☎ 634 455. An Italian-trained dentist who speaks Italian and some English.
Orthodent Strahinjića bana 33; ☎ 188 327

Sava dent Krunska 6a; ✎ 3238 028
Super dent Sazonova 116a; ✎ 404 350
Zepter Dental Clinic Kralja Petra 32; ✎ 3283 880, 3283 881, 3283 882

There are **24-hour dentists** on duty at Obilić venac 30; ✎ 635 236, and Ivana Milutinovića 15; ✎ 4441 413.

Pharmacies (24 hour)
Prima 1 Nemanjina 2; ✎ 3610 999, 644 968. Open every day of the year.
Sveti Sava Nemanjina 2; ✎ 643 170
Zemun Glavna 34; ✎ 618 582

RELIGIOUS SERVICES
The majority of Belgrade's churches are Orthodox although there are a few Catholic, Baptist, Reformist and Adventist churches in the city too. The Tourist Organization of Belgrade can give advice on service times. There is just one place for Muslim worship, the Bajrakli Mosque (*Gospodar Jevremova;* ✎ *2622 428*) and a solitary synagogue at Maršala Birjuzova 19.

TOURIST INFORMATION
The main branch of the helpful **Tourist Organisation of Belgrade** (TOB) is down the underpass at the bottom of Kneza Mihaila in Terazije Passage near the 'Albanija' building (✎ *635 622;* f *635 343* [4 F8]). It is open Monday to Friday

09.00–20.00, Saturday 09.00–17.00 and Sunday 10.00–16.00. There is a smaller branch nearby at Kneza Mihaila 18 (☎ 2629 992 [3 E6]), which is shared with the **National Tourist Organisation of Serbia** and is open Monday to Friday 09.00–21.00, Saturday 09.00–17.00 and Sunday 10.00–16.00. Another branch is at the Central Railway Station, which has a useful exchange office next door (☎ *3612 732, 3612 645; open Monday to Friday 09.00–20.00, Saturday 09.00–17.00, Sunday closed*). In addition, TOB have a counter at Belgrade Airport (☎ *601 555 or 605 555, ext 2638*), which is open daily between 09.00 and 20.00 to meet incoming flights. All of these can issue city maps, hotel listings and a copy of *Welcome to Belgrade* magazine, as well as advise on current events in the city. The *This Month in Belgrade* booklet is also useful. TOB has its own useful and informative website at www.tob.org.yu.

For more general information about Serbia as a whole the National Tourist Organisation of Serbia (NTOS) also has useful information on its website at www.serbia-tourism.org.

LOCAL TOUR OPERATORS

The **Tourist Organisation of Belgrade** run a couple of good-value bus tours: a city sightseeing tour that leaves every Sunday at 10.00, lasting 90 minutes and costing 200din, and a three-hour guided tour to the Vinča archaeological site that leaves on Saturdays at 11.00 and costs 280din. Both tours depart from near their head office at Trg Nikole Pašiča. They can also arrange guided walking tours of the

Belgrade fortress and Stari Grad and coach tours of Belgrade's churches and Old Zemun. The tourist office run regular river pleasure cruises and can book railway trips and group visits to the Royal Compound at Dedinje (see *Sightseeing*, pages 237–9). If you wish to travel beyond the city TOB also have a number of day trips available: a wine tour to the Fruška Gora, an excursion to the naïve art centre of Kovačica and a tour to Manasija Monastery.

Argus Tours Svetog Save 6; ℘ 4444 463, 3443 297, 3443 172; e info@argus.co.yu; www.argus.co.yu. Mostly deal with outbound travel but can arrange two-day Vojvodina tours as well as air tickets.

Belgrade Sightseeing is a tourist service headed by Branko Rabotić, a licensed guide who speaks English, Serbian and Greek. Mr Rabotić is very knowledgeable about Belgrade's history and organises a range of private tours and city walks, as well as multi-day excursions further into the Serbian countryside. Prices are available on request but should be in the order of €80 and up for the Belgrade Highlights Tour, which includes a Belgrade sightseeing tour by car and a walking tour. In addition, short walking tours around the Old Town are available from about €30 per group. Belgrade Sightseeing is also able to provide hotel booking and airport transfer services. Contact details: Mr Branko Rabotić MA; ℘/f 4461 153; GSM (+38163) 854 2648 (calls to GSM from inside Serbia 063 854 2648); e rabotic@EUnet.yu. The website is highly informative with Serbian-language and hotel-booking links: http://solair.eunet.yu/~rabotic. Alternatively, try http://rabotic.tripod.com.

Belgrade Tourist Guide Association Kalemegdan Fortress Information Centre; ✆ 3547 865; f 622 452 [1 A2] This is a collective of trained multi-lingual guides who can guide you around the fortress or further afield in the city and beyond. Their prices start at about 1,500din for a 90-minute fortress tour.

Five Star Travel Studentski trg 10; ✆ 3284 651, 3285 078; f 636 619; e fivestar@tehnicom.net. Five Star Travel organise Danube cruises with wine tasting as well as overnight 'Blue Train' excursions to Vrnjačka Banja.

Glob Metropoliten Tours Dositejeva 26; ✆ 2626 899, 2622 620; f 2181 181; e glob@metropoliten.com; www.metropoliten.com. This company's excursions include Belgrade musical weekends, walking tours and two-day monastery trips. They can also arrange tickets and car hire.

Jolly Travel Kneza Miloša 9; ✆ 3232 393; f 3341 843; e office@jolly.co.yu; www.jolly.co.yu. Jolly mainly deal with domestic travel needs but they can arrange tours for visitors in Belgrade and beyond, and assist with car hire and booking airline tickets.

Putnik Dragoslava Jovanovića 1; ✆ 3232 911, 3230 699, 3240 022; f 3242 278, with another branch at Terazije 27; ✆ 3232 473; www.putnik.com. Putnik used to be the Yugoslav state tourist agency but the company has now been bought by a Serbian-American who is keen on modernising and expanding its operational base. Putnik can organise city tours for individuals or small groups and boat tours with dinner and folk music for groups of 30 or more.

Top Tours Bulevar Kralja Aleksandra; ✆ 2450 452; f 2452 590; e toptours@eunet.yu; www.toptoursad.com. This operator runs a number of sightseeing excursions of the city in addition to tours to Vojvodina and the monasteries of central Serbia. They can also organise weekend stays in Belgrade and airport transfers.

Zepter Passport Travel Company Kralja Petra 32; ℄ 3281 414; f 3288 368; e travel@passport.zepter.co.yu [1 C4] Run half-day tours to the naïve art centre of Kovačica and one-day tours to the monasteries of Fruška Gora.

For the purchase of tickets, both **BAS** at the bus station (℄ 638 555) and **Turist Biro Lasta** (*opposite at Milovana Milovanovića 1;* ℄ 641 251) sell bus tickets, as well as **Putnik**. Train information and tickets may be obtained from the English-speaking staff at **KSR Beogradturs**, Milovana Milovanovića 5 (℄ 641 258), avoiding the crush and possible communication difficulties at the station itself. They do not charge commission. They also have a branch at Dečanska 21 (℄ 3235 335).

RIVER PLEASURE CRUISES

River services between Belgrade and other Serbian towns used to run in the past and there is some hope that pleasure cruises may restart in the next year or two.

The Tourist Organisation of Belgrade runs local river cruises during the summer months, beginning at the quay by the Hotel Jugoslavija. The boats sail past Lido beach in Zemun, around Veliko Ratno Island in the confluence of the two rivers, and past the 'May 25' Sports Centre in Dorćol; then they turn south to pass Kalemegdan Fortress and the Orthodox Cathedral, heading under the Sava River bridges as far as Ada Ciganlija Island before returning north past the Museum of

Contemporary Art to the quay. Boats leave at 16.00 and 18.00 on weekends, and at 18.00 during the week; there is no service on Mondays. The trip takes approximately 90 minutes and costs 300din for adults, 150din for children aged six to 14, and free for children less than six years old. They also run occasional nighttime trips with onboard music and refreshments.

RAILWAY LEISURE TRIPS

On some summer weekends, excursions with the *Romantika* steam train take place between Belgrade and Sremski Karlovci, near Novi Sad. The *Romantika* departs from Belgrade at 08.45 and returns to arrive back there at 19.55. The Magelan Corporation Tourist Agency of Novi Sad arranges tours that can be pre-booked to meet the train at Sremski Karlovci, visiting the Peace Chapel, the Krušedol and Gregteg monasteries and the museum house at Neradin. Lunch is also included. Return train tickets cost between 370 and 560din, depending on class; for children between four and 14, 300din. The excursion costs 800din for adults, 500din for children.

Another summer steam excursion operates in summer between Belgrade and Smederevo, leaving Belgrade at 08.15 and arriving in Smederevo at 10.45, where a tour can be arranged of the town and its museums before the train returns to Belgrade at 18.00, arriving at 20.15. Lunch can also be booked at a traditional restaurant 5km from the town with transport to and from provided.

For the precise dates of these weekend excursions enquire at a TOB office. The tours can be booked at several travel agents, including branches of Putnik and KSR

TITO'S 'BLUE TRAIN'

One possibility for the future may be to take a trip using Tito's famous 'Blue Train'. This has recently been rescued from an engine shed in the suburb of Rakovica and refurbished for commercial use. The train was considered to be one of the world's most luxurious when it was built in 1947 and Tito used it to travel around Yugoslavia promoting socialism from his 'hotel on wheels'. He also used it to entertain world leaders like Brezhnev, Arafat and Nehru. From his first journey until the end of his life Tito negotiated with over 60 world statesmen, and travelled more than 600,000km, on this train. Its last journey was in 1980 when the train was used to bring his coffin along mourner-lined tracks all the way to Belgrade from Ljubljana.

Serbian Railways have recently decided that it is time the train earned a living once more. The first tourist trip took place on 31 December 2004 between Belgrade and the spa of Vrnjačka Banja. The train remains as luxurious as ever, retaining exactly the same fittings and furnishings as in its 1950s' heyday, all in Art Deco style with mahogany panelling, carpets and plush silk. Although currently there are no regular excursions the train is now available for lease (at around €2,500 a trip) for glamorous journeys to Subotica, Užice and Vrnjačka Banja.

Beogradturs and Agencija Romantika Travel at Balkanska 52–54 (↘ *683 056, 683 046*).

ADVENTURE TOURS BEYOND THE CITY

You might wish to combine your time in the city with something more energetic in the beautiful Serbian countryside.

Magelan Corporation Zmaj Jovina 23, Novi Sad; ↘ 021 420 680, 4722 028; e office@magelancorp.co.yu; www.magelancorp.co.yu. Magelan run eco-adventure and birdwatching tours in Vojvodina. They are based in Novi Sad but can organise trips starting from Belgrade too.

ACE Cycling and Mountaineering Centre B Krsmanovica 51/8, Niš; ↘ 064 2476 311, 018 47 287; f 018 43 197; e info@ace-adventurecentre.com; www.ace-adventurecentre.com. Based in Niš but able to arrange transport from Belgrade, ACE have a variety of cycling, hiking and mountain-biking tours to choose from. They can also design a bespoke tour according to their clients' specifications.

Tito's 'Blue Train'

Local transport

AIRPORT TRANSFER

Belgrade's Surčin Airport (*code: BEG; for enquiries, ☏ 601 555, 605 555*) lies 20km west of the city. After passing through immigration you enter the arrivals hall that has a money exchange, an ATM machine and a tourist information counter. The airport taxi drivers will conjure a price of between €15 and €30 to go into town, whereas the true cost should be something more like €8–10 for the 30-minute journey. Rather than leaving it to chance, it is a much better idea to get the tourist information counter at the arrivals hall to phone a taxi for you. The alternative is to take the bus, which is almost as easy. There are two options: city bus 72, which leaves every 20–30 minutes from outside the main terminal building and terminates at Zeleni venac close to Terazije and Kneza Mihaila, or the official JAT bus that departs every hour from 07.00–20.00, and which will take you to the Hotel Slavija at Trg Slavija downtown, stopping in Novi Beograd and the railway station (probably the most useful stop for most of Belgrade's hotels) along the way. The city bus costs just 50din, the JAT bus 160din.

Getting a taxi to take you from the city centre to the airport for a fair price is far easier. Once again, you could take the bus: JAT buses leave from the Hotel Slavija on the hour from 05.00 until mid evening.

Arriving by train or bus brings you right into the city centre itself, as both the **main railway station** (Železnička Stanica Beograd) and the **central bus station**

(Beogradska Autobuska Stanica, БАС in Cyrillic) lie next door to each other on busy Karađorđeva, one of Belgrade's main thoroughfares. Both stations possess a *garderoba* – a left-luggage office – and currency-exchange facilities, and there is also a small tourist office at the entrance to the train station (*open Monday to Friday 09.00–20.00, Saturday 09.00–17.00, Sunday closed*). Currently there are no ATM machines at either of the stations but both have exchange offices for cash.

Unless you have elected to stay in New Belgrade across the river, it will be a relatively short, uphill walk from here to your chosen hotel. The taxis parked up in front of the stations are more likely to agree to use their meter than those at the airport but if they do not agree to this, then it is easy enough to flag down one that is passing. The fare to any of the central hotels should be little more than €2. Alternatively, any one of trams number 2, 11 or 13 passing right to left in front of both stations will take you up to Kalemegdan Park, a short distance from Studentski trg. The fare is 30din if you pay the driver or 20din if you buy a book of tickets from one of the snack booths at the bus station beforehand. Be aware that the tram may be crowded and could be a trial if you are carrying much luggage.

International train services to and from Serbia terminate and depart from the main railway station, although some trains may stop at suburban stations on the way as well. Through-tickets may be bought on services to Zagreb, Budapest, Ljubljana, Thessaloniki, Skopje and Bucharest, or even to more far-flung destinations like Moscow or Istanbul. International buses run as far as Scandinavia and Istanbul. For international journeys, trains are generally a better bet but for domestic journeys within Serbia buses are usually faster and more reliable, the exception being the marvellously scenic train journey to Bar on the Montenegrin coast.

In planning your exit from Belgrade, either station will give you an opportunity to get to grips with the Cyrillic alphabet, although the train station does have boards in Latin script announcing *Dolasci* – arrivals – and *Polasci* – departures.

For information and reservations:

Bus station ↘ 636 299
Railway station ↘ 636 493

BUSES AND TRAMS

Belgrade has a comprehensive bus, trolleybus and tram network, which is cheap but invariably crowded at rush hour. One of the most useful routes for visitors is the tram service that runs between the Old Town and the bus and railway stations – the aforementioned numbers 2, 11 and 13 – as well as the trolleybuses that connect Trg Slavija with Kalemegdan – numbers 19, 21, 22 and 29. Do not neglect to buy a ticket and make sure that you get it cancelled in the machine on board as you will run the risk of having to pay a fine if caught. A ticket purchased in bulk from a booth costs only 20din. It costs 30din if you pay the driver.

Bus routes

These have the most extensive coverage, plying every corner of the city on both sides of the Sava River.

Local transport

USEFUL BUS, TRAM AND TROLLEYBUS ROUTES

There is such a confusing network of buses, trams and trolleybuses in Belgrade that trying to use it may seem more trouble than it is worth; after all, taxis are plentiful and inexpensive. There are, however, a few routes that are extremely convenient and service those travellers whose needs are those of a sightseer rather than a commuter.

Tram 2, 11, 13 Karađorđeva (railway/bus station) to Pariska (Kalemegdan)
Tram 3 Tašmajdan Park to Rakovica Monastery
Tram 7L Tašmajdan Park to Jurija Gagarina and Buvlja pijaca (New Belgrade)
Trolleybus 19, 21, 22, 22L, 29 Trg Slavija to Trg Republike
Trolleybus 41 Studentski trg to Bulevar Mira ('House of Flowers')
Bus 31 Studentski trg to Bulevar JNA (St Sava's Church)
Bus 15, 84, 704E, 706 Pijaca 'Zeleni venac' to Hotel Jugoslavija and Zemun
Bus 72 Pijaca 'Zeleni venac' to Surčin Airport
Bus 1A Pijaca 'Zeleni venac' to Ada Ciganlija

Trolleybus routes

These are more limited and run mostly between Stari Grad, Trg Slavija and the southwest of the city. Trolleybuses do not operate in New Belgrade.

Tram routes

Cranky old trams trundle along a few well-placed routes that link the city centre with Stari Grad. There are also a couple of routes that delve into the city's southern extremities (Tram number 3 terminates near Rakovica Monastery). A single line crosses the Sava into New Belgrade.

TRAINS

Beovoz is a limited local service within the city that runs – mostly underground – between Železnička Kolonija at Zemun-Novi Grad, Novi Beograd, Nova Železnička 'Prokop' (sometimes referred to as 'Beograd Central') near Hajd Park, Karađorđev Park and Beograd-Dunav by Pančevački most on the south bank of the Danube. These city stops lie on a line that connects the city with Pančevo to the northeast and Batajnica to the northwest. Belgrade's main railway station is *not* part of this network. Trains run at more or less hourly intervals to connect these two towns, with a more frequent service running between Belgrade Pančevački most and Pančevo.

TAXIS

For many, taxis are a better option than buses or trams for getting around town. Not only are they cheap but their appeal is strengthened with the knowledge that, with the exception of the airport-based operators, cab drivers in Belgrade are usually honest and helpful, although those lurking in wait outside the train and bus

THE UNDERGROUND THAT NEVER WAS

At the edge of Ćirila i Metodija Park in the city centre, under the whiskery gaze of Vuk Karadžić whose statue graces the western corner, are several entrances that lead down to what appears to be an underpass. But there is more to this than you might imagine: this is the location for the only station on Belgrade's metro. The station, known simply as Vukov spomenik ('Vuk's Statue') was to be part of an underground system that never came to fruition, and which, as things turned out, ended up being one of the city's biggest white elephants. It was built during the Milošević period in 1995 as the first component of what would be a comprehensive underground network but the turn of events in Serbia in the late 1990s resulted in the country having far more pressing needs than that of a highly expensive underground railway. The part that was completed is well worth seeing, even if it is a bit surreal. A number of entrances lead down to a stylish atrium in brushed steel from where escalators plummet down further to the platform. The station has since found use as a stop on the Beovoz line that plies between Zemun and Pančevo.

stations are more likely to overcharge than one hailed on the street. A typical fare for a short city ride is 100–150din. There are a few cowboys of course, but a genuine registered taxi can be recognised by a clear plastic sign on the roof, a functioning meter and a sticker in the window displaying its rates. They are marginally more expensive at night and on Sundays. Dependable companies which may be called up are: **Alfa** (✆ 4441 113), **Alo** (✆ 5322 888), **Bell** (✆ 2351 212), **Beltaxi** (✆ 9808), **Beogradski** (✆ 9801), **Beotaxi** (✆ 970), **Lux** (✆ 3248 888), **Palma** (✆ 3162 020), **Plavi** (✆ 555 444), **Pink** (✆ 9803), **Naxi** (✆ 157 668), **Yellow Cab** (✆ 970), **Zeleni** (✆ 3246 088) and **Žuti** (✆ 9802).

CAR HIRE

Unless you plan to travel beyond Belgrade, driving in the city is probably best avoided as the city is easily covered by a combination of foot, bus, tram and cheap taxis. Like most big cities, secure parking can be a headache and not all hotels have their own car park. Parking is zoned in the city – red, yellow and green – with red being the most limited in time allowed. In the green zone you may pay for up to three hours' parking; in the red, just one. Tickets may be bought from kiosks in all three zones, or from a meter in the red zone.

Even outside the city driving can be pretty nerve-racking due to the lack of road signs and abundance of speed-crazed impatient drivers and vigilant traffic police. Speed limits of 60km/h in town, 80km/h on main roads and 120km/h on highways are strictly enforced. There is also a strict limit on the amount of alcohol permitted in the blood, currently 0.05%. A full driving licence and Green-Card insurance are necessary.

Avaco Trmska 7; ✆ 2433 797; f 3440 412 (08.00–16.00); m 381 64 184 5555; e avaco@yubc.net; www.avaco.co.yu. Their office is located off Bulevar Revolucije, with cars from around €30 per day for long-term hire, more for shorter periods. Minimum age is 21; at least two documents with photo and a deposit of €500–1,000 are required. Open 24 hours.

Avis www.avis.co.yu. Branches at: Bulevar Kralja Aleksandra 94 (✆ 433 314), Obilićev venac 25 (✆ 620 362), Hotel Intercontinental (✆ 3112 910), Maksima Gorkog 32 (✆ 4442 027) and at Belgrade Airport (✆ 2286 133).

Auto-Rent Belgrade Airport; ✆ 2286 388, 601 555 ext 3534; m 063 349 341; www.carrental.co.yu. Rent cars with drivers as well as self-drive.

Budget Hotel Hyatt Regency, Milentija Popovića 5; ✆ 137 703. At Belgrade Airport; ✆ 601 555, ext 2959.

Eminence 29 Novembra 15; ✆/f 3239 603; 24-hour m 063 397 266. Cheap rates for long-term hire (Yugo or Zastava).

Ineco have branches at Topličin venac 17 (✆ 639 319), Južni bulevar 40 (✆ 2452 160) and Belgrade Airport (✆ 601 555 ext 2732).

Putnik-Hertz have three city branches: Kneza Miloša 82 (✆ 641 566, 683 742), Belgrade Airport (✆ 2286 017) and Palmira Toljatija 9 (✆ 695 225, 3193 805). For reservations, phone 2659 567 or 2684 443.

YUTim rent-a car (previously Kompas Hertz) ✆ 692 339; f 609 730; e yutimrac@eunet.yu; www.yutim.co.yu. Branches at Bulevar Nikole Tesle 3, Hotel Jugoslavija and Belgrade Airport.

TOUR BUSES

Tours of the city by bus can be arranged through the **Tourist Organisation of Belgrade** at any of their offices. They run a sightseeing tour of the city by bus every Sunday at 10.00 leaving from Trg Nikola Pašića.

Top Tours AD Bulevar Kralja Aleksandra 130; ☏ 2450 452; f 2452 590;
e marija@toptoursad.com; www.toptoursad.com. These run regular three-hour bus tours of Belgrade's major sights.
Putnik Dragoslava Jovanovića 1; ☏ 3239 063, 3247 139; e gkonopek@putnik.com;
www.putnik.com. Putnik can arrange city tours by coach or by minibus according to the number of passengers.

CYCLING

As a rule, central Belgrade is not a great place for bicycles, as the combination of cobbled streets, tramlines and unheeding drivers make cycling more of a trial than a pleasure. There are places in the city, however, where leisure cycling is highly popular and where purpose-built tracks make it both safe and enjoyable. Such areas include the 8km track that borders the lake at Ada Ciganlija, parts of Kalemegdan Park, Košutnjak Park, and the promenades that run along the Sava and Danube riverfronts.

Belgrade has 35km of official cycle paths that stretch along two routes. Route A goes from the marina at the waterfront at Dorćol along the east bank of the Sava

River to Ada Ciganlija. Route B follows a circuit of New Belgrade between the Hotel Jugoslavija and Blok 45 to the south. Route A connects with Route B at Brankovo most, where there is now a bicycle lift to carry bikes up from the river cycleway to the higher level of the bridge.

Bicycle hire is available at several places along these designated paths: by the Hotel Jugoslavija in New Belgrade, a little further on in Zemun opposite Lido beach, in Dorćol by the '25 Maj' Sports Centre, and on Ada Ciganlija at the east end of the lake near the causeway.

Local transport

Accommodation

HOTELS

Most of Belgrade's hotels remain in state ownership and, although most have obliging and enthusiastic staff, a few of them tend to perpetuate the stereotypes of the socialist-era school of management. At the higher end of the market, the majority are perhaps geared more towards expense account-funded business conventions than to the tastes of foreign tourists. Nevertheless, Belgrade's better hotels are invariably spacious and comfortable.

Of late, there has been a welcome trend of new privately funded hotels opening up in the city. These are welcome additions to Belgrade's existing hotel stock and hopefully, in the future, a few more middle-range options will swell the ranks too. In addition to this, some of the older, established state-run hotels have been taken into private ownership and undergone renovation.

There is a degree of overlap between the mid-range and budget categories listed below. The stars awarded in each category should be taken with a pinch of salt, especially at the bottom end of the market, although the categorisation tends to be applied much more rigidly with the more recently opened, privately owned hotels.

As a rule, budget travellers are not particularly well catered for, although there are a couple of real bargains that should be reserved in advance. During busy periods such as the October Book Fair, budget-priced rooms are particularly hard to find. It is usually safer to book well ahead. There is a residency tax to pay of 84din a day that cheaper hotels tend to include in the price but more expensive ones usually do not.

Although accommodation must be paid for in dinars, prices are often quoted in euro – as indeed, they are below – to avoid amending rates according to fluctuations in the dinar.

In or near the Old Town
Luxury

Aleksandar Palas***** Kralja Petra I 13–15; ☎ 3305 300, 3305 326; f 3305 334; e aleksandar@legis.co.yu; www.aleksandarpalas.com [1 B4]

The Aleksandar Palas is a recently opened, privately owned luxury hotel that is under the same ownership as the adjoining Que Pasa? restaurant and is a member of the Great Hotels of the World alliance. Perfectly situated close to the Orthodox Cathedral, Kalemegdan Park and the pedestrian shopping street of Kneza Mihaila, the Aleksandar Palas offers just 9 luxurious apartments with facilities such as king-size beds, cable TV, DVD, internet lines and home cinema system. Each apartment has a bedroom, a tastefully furnished living-room and a bathroom. The bathrooms come complete with state-of-the-art shower cabins that include Turkish bath and Finnish sauna facilities. Because of its relatively small size, the hotel gets booked up weeks ahead and so it is best to make an early reservation here. The weekday suite rates (Mon–Fri) are €260 for apartments 1–8 and €360 for apartment 9, which is a duplex; the weekend rate is €220, with the duplex costing €320. Rates may be higher at times of high demand.

Upmarket

Le Petit Piaf*** Skadarska 34; ↘ 3035 252; f 3035 353; e office@petitpiaf.com; www.petitpiaf.com [4 H6]

Le Petit Piaf is a privately owned central hotel that first opened for business in September 2004. It is situated in the heart of Skadarlija behind the house of the writer and painter Đura Jakšić. The three stars do not do justice to the hotel's true status as, in many ways, the facilities and service at this small hotel are superior to some of those awarded four stars. For the time being the hotel has a bar, a restaurant and 2 terraces but it is looking to expand in the future. There are 7 dbl rooms and 5 suites, each with cable TV, internet access, direct phone lines and air conditioning. Rates are € 151 for sgl occupancy and € 181 for dbl; apartments are € 184–220. Most credit cards are accepted.

Majestic**** Obilićev venac 28; ↘ 3285 777; f 3284 995; e majestic@eunet.yu; www.majestic.co.yu [3 E7]

The Majestic enjoys an excellent, central location just off pedestrian-only Kneza Mihaila and close to a concentration of bars, clubs and restaurants. Some of the rooms have been recently renovated. The Majestic has a restaurant, a coffee shop, a summer terrace and garage. The hotel has 76 rooms in total (46 sgls, 26 dbls and 4 triples) at € 65–115. Also, 6 large apartments with rooftop terrace at € 120–150.

Moskva**** Balkanska 1; ↘ 2686 255; f 688 485; e recepcija@hotelhotelmoskva.co.yu; www.hotelmoskva.co.yu

Right in the heart of the city, the Hotel Moskva is actually one of Belgrade's most beautiful buildings with a very attractive Art Nouveau façade and lots of period charm. This well-appointed hotel, built in 1906 and reconstructed in 1973, is one of central Belgrade's better-known landmarks. There are genuine antiques in some of the rooms, while others are rather more prosaically furnished. The lobby is deceptively small, but the rest of the hotel is airy and spacious with high ceilings. Restaurant, aperitif bar, banquet hall, patisserie, business lounge, limited parking. There is an atmospheric coffee shop at street level. There are 132 rooms in total, with sgls starting at €56 and dbls from €92. Triple rooms and apartments are also available.

Palace**** Topličin venac 23; ✆ 185 585, 637 222; f 184 458; e office@palacehotel.co.yu; www.palacehotel.co.yu [3 C6]
This is another of the older city-centre hotels, in this case dating back to the 1920s. The Palace has an elegant façade, which is brightly lit at night, and 2 restaurants (the Classic in the lobby, and the Belgrade Panorama on the sixth floor that offers excellent city views) as well as bar, exchange office, casino, garage with car-wash service and all standard business facilities. The hotel has been recently privatised, with most rooms now refurbished or renovated; 71 rooms from €60–80, and 15 suites at €100.

Mid-range
Kasina*** Terazije 25; ✆ 3235 574/5; f 3238 257; http://kasina.stari-grad.co.yu [4 F8]
The Kasina has a very central location, close to Balkan and Moskva on Terazije, one of Belgrade's busiest thoroughfares. The sgl rooms are quite small but the dbls are good value.

A good bar and pavement café serves beer from its own small brewery. No private parking. All 84 rooms have recently been renovated. Sgls start at €33; dbls €55. There are also a few well-renovated apartments.

Union*** Kosovska 11; ☏ 3248 022, 172; f 3224 480; e h-unionoffice@bvcom.net; www.hotelunionbelgrade.com [4 H8]
Five minutes' walk from Trg Republike and the Serbian Parliament, this is a comfortable, well-kept hotel with helpful, obliging staff. The Union has recently been renovated and passed into private ownership. The larger dbls are particularly pleasant and represent very good value. All rooms have cable TV and free internet access is available on request. With 22 sgls, 28 dbls, 4 three-bed suites and 6 twin suites. The hotel's restaurant has live music some nights. Parking is available. Sgls are €33–37; dbls €51–69; triples €81; apartments €83–94. A 30% discount is offered at weekends.

Budget
Balkan** Prizrenska 2; ☏ 2687 466; f 2687 541 [4 F8]
This is another old central hotel, directly opposite the Moskva. An old-fashioned atmosphere pervades the Balkan with its smoky lobby area, smallish rooms and 1970s' décor. Nevertheless, it represents good value for money: given the hotel's bustling central location, the rooms are remarkably quiet, and the view from the upper floors is equal to that of the Moskva opposite but costs just half as much. The hotel has its own restaurant but the coffee-shop facilities across the road at the Moskva are more inviting. Sgls are €25; dbls €37.

Hotels

Royal * (formerly Toplice**, pronounced: *Taup-leetse*) Kralja Petra 56; ☎ 2634 222; f 626 459; e toplice@net.yu; www.hotelroyal.co.yu [1 D3]

Still occasionally referred to by its former name by some, this is actually Belgrade's oldest existing hotel, dating from 1886. The hotel has a superb location on a quiet street that runs across the top of Kneza Mihaila, close to many restaurants and bars, museums, Kalemegdan Park and Belgrade's solitary mosque. The Royal has its own restaurant, lobby bar (with cheap beer) and exchange facilities. This is a good inexpensive three-star choice but book well ahead. All of the reception staff speak English and are generally courteous and helpful. The year 2005 heralded the introduction of cable television and, although prices may have increased a little here of late, the service has improved too. There are 105 rooms: sgls €22–24, depending on facilities; dbls €30; triples €42; apartments €42–55. Room rates include a rudimentary breakfast of eggs, coffee and bread, served in the basement restaurant to a musical soundtrack that can include anything from Louis Armstrong singing *Wonderful World* to opera classics.

In the city centre
Upmarket
Slavija Lux**** Svetog Save 2; ☎ 2441 120; f 3442 931; e slavija_hotels@jat.com

Located 1km south of the city centre and railway station, towering over the thunderous traffic circling Slavija Square, and looking more like an office block than a place to sleep, this is notably more downmarket than those listed above. Owned and run by JAT, the national airline, the 'Lux' has rather a careworn feel to it. Sgl rooms cost €115; dbl rooms €153; apartments €185–203.

Mid-range

Metropol*** Bulevar Kralja Aleksandra 69; ↘ 3230 910, 919; f 3232 991;
e metropol@sezampro.yu

The Metropol is a pleasant 1950s' hotel, 1km from the city centre, next to Tašmajdan Park. This hotel had plenty of prestigious visitors in the 1960s and 1970s but its popularity has now been eclipsed somewhat. Marble lobby with an attractive aperitif bar, restaurant, garage, café, hairdresser, travel agency, guarded parking. The Metropol has a total of 211 rooms at 3,600–8,000din, as well as 6 suites at 16,000din. Levels II, VII and VIII are the most expensive.

Park*** Njegoševa 4; ↘/f 3234 722; http://park.stari-grad.co.yu

The Park lies about 1km from the city centre, within walking distance of the Belgrade Palace, the Student Cultural Centre, and the Nikola Tesla and Natural History museums, in a street full of designer cafés and bars. Some of the lower rooms may be noisy due to rush-hour traffic. The hotel has its own restaurants, bar and garage. There are 50 sgl rooms at €43–56, 70 dbls at €72–92, and 2 apartments at €132.

Rex*** Sarajevska 37; ↘ 3611 862, 3613 949; f 3612 965; e reservation@hotelrex-belgrade.com; www.hotelrex-belgrade.com

Another of the small concentration close to the railway station, this hotel was formerly known as the 'Turist' and originally more geared towards businessmen than tourists, despite the name. The hotel passed into private ownership in 2003 and many rooms have since been pleasantly renovated. Facilities include restaurant, coffee bar with terrace, conference hall and parking. With 37 sgls, 51 dbls and 2 suites in total, sgl rooms cost €55 in a renovated room, while dbls are €77; suites cost €104–132. Un-renovated rooms are available at a lower rate.

Budget

Astorija*** Milovana Milovanovića 1a; ☎ 2645 422; f 686 437; e astorija@astorija.co.yu; www.astorija.co.yu

The Astorija is located opposite the train and bus stations in a noisy, uninspiring part of town. The hotel has a restaurant, coffee shop, bar and parking spaces for its guests. The Astorija has 81 rooms in total, at prices of €25 for sgls, €40 for dbls and €66 for apartments.

Beograd** Balkanska 52; ☎ 2645 199; f 2643 746

Another one located near the railway station, the Beograd is one of the city's more basic hotels and could do with renovation. It has a restaurant and bar. There are 77 rooms in total: sgls €20; dbls €30; triples €42.

Bristol** Karađorđeva 50; ☎ 2631 895; f 637 453

Close to the bus station, with a restaurant, souvenir shop and bar, this is a reasonable budget choice. Credit cards are not accepted. Sgl rooms cost €20; dbls €34.

Centar (B category) Savski trg 7; ☎ 644 055; f 657 838

Not to be confused with the 'Central' in Zemun, the Centar is directly opposite the railway station, so handy for late-night/early-morning connections. The hotel has a dark, dingy brown lobby with helpful reception staff. It is quite basic and very 1970s in style, but reasonable value for the money. Because of its low price this hotel tends to get block-booked for months on end but, if you can get in, sgls go for around €12; dbls for around €18.

Dom** Kralja Milutina 54; ☎ 685 696; f 683 872; e hoteldom@eunet.yu
The Dom is situated a little way from the city centre, across the road from the Russian Embassy. Sgls go for €20; dbls €28–42.

Excelsior** Kneza Miloša 5; ☎ 3231 381; f 3231 951; e hotelexcelsior@beonet.yu; www.hotelexcelsior.co.yu
This is located close to the Parliament building, with restaurant, coffee shop and small conference hall. With a total of 80 rooms, sgls cost €28 and dbls €41.

Pošta** Slobodana Penzića Krcuna 3; ☎ 3614 260; f 643 961
As its name implies, this is found opposite the post office, over the road at the side of the railway station. The Pošta is a serviceable, if rather basic, hotel with its own inexpensive restaurant. Sgl rooms can be had for €20; dbls €30.

Prag*** Narodnog fronta 27; ☎ 3610 422; f 3612 691; e hotelprag@sezampro.yu; www.hotelprag.co.yu
Located in a small street halfway up the hill between the station and the Old Town, the Prag has its own restaurant, exchange office and bar. There are 116 rooms in total, with sgls costing €26–34, dbls €48–63 and triples €70–73.

Slavija 'A'** Svetog Save 1; ☎ 2450 842; f 2431 517; e slavija_hotels@jat.com
This hotel is the poor relation of the Slavija Lux. Like its more luxurious twin – the tower

next door – the Slavija 'A' is owned by JAT and the hotel serves as the drop-off and departure point for airport buses. Still, at least it has plenty of rooms in a crisis, with sgls available at €33 and dbls at €44.

Splendid*** Dragoslava Jovanovića 5; ☎ 3235 444; f 3243 298; e reservation@splendid.co.yu; www.splendid.co.yu

Dating from 1937, this hotel has a city-centre location, a small lobby and attached café-bar, parking and exchange office, but no restaurant. Splendid by name and splendid by nature if you can trust the sign by the door that proclaims, 'You can touch the star with us'. You can also get your legs shaved in the salon next door should the urge take you. A cluster of travel agencies are located nearby, including Putnik, whose staff make good use of the hotel's lobby bar. There are 18 sgls at €26–32 and 31 dbls at €39–46.

Taš** Beogradska 71; ☎ 3243 507; f 3238 027

Located to the east of Tašmajdan Park, above a sports centre, this offers restaurant, casino and parking amongst its facilities. Sgls are €26; dbls, €36.

Away from the centre
Upmarket
Best Western M**** Bulevar JNA 56a; ☎ 3972 560; f 3095 501; e office@hotel-m.com; www.hotel-m.com

About 4km from the city centre, in a wooded residential area close to the FC Red Star football stadium, this is, perhaps, best suited to business travellers and those travelling in groups or with their own transport. This modern, comfortable hotel, near the quiet upmarket Dedinje area, joined the Best Western group in 2000 when it was completely overhauled and renovated. Facilities include conference halls, nightclub, restaurant, aperitif bar, free parking facilities and hair salon. The 'M' has 173 spacious rooms at €110–130 for dbls, €85–110 for sgl occupancy; apartments €156–181.

Šumadija**** Šumadijski trg 8; ℩ 3551 161, 3554 255; f 3554 368; e office@hotelsumadija.com; www.hotelsumadija.com
This is another four-star choice located well away from the city centre at Banovo Brdo, halfway between Ada Ciganlija and Košutnjak, 7km from the city centre but just 2km from Sajam fairground. With 3 conference rooms and a business centre, the hotel is as much geared to business visitors as it is to tourists. All rooms were completely renovated in 2005 and are well appointed, with satellite TV, minibar, air conditioning and internet access. The hotel has a total of 74 rooms and 4 apartments, which cost €99 for sgls, €109–119 for dbls, and €149–159 for apartments. Weekend rates are about 20% lower.

Budget
Hotel N** Bilećka 57; ℩/f 3972 183; e office@hotel-n.co.yu; www.hotel-n.co.yu
At 5km from the centre, in the quiet suburb of Voždovac, this is also a long way out. With its own restaurant, parking and coffee shop, it claims 'Your pleasure is our idea'. Sgl rooms cost €24; dbls €37.

Mihailovac* Požeška 31; ☎ 3555 458; f 3555 127; e lvisa@verat.net
At Banovo brdo, 5km from the city centre, with a restaurant, parking and coffee terrace.
Sgls €25; dbls €30; triples €40.

Nacional*** Bežanijska bb; ☎ 601 122; f 601 177; e nacional@bitsyu.net;
www.hotelnacional.co.yu
Located 8km from the city centre on the E-70 highway, and reasonable value for those with
their own transport. The Nacional boasts a restaurant, aperitif bar and conference hall.
There is parking for guests. Rooms cost around €22 for sgls; €33 for dbls.

Srbija** Ustanička 127c; ☎ 2890 404; f 2892 462
This is another hotel, 4km from the city centre, that caters mostly for businessmen. It has a
restaurant, a bar, parking, disabled facilities, conference hall and non-smokers' rooms. No
credit cards are accepted. Rooms cost €24–35 for sgls; €33–50 for dbls.

Trim** Kneza Višeslava 72; ☎/f 3540 669
In Košutnjak, 9km from the city centre. Conference hall, restaurant, parking, TV, minibar. Sgls
€32; dbls €46.

New Belgrade and Zemun
Luxury
Beograd Inter-Continental***** Vladimira Popovića 10; ☎ 3113 333; f 3111 402;
e ihcbegha@eunet.yu

This top hotel, close to the Hyatt, is one with real historical connections for Balkans buffs. It was here that gangster, bank-robber, nationalist hero and alleged war criminal Arkan was killed by unidentified gunmen in January 2000 but don't let this put you off staying there – Arkan was hardly a typical guest. The Inter-Continental boasts an enormous lobby, several restaurants, sports centre, swimming pool, solarium, nightclub, tennis courts and the biggest banquet hall in the city. A very good buffet breakfast is included in the price. Altogether, the hotel has a total of 415 rooms and suites, some non-smoking, at rates of €185–225 per room; apartments €290. There is a slight reduction for sgl occupancy and rooms may also be available at the special promotional weekend rate of €90.

Hyatt Regency Beograd***** Milentija Popovića 5; ☎ 3011 182; f 3112 234; e admin@hyatt.co.yu; www.regency.belgrade.hyatt.com
This is close to the Inter-Continental, 1km from the city centre in Novi Beograd, next to the Sava Congress Centre, a modern concert and conference venue. Used by embassies for visiting VIPs, as well as by visiting businessmen and discerning tourists, the Hyatt interior welcomes you with a massive marble lobby area that resembles a classical temple. Beneath this is a lower lobby with an imaginative 'jungle theme' planting with a flowing water feature. Surrounding this sybaritic oasis is a number of smart fashion and gift shops, a gym and car rental. The rooms are spacious and elegant, with excellent views of the city from the upper floors, while the service is just the right balance between friendly and formal. The Hyatt has two good restaurants – Focaccio and Metropolitan Grill – and large tea room. Other facilities include: business centre, solarium, fitness centre with swimming pool,

Hotels

disabled facilities. Breakfast is not included in the basic price but Serbian, American or Continental varieties are all available with plentiful fresh juice and foreign newspapers. The hotel has a total of 308 rooms and suites for €225–325, slightly less for sgl occupancy; also, 43 apartments and suites with prices on request.

Zlatnik***** Slavonska 26, Zemun; ☏ 3167 511; f 3167 235; e office@hotelzlatnik.com; www.hotelzlatnik.com
Zlatnik is a new, privately owned hotel located in Zemun, 7km from Belgrade city centre. This modern hotel has 2 restaurants – national and seafood, both of which are highly rated – a conference hall and business centre, a gift shop and an aperitif bar. All rooms have air conditioning, cable TV, internet access and safe deposit boxes. Both garage parking and non-smoking rooms are also available. Sgls cost €120; dbls €146; apartments €160–296. Most credit cards are accepted.

Mid-range
Jugoslavija*** Bulevar Nikole Tesle 3; ☏ 2600 222; f 3194 005; e hotelyu@sezampro; www.hoteljugoslavija.com
In New Belgrade, on the banks of the Danube, 3km from the city centre. A good location if you have business in New Belgrade or intend to spend a lot of time visiting the numerous floating restaurants, cafés and nightclubs moored nearby. There is another Arkan connection here, in that he allegedly used to own the hotel's casino. This may or may not account for NATO bombing it in 1999, destroying the swimming pool, conference hall and some of the

rooms. The Chinese Embassy nearby was also famously hit in the same raid. This vast complex houses restaurants, cocktail bars, a post office, a hair salon and souvenir shops. Disabled facilities. There are 130 rooms at prices from €50–112 and 18 apartments at €136–192. The higher elevated rooms at levels VI–VIII are the more expensive ones.

Skala*** Bežanijska 3, Zemun; ☏ 3075 032; f 196 605
Located 6km west from the city centre in Zemun, a separate town that effectively serves as a suburb of Belgrade. This small hotel is privately run, with quiet, well-furnished rooms grouped around a covered courtyard. It has its own restaurant and garage. There are 16 rooms with satellite TV, minibar and air conditioning. Sgls are around €50; dbls €70.

Budget

Central (B category) Glavna 10, Zemun; ☏ 191 712; f 196 165
This is located 6km from central Belgrade and so is only 'central' in the sense of being in the middle of Zemun. The hotel has a restaurant; credit cards are not accepted. When I enquired about a room here the woman at the reception desk was very friendly but pointed out that the hotel had no heating – an important consideration in the cold winter months. There are 10 sgl rooms at €15; 18 dbls at €22; triples at €26.

Imperium*** Partizanska 19a, Zemun; ☏ 193 837; f 3164 773
This is a small, new guesthouse in Zemun with just 9 dbl rooms and one sgl. It is 6km from Belgrade centre, close to Zemun-Novi Grad railway station and the motorway north and west. Bed and breakfast costs about €20 per person.

Lav** Cara Dušana 240, Zemun; ✆ 3163 289; f 3162 648
Another budget choice in Zemun, 7km from the city centre, with its own restaurant and
private parking. Sgls €25; dbls €29;triples €39.

Putnik*** Palmira Toljatija 9; ✆ 697 221, 3191 444; f 692 534
In Novi Beograd, 4km from the city centre. In keeping with its surroundings, the Putnik is a
large concrete edifice that functions very much as a business hotel. It has two restaurants,
café-bar and exchange office, and a total of 83 dbls, 31 sgls and 6 suites along with plenty of
parking space. Rooms cost €20–35.

HOSTELS

Small privately owned hostels are mushrooming in Belgrade, offering cheap
accommodation for those who do not crave too much privacy. Most of these offer
similar facilities: dorm beds, kitchens, internet access, luggage storage and lockers.
Generally there is no curfew, which may be seen as an advantage or disadvantage
depending on how well you sleep. It should be noted that some of the
establishments below are only open seasonally.

Most of those listed below can be pre-booked on the internet at www.hostels.com,
www.hostelworld.com, www.hostelz.com or www.hostelbookers.com.

Black Kangaroo Kraljice Natalije (formerly Narodnog fronta) 39
A hostel located fairly close to the train station, with mixed dormitories at €12 per
person.

Hostel BG747 Novi Beograd, Aleksandra Dubčeka (formerly Tvornička) 58 (directly opposite Luda Adamiča 30); ☏ 319 3980; e bghostel@sezampro.yu; www.bg747.com
Located in New Belgrade not far from Hotel Jugoslavija and just a five-minute walk from Zemun, this is a good choice for self-catering families. There are 10 twin bedrooms each with their own bathroom and small kitchen. Free parking is available and free pickups are offered for groups of 3 or more. Beds cost €12 per person.

Jelica Milovanović Krunska 8; ☏ 3248 550, 3220 762; www.hostels.org.yu
This hostel has a good central location, close to the Parliament building. It should be booked in the same way as above as you are supposed to be a member of Hostelling International to stay here. However, an International Student Card might just do the trick. This is a good deal if you are here at the right time of year. The hostel is clean and newly renovated, and has 3–4 bedded rooms with showers, and 4–8 bedded rooms without. In the 3- or 4-bed rooms it costs €11 per bed; in the 4–8 bed rooms, €9 per bed. Group bookings can also be made at €9 per bed. There are also 4 private rooms – 2 sgl and 2 dbl – at a slightly higher rate. Facilities include a computer room, gym and a library. *The hostel is open sporadically, mostly during holiday periods: from 22 Dec–13 Jan, 1–4 Mar, 1–7 May and 22 Jun–31 Aug. Reception is open 08.00–12.00 and 17.00–23.00.*

King Aleksandar I Bulevar Kralja Aleksandra 75; ☏ 401 800, 3400 440; f 401 536; e kraljaleksandarhostel@yahoo.com; www.belgradehostels.com/kai/kai.htm
A large hostel located a 20-minute walk from the city centre. Open during the summer only from 1 Jul to 1 Sep. Sgl €18; dbl €14; triples €12; dorm €11 per person.

Open Belgrade Gospodar Jovanova 42; ✆ 064 258 8754, 064 167 6944, 064 150 5233;
e openbelgrade@gmail.com; www.openbelgrade.com
This is a new laid-back hostel with just 9 beds in an old house in Dorćol close to the city
centre. Beds cost €11 if booked through their own website. They also have a city
apartment for rent.

Star Hostel Kolarčeva 3; ✆ 063 196 7961
Located in a third-floor flat very close to Kneza Mihaila and Trg Republike, with a 6-bed
dormitory and a sgl for €10–12 per person per night with breakfast.

Studentski Grad (Student City) 'Dom I' Tošin bunar 143–151, Novi Beograd; ✆ 604 578
This student residence, which unfortunately is situated a long way from the action, provides
hostel accommodation during summer only, from 1 Jul to 30 Sep. The charge is around €11
for bed and breakfast.

Three Black Catz Čika Ljubica 3 [4 F6]
This small, unofficial hostel is just off Trg Republike at the very heart of the city. The Three
Black Catz is basically just a 6-bed dormitory and a communal living room. Facilities include
DVD and cable TV, and the youthful staff can advise on clubs and bars in the city. The hostel
offers security lockers, internet access, free coffee and the use of a kitchen. With dormitory
beds, no curfew and 24-hour reception it is squarely aimed at younger travellers and
represents good value if you do not object to felines or the slightly hugger-mugger
atmosphere of the place. Currently there is just one cat in residence. Bed with breakfast
costs €12 per person.

Accommodation

A final option might be the Youth Hostel 'Lipovačka Suma' (*Lipovačka, Barajevo;* ↘ *830 2184;* f *830 2134*). Unfortunately this is located 15km from the city centre. The good news is that beds cost only €5 per person and it is open all year round.

PRIVATE ACCOMMODATION

This is very hard to find in Belgrade. There may possibly be a few individuals hanging around the railway station who sidle up and offer you the option of a private room. Great discretion should be shown as these may turn out to be poor value. At least check the room out first before committing yourself or handing any money over.

CAMPING

There is nowhere to pitch a tent anywhere near the city centre although you may wish to consider the following:

Auto-kamp 'Košutnjak' Kneza Višeslava 17; ↘ 3555 127; f 3547 345
This is close to Topčider Park, to the south of the city centre. They do not have places for tents but have bungalows available for €20–35. The site is in a pleasant, leafy suburb and has plentiful sports facilities.

The nearest campsite outside the city is at **Dunav** at Batajnički put, Zemun (↘ *199 072;* f *610 425*) 12km northwest of the city centre. They charge 90din to camp, 90din for a car, 120din for a tent or a trailer and 120din to be connected to an electricity supply. They also have bungalows to rent for 900din.

Camping

Eating and drinking

FOOD AND DRINK

The long Ottoman occupation has clearly had some influence on Serbian food, especially in the wide range of grilled meats available. A typical meal might consist of *kajmak* – a sort of salty, cream-cheese spread – with bread to start, then a grilled meat like *čevapčići* with a salad. Fresh fruit is as likely to conclude a meal as any sweet dish. While wine is often chosen to accompany a meal, something stronger like a glass or two of *šljivovica* might well precede it as an aperitif. For many Serbians, lunch (*ručak*) is the main meal of the day, followed by something a bit lighter for dinner (*večera*).

For starter courses, smoked meats are a popular choice, with *dalmatinski pršut*, a lightly smoked ham, or *užički pršut*, a hard, smoked beef, frequently offered on menus. A delicious dip that can be spread on bread in the same way as *kajmak* is *ajvar*, made from spiced peppers and oil.

For the main course, the most popular meat dishes are *pljeskavica* (meat patties, usually a mixture of pork, beef and lamb, sprinkled with spices, then grilled and served with onion), *ražnjići* (shish kebabs of pork or veal), *čevapčići* (spiced minced meat kebabs), *leskovački čevapčići* (kebab with peppers), *mešano mesto* (mixed grill), *karađorđeva šnicla* ('Black George's schnitzel'), *medaljoni* (veal steak), *ćulbastija* (grilled veal or pork), *jagnjetina na ražnju* (spit-roast lamb), *jagnjeće pečenje* (roast lamb), *kapama* (lamb stew), *kolenica* (leg of suckling pig) or *kobasice* (sausages). Other

Serbian dishes combine meat with vegetables, as in *sarma* (minced beef or pork mixed with rice and stuffed inside pickled cabbage leaves), *podvarak* (roast meat with sauerkraut), *punjene tikvice* (courgettes stuffed with meat and rice), *đuveč* (pork cutlets baked with spiced stewed peppers, courgettes, tomatoes and rice) and *punjene paprike* (peppers stuffed with minced meat and rice).

Accompaniments to the above might include a *šopska salata* (chopped tomatoes, onions and cucumber with grated white cheese), a *mešana salata* (mixed salad – rather variable) or a *srpska salata* (tomatoes, onions, peppers and parsley); alternatively, you might choose something cooked like *pečene paprike* (roast peppers with garlic and oil).

Fish (*riba*) dishes can be very good but generally are more expensive than meat, as fish has to be brought a considerable distance from the coast. As well as seafood, freshwater fish are widely available too, and just as popular, especially *pastrmka* (trout) and *šaran* (carp).

If all of this sounds too much then you will be relieved to know that a wide range of international food is readily available in Belgrade and it is quite possible to spend some time here without ever sampling the national cuisine – it would be a pity though.

Snack food
Some of the tastiest food in Belgrade is that sold on the street and from bakeries. Apart from the ubiquitous *pljeskavica, senvić* and hamburger outlets, there are also

WHAT? NO MEAT? – VEGETARIANS IN BELGRADE

Serbs enjoy eating meat in as many ways as they can think of cooking it. This passion for animal flesh has resulted in a cuisine that can be daunting for vegetarians and health-food aficionados. If you are vegetarian you will need to declare, *'Ja sam vegetarijanac'* if you are a man, or *'Ja sam vegetarijanka'* if female. It's probably better to be more specific and say, *'Ne jedem meso'* – 'I don't eat meat' – perhaps adding, *'Ne jedem pileće meso, ribu ni šunku'* – 'I don't eat chicken, fish or ham' – just to be on the safe side.

Once you have clarified what you do *not* want to eat you can then try and work out what is available. There will always be salads – *šopska* or *srpska* – and probably roast peppers, *pečene paprika*. Eggs in various forms – omelettes etc – can usually be ordered, as can side dishes of vegetables, usually potatoes, French fries (*pomfrit*) and beans. If you are in luck, there will also be some freshly baked products on offer – *gibanica* (a sort of cheese and egg pie baked with filo pastry) or *zeljanica* (similar to *gibanica* but with chard, rather like the Greek dish *spanikapita*). These are usually served as starters but they are quite filling on their own. Other starters to consider are *ajvar* (a roast pepper and garlic purée) and *kajmak*, both delicious spread on fresh bread. Most places that serve pizzas and/or pancakes will also be able to provide a vegetarian option.

many establishments that sell *burek* (cheese or meat pies, sometimes with apple to cut the grease a bit). *Burek*, which is of Turkish origin, is often eaten with yoghurt and is more usually on sale in the mornings. Other popular snack choices are *gibanica*, a mouth-watering, flaky sour cherry strudel called *pita sa višnjama* and sometimes a range of mini pizzas. All of these are cheap and delicious, and an excellent choice for breakfast or a snack; servings are always generous.

Sweets and pastries

Many *poslastičarnica* (confectioners) offer table service and fresh coffee, together with a tantalising selection of delicious cakes (*torta*) and pastries (*kolač*) to choose from: the strudels (*štrudla*) in particular are quite wonderful. *Štrudla sa jabukama* is apple strudel, and *štrudla sa višnjama* is filled with sour cherries. Ice cream (*sladoled*) is as popular as it is in Italy and is available in just as many flavours. Another Serbian favourite is pancakes (*palačinke*), which come in a range of inventive sweet and savoury fillings.

Hot beverages

Coffee comes in a bewildering variety of forms: strong thick Turkish coffee (*Turska kafa*), cappuccino, espresso, Nescafé, iced coffee, flavoured coffee – everything, that is, apart from decaffeinated coffee, a concept that is not really understood in this part of the world. However you ask for it, it is invariably excellent. When ordering Turkish coffee, sugar is usually added at the beginning of the brew and so it is customary to

Food and drink

specify the amount of sweetening that you require (medium is *sredina*), although with foreigners they quite often let you add your own to taste. Tea (*čaj*) is also available but it usually tastes fairly weak and insipid to the British palate. For tea with milk, ask for *sa mlekom*, with lemon, *sa limunom*. Fruit and herb teas are also popular.

Alcoholic drinks

Many Serbian wines are very palatable. The best are probably the white wines (*belo vino*) that come from the Sremski Karlovci region in Vojvodina, but Serbia has a range of wines that come from various grape-producing regions such as Vršac and even Kosovo. Some red wines (*crno vino*) also come from Montenegro. Wine can be bought in restaurants and cafés by the bottle, by the glass or in carafes of various sizes. In a supermarket, a bottle of domestic wine will cost something in the order of 150–600din; in a restaurant, maybe double this.

Serbians are proud of their wines but generally more enthusiastic about the range of alcoholic spirits they produce. Experimentation with these products can be something of an adventure. *Šljivovica* is a sort of brandy traditionally made from plums, but *rakija*, which is normally a spirit made from grapes, tends to be used as a generic term for any sort of strong liquor. *Konjak* is, as its name implies, cognac, and *lozovača*, another form of grape brandy.

Beer (*pivo*), both draught and bottled, is very popular both as a drink in its own right and as an accompaniment to a meal. The most popular brands are probably Jelen, BIP (Beogradska Industrija Pivara), BG (Beogradsko Pivo), Weifert and

Montenegrin Nikšičko. Imported bottled beers, like Amstel, Heineken, Slovenian Laško and Efes from Turkey, are always more expensive: their popularity seems to owe more to their being a status symbol rather than anything to do with flavour.

Non-alcoholic drinks

Besides the usual Fanta, Sprite and Coca-Cola, a wide range of bottled fruit drinks is available, as well as the real thing in season. *Sok od pomorandža* is orange juice; *sok od jagode*, strawberry; and *sok od jabuka*, apple juice. Bitter lemon is also highly popular and for my money far more thirst-quenching than the other carbonated drinks. Although tap water is perfectly safe to drink, mineral water (*mineralna voda*) is easy to find.

RESTAURANTS

Belgrade abounds with restaurants, cafés and bars for all tastes and pockets. Cheapest and most plentiful are the ubiquitous fast-food places that sell *čevapčići, burek, pljeskavica* etc. Most of the 'international' cuisine is actually Italian, although Belgrade has representatives from all over the globe – French, Chinese, Japanese and even Indian are all represented.

Restaurants tend to be clustered in certain areas of the city, as do the café-bars. In the old city, many cafés, bars and restaurants line the pedestrian thoroughfare of Kneza Mihaila, as well as the side streets that lead off from it. In particular, Obilićev venac, by the Metropol hotel, has almost totally given itself over to stylish theme-bars, the haunt of young folk mostly, and the place to be seen sipping your cappuccino. Many of the bars also serve light snacks: pancakes, sandwiches, ice creams and the like. For heavier fare, there is a dense concentration of Serbian 'national' restaurants that run all the way along the short length of Skadarska, although this area is much busier during the summer months than the rest of the year. Similarly, the lines of boat restaurants moored along the Danube and Sava tend to be most active when nights are warm and at their shortest. A little further afield, and a pleasant choice for a summer's evening, is the neighbouring town of Zemun with its own concentration of fish restaurants lining the river frontage there.

Away from Stari Grad and the city centre, restaurants and cafés tend to be more spread out. Even here, there are pockets of activity that lure people out in the evening, an example being the concentration of smart café-bars along Njegoševa close to the Park hotel. The latest area for development over the past couple of years has been Strahinjića Bana, locally known as 'Silicon Valley', which runs parallel to Kneza Mihaila and stretches from Dorćol to the bottom of Skadarska. This is very much the place to be seen, especially if you are the owner of a smart car and wish to park it ostentatiously close to your chosen venue. Most of the cafés along here are themed in someway and, although some of them are quite busy during the daytime, it is after dark that the area really comes into its own.

There is a tremendous overlap between the categories listed below and it is perfectly acceptable to order just a coffee or a beer in many restaurants. Similarly, many cafés serve light snacks and function as an easy combination of café, cocktail bar, snack bar and trendy nightspot simultaneously. You can even buy a beer in most *poslastičarnica*. There are few pubs proper but a plethora of places to have a drink. Because of the aforementioned overlap, the *Entertainment and nightlife* chapter should also be consulted on matters of night-time food and drink.

In the Old Town

Beogradska panorama 6th floor of Hotel Palace, Topličin venac 23; ❧ 186 866 [3 C6]
As you might expect, there is an excellent city view from up here. *Open 19.00–01.00.*

Big Bull Vase Čarapića 9; ❧ 183 088; f 634 156 [3 E5]
There is a clue in the name: this is one for meat eaters. In fact, Big Bull is so meat-oriented that the entrance is actually through a butcher's shop, which guarantees freshness at least. A large sign in English in the shop above announces 'Domestic cuisine' and points downstairs. Seating is at large bench tables in a cellar with simple, modern décor. Adventurous carnivores might wish to try *teleća glava u škembići* ('calf's head in tripe') or *beli bubrezi* ('sex glands'); those of a nervous disposition would do best to stick with the excellent grilled meats on offer like *čevapčiči* and *pljeskavica*. Excellent value if you are a meat eater and do not mind the slight lack of conviviality. Good service and very reasonably priced, with main courses at 125–400din.

Daka Đure Daničića 4; ❧ 3222 068 [4 K7]
Not to be confused with 'Dačo', this is an exclusive restaurant with a lovely garden. It is located through an entrance opposite the junction with Šafarikova. Dinner for two with wine should come to around €60.

Edison Inex café Trg Republike 5; ☏ 621 940 [4 F7]
On the 2nd floor above the Edison Inex coffee and cake shop is an unnamed pizzeria. The
sign simply says: '*Restoran-Picarija-Postlastičarnica*'.

Freska Vuka Karadžića 12; ☏ 3284 893 [3 C6]
This is an Italian place next door to Vuk with lower prices but also considerably lower
standards of food and service.

Grčka kraljica (Greek Queen) Kneza Mihaila 51; ☏ 638 963 [1 B4]
As the name suggests, there is a vaguely Hellenic theme to the food here. There is a
pleasantly bright dining room inside, or you can eat outside and observe the evening *korso*
along Kneza Mihaila. *Open 09.00–midnight.*

Kalemegdanska terasa Belgrade Fortress, Mali Kalemegdan 7; ☏ 623 839 [1 A1]
This is a fine and fairly pricey restaurant serving international cuisine for those who like to
surround themselves with history while they eat. Situated just behind Belgrade Zoo, there
are views of both the Danube and Sava rivers from here, and so undeniably a romantic
spot. This restaurant has a fairly strict dress code ie: no shorts and sandals. Live music is
provided some nights. *Open 12.00–01.00.*

Kapric Kralja Petra 44; ☏ 625 930 [1 D3]
This smart pasta place, just off Kneza Mihaila, is one of Belgrade's top Italian restaurants.
Prices are quite reasonable for the quality of food that is offered.

Klub književnika Francuska 7; ☏ 627 931 [4 G6]
This place, The Writers' Club, is an institution that dates back to the Tito era when Belgrade's government-approved literati would meet here to discuss metaphors over *kajmak* and glasses of *šljivovica*. The entrance to this grand stucco mansion is through a gate on the street that has a plaque next to it that reads: 'Association of Literary Translators of Serbia'. The dining room is downstairs. White-jacketed waiters help to complete the impression of a bygone age. The roast lamb with potatoes is heartily recommended. No literary credentials required. *Open 08.00–01.00.*

Kolarac Kneza Mihaila 46; ☏ 638 972, 636 987 [3 C5]
Many meaty Serbian choices at low prices are available in this restaurant favoured by locals and family groups. Good value and good, solid food, it's also a good place to stop for a beer at the outside tables. *Open 08.00–midnight.*

Košava Kralja Petra I 36; ☏ 628 281, 627 344 [1 C4]
A small atmospheric and cheerful *trattoria* with 2 small rooms on different levels, located just off Kneza Mihaila, near the Royal hotel. The menu offers authentic Italian food, including pastas and pizzas, as well as meat dishes like goulash. Excellent selection of homemade breads, and good salad dishes too. The service is friendly and attentive, and prices are quite moderate. *Open 10.00–01.00.*

Ottimo Studentski trg 10; ☏ 189 514 [3 E5]
A small Italian restaurant with a good range of pasta dishes, a pleasant atmosphere and

good service. The outside raised dining area next to the park is decorated in the style of a rural Italian home. *Open 10.00–midnight.*

Park Pariska 20; ☎ 621 636 [1 C3]
This national restaurant is just across Pariska facing Kalemegdan Park. There is a large outdoor terrace and a good choice of the usual Serbian dishes. This is a good place to have a quiet beer, too, away from the more frenzied atmosphere of nearby Kneza Mihaila. *Open 09.00–midnight.*

Peking Vuka Karadžića 2; ☎ 181 931 [3 D5]
Not surprisingly, the Peking is a Chinese restaurant, ideal for those hankering to order their food by numbers. As well as Chinese specialities like pork in sweet and sour sauce, it also serves Serbian dishes. This is rated as a four-star restaurant, so it is fairly expensive. *Open 11.00–23.00.*

Porto Francuska 52; ☎ 3225 624
Porto is a high-class seafood restaurant that serves marine specialities such as octopus salad and fish in salt. Prices are on the expensive side. *Open 12.00–01.00.*

Proleće Vuka Karadžića 11; ☎ 635 436 [3 C6]
This is a fairly standard national restaurant close to Kneza Mihaila with low prices and friendly service. *Open 10.00–23.00.*

Royal Knez Kneza Sime Markovića 10; ☎ 631 545; www.royalknez.com [3 C6]
Housed in an old building close to the Saborna Church and Princess Ljubica's mansion, the food here is international. *Open 12.00–midnight.*

'?' (Znak pitanje) Kralja Petra I 6; ℡ 635 421 [3 B6]
The '?' is actually one of very few 19th-century buildings still standing in the city but, instead of being a museum piece, it remains an authentic local restaurant, refreshingly un-themed and without a hint of pretence. To eat, you sit on low wooden chairs around equally low, wooden tables. There is a battered English menu of sorts and the food, the usual range of Serbian grilled meat and salads, is filling, wholesome and encouragingly cheap. The whole experience is so unforced and authentically Serbian that you feel that you could be in an Emir Kusturica film. *Open daily 07.00–23.00. It does not serve food on Sunday evenings.*

Que Pasa? Kralja Petra I 13–15; ℡ 3284 764; www.que-pasa.co.yu [3 B5]
On the way down the hill towards the '?', this could not be more different in character if it tried. Que Pasa? is a smart, trendy café-restaurant with a self-conscious Spanish/Latin-American theme. Light snacks or more substantial meals are available, like pancakes and *tortillas*. This is very much a haunt of Belgrade's beautiful people, with fairly high prices to match. The numerous monitors showing Fashion TV tend to be quite distracting and obtrusive. Occasionally, live music provides a more harmonious accompaniment. *Open 09.00–02.00.*

Srpska kafana ('Serbian Tavern') Svetogorska (Lole Ribara) 25; ℡ 3247 197 [4 K8]
Founded in 1936, this is a centrally located national restaurant with heavy wooden chandeliers rather like cartwheels. Menus in English and Cyrillic offer the usual range of Serbian dishes at good prices. The atmosphere and décor is homely and a little less pretentious than its Skadarlija equivalents. This restaurant is quite popular with Belgrade's

expatriate community, as well as with actors from the nearby theatre. *Open 07.00–02.00; 07.00–23.00 on Sundays.*

Teatroteka Jevremova 19; ☎ 624 222 [1 E3]
This is a traditional restaurant tucked away behind the Museum of Theatre Art next to the Vuk and Dositej Museum in Dorćol.

Vuk Vuka Karadžića 12; ☎ 629 761 [3 C6]
Good, if fairly pricey grilled meats on a pleasant, breezy summer terrace just off Kneza Mihaila. *Open 09.00–23.00.*

Zepter Club Kralja Petra 32; ☎ 3281 414; f 4183 988 [1 C4]
Unusual for Belgrade, this is a stylish, post-modern restaurant located in the courtyard of the metal-and-glass, post-modern Zepter building. Zepter Club serves international food at quite reasonable prices.

Skadarlija
Alexandar Cetinjska 15; ☎ 3227 401 [4 J5]
This is actually a beer garden but it also serves a wide range of light dishes and is a good choice for lunch on a warm day.

Chez Tristan Skadarska 34; ☎ 3035 252 [4 H6]
This small, elegant restaurant belongs to Le Petit Piaf hotel and exudes a calm modernity when compared with most of the other restaurants in the vicinity. There is a good range of

international dishes, expertly cooked, and a large wine list. Special musically themed evenings are sometimes staged here. *Open 12.00–midnight daily.*

Dva jelena Skadarska 32; ☎ 3234 885; f 3238 363 [4 H6]
One of many 'national cuisine' restaurants on this street, the 'Two Deer' is an institution that dates back to 1832. With two large, smoky dining halls that can cater for large groups this restaurant is often the location for the 'folklore evening' attended by visiting tour groups. Like all Skadarlija restaurants, it is a tad overpriced – you pay for the atmosphere and the musical accompaniment – but the Two Deer is really not 'too dear' for what you get: the food is wholesome and filling and the choice of wine is good. *Open 09.00–midnight.*

Guli Skadarska 13; ☎ 3237 204 [4 H5]
This is a small Italian place with its own pizza oven, a vaulted roof and bench seating. Authentic pizzas are served on wooden platters. *Open 11.00–01.00.*

Ima dana Skadarska 38; ☎ 3234 422 [4 H5]
Ima dana is a four-star national restaurant and perhaps the most exclusive of the choices on this street, with two restaurant halls and a covered terrace. A wide selection of appetisers is available, along with popular national dishes like *karađorđeva šnicla. Open 11.00–01.00.*

Šešir moj ('My hat') Skadarska 27; ☎ 3228 750 [4 H6]
Certainly the most attention-grabbing restaurant of this street with a fantastic floral display around the entrance, Šešir moj offers more in the way of vegetarian choice than most others in Skadarlija. *Open 11.00–midnight.*

Tri šešira ('Three hats') Skadarska 29; ☎ 3247 501 [4 J5]
This large, four-star restaurant, one of the most popular along this street, is probably also one of the best. House specialities include *sarma*, stuffed pickled cabbage leaves, and *proja*, corn bread. There is also live music, of course. *Open 09.00–01.00.*

Velika Skadarlija Cetinjska 17; ☎ 3234 983 [4 J5]
At the bottom of Skardalija, on the corner, with a large dining hall that is often popular with wedding parties. *Open 09.00–midnight.*

City centre

Byblos Kneginje Zorke 30; ☎ 064 610 6542
Close to the Slavija roundabout, Byblos is a Lebanese restaurant that specialises in *mezze* dishes.

Casa Makenzijeva 24; ☎ 4460 866, 4460 684
Casa is an elegant restaurant, located in a 19th-century house, which offers dishes from a variety of Italian regions.

Kalenić Mileševska (Save Kovačevića) 2; ☎ 450 666
As its name suggests, this national restaurant is located close to Kalenić market on the corner with Maksima. There is a large dining hall with wood panelling inside, as well as some tables on a terrace facing the street. Kalenić comes recommended by many for its traditional Serbian cooking. *Open 08.00–midnight.*

Makao Starine Novaka 7a; ☏ 3236 631
Close to Tašmajdan Park, this pleasant restaurant serves *dim sum* and a wide range of excellent Chinese food. The ambience is good and the prices are very reasonable.

Mamma Mia Resavska (General Ždanova) 70; ☏ 684 857
Italian, obviously, and Belgrade's only four-star Italian restaurant; close to the British Embassy. *Open 08.00–midnight.*

McDonald's Brankova; ☏ 630 105 [3 D8]
There are nine McDonald's in Belgrade, and this branch of the familiar icon of our globalised world sits on a terrace above Zeleni venac, the terminus for many of the city's bus routes. Unusually, there is air conditioning and a no-smoking policy in operation inside. The nearby, and much larger, branch on Terazije offers free internet access as one of its perks.

Orač Makenzijeva (Maršala Tolbuhina) 81; ☏ 4440 507
On the corner of Makenzijeva and Mutapova at Vračar, this is a Serbian grill restaurant with very reasonable prices.

Orao 29 November 28; ☏ 3228 836, 3224 231 [4 I6]
This pizzeria provides a wide range of both national and Italian dishes that are good value and come with prompt service. The outside terrace, however, is extremely noisy with the constant stream of heavy traffic thundering down this major thoroughfare. There is another branch at Bulevar Kralja Aleksandra 142; ☏ 4443 031, 4441 606. *Both restaurants offer 24-hour service.*

Polet Kralja Milana 31; ☏ 3232 454

On the corner with Njegoševa, close to the Park hotel, this has good, inexpensive seafood dishes, along with some pasta dishes and, of course, meat. The lower restaurant vaguely resembles the inside of a passenger ship with fitted brass rails but no lifebuoys or portholes. Polet is popular with the local business community and is a good choice for lunch. *Riblja čorba*, 80din. *Open 08.00–23.00.*

Resava Resavska 24; ☏ 3233 192

This is another high-class Italian restaurant quite close to the British Embassy. *Open 12.00–midnight.*

Studio B Masarikova 5; ☏ 3613 886

This restaurant is discreetly hidden away on the 5th floor of the Beogradjanka ('Belgrade Girl') building with a lush, albeit slightly dated, interior. A cheap, set lunch menu is available.

Tabor Bulevar Kralja Aleksandra 348; ☏ 412 464

Tabor is a four-star Serbian restaurant that puts on live music for its diners. *Open 10.00–01.00.*

Trandafilović Makenzijeva 63; ☏ 430 230

This city restaurant, within walking distance of St Sava's Church and Kalenić market, specialises in Serbian national cuisine and attracts many well-known Belgraders, politicians and lawyers. The leafy garden, an excellent place to be in summer, is shaded by an old oak tree that is protected by law.

Zorba Corner of Starine Novaka and 27 Marta; ☎ 337 6547; www.zorba.co.yu
Zorba is a small Greek taverna with very reasonable prices.

Elsewhere in the city
Amigo Mladena Stojanovića 2a; ☎ 663 366
This is a Mexican-style restaurant in the Dedinje area.

Dačo Patrisa Lumumbe 49; ☎ 781 009, 782 422
This gem is hidden away in the Karaburma district of the city's northeast suburbs. The décor and layout is that of a traditional Serbian farmstead, both inside and out, reflecting the roots of the proprietor who hails from Guča in the Šumadija region of central Serbia. There are exhibits of farming implements to examine between courses, a gift shop where you can buy souvenirs like Serbian headgear and pottery, and rustic touches such as loudspeakers mounted in wine barrels. In terms of food, Dačo offers a wholesome and wide range of authentic Serbian and Montenegrin dishes at very moderate prices. There is an English menu, which is quite charmingly illustrated, and most of the staff speak English too. Helpings are very large, served in rustic clay dishes, and for the adventurous there is a whole range of fruit-flavoured *rakija* to experiment with. A recommended first course is the 'Village Starter', which is a selection of meats, cheeses and pâté served with corn bread. Vegetarians are well-catered for too, with plenty of delicious non-meat dishes on the menu. It is always best to book a day ahead here. A taxi from the centre or Stari Grad should cost just €2–3. *Open 10.30–midnight, but closed on Mondays.*

Đorđe Šekspirova 29; 📞 2660 684; www.restorandjordje.co.yu
Đorđe is a very smart restaurant in the well-to-do suburb of Dedinje that serves a wide range of international dishes.

Frans Bulevar JNA 18a; 📞 641 944, 642 439
A smart restaurant with a summer garden that serves international cuisine, mostly French and Italian. Despite its unenviable location beside one the city's major thoroughfares, the restaurant is very popular and so it is always best to book at least a day ahead.

Iguana Bozidara Adzije 30; 📞 2443 383
This small restaurant in a quiet street in the Vračar district, quite close to the Vuk monument, has no outside sign to advertise itself. With an ever-changing menu depending on whatever is fresh and good at Kalenić market, the food is inventive and Mediterranean, perhaps even Australian, in character. The décor is simple and well lit. The owner has recently returned to Belgrade with his young family after 15 years in Melbourne. *Open 20.00–midnight.*

Indian Palace Ljubićka 1b; 📞 3446 235; www.indianplace.co.yu
Well away from the city centre, in the suburb of Dušanovac, this stylish restaurant serves the sort of mouth-watering northern Indian food that is familiar to British taste buds. Despite an awkward location, this restaurant is a very worthwhile target for curry addicts. Such is the exoticism of Indian cuisine in Belgrade that prices here are fairly expensive. *Open 12.00–midnight; closed on Tuesdays.*

JAT Airlines splav Ada Ciganlija; ☎ 254 577
A curiosity this one: a floating raft restaurant on Ada Ciganlija run by Serbia's national airline. It is found on the north shore of the island facing New Belgrade, just to the east of where the passenger ferries leave to cross the Sava to reach Blok 70. Not pre-packaged airline food as you might expect but traditional Serbian dishes at very low prices. The restaurant is popular at lunchtime with day trippers to Ada Ciganlija and off-duty policemen.

Priroda Batutova 11; ☎ 411 890
A real rarity, this one: a macrobiotic restaurant next to the 'Hajduk' football ground in Zvezdara that promises organically grown food and unrefined ingredients.

Rubin Kneza Višeslava 29; ☎ 3910 987
On top of the hill in Košutnjak, it is probably worth coming here for the view alone.

Zaplet Kajmakčalanska 2; ☎ 404 142
Directly opposite Café Square in Vračar district, this fashionable, elegant restaurant has a modern menu that combines elements of both Serbian and Mediterranean cuisine.

New Belgrade and Zemun
Bahus Bulevar Nikole Tesle; ☎ 673 437
An expensive floating restaurant behind the Hotel Jugoslavija that is air conditioned in summer and heated in winter. The emphasis is on fresh fish. You can study their menu online

at www.bahus.co.yu. Bahus refers to the Greek god of indulgence rather than any pre-war German school of art. *Open 10.00–01.00.*

Campo de Fiori Dubrovačka 10, Zemun; ☏ 613 948
A delightful *trattoria* with authentic-tasting Italian food that is located on a quiet street in Zemun away from the waterfront. *Open 12.00–midnight.*

Cica Omladinskih brigada 3b, Novi Beograd
Considered by some as the best place for *čevapčići* in the city, Cica, located just across from New Belgrade city hall, has only about 8 tables but receives a constant progression of customers throughout the day and night. The portions are very large and the prices very low. There is also a take-away window. *Open 24 hours a day.*

Danubius Kej Oslobođenja 57, Zemun; ☏ 617 233
This waterfront café-restaurant in Zemun serves *riblja čorba*, fish and grilled meats, all at very reasonable prices. There are several similar restaurants close by that also serve fish dishes in a riverside setting.

Dijalog Ušće bb; ☏ 2224 847
A restaurant on the waterfront in New Belgrade conveniently situated close to the Museum of Contemporary Art. *Open 09.00–01.00.*

Focaccia Milentija Popovića 5 (Hyatt Regency hotel); ☏ 3011 143
Located in one of Belgrade's smartest hotels and, as you might expect, one of Belgrade's most elegant restaurants too, with a very good selection of international wines. If you are

really pushing the boat out, expense-wise, you could do far worse than eat here. Alternatively, Sunday brunch is a relative bargain and a good place to bring children as there is a large play area for them. *Open 19.00–23.00; Sunday brunch 12.00–17.00.*

Gardoš Kula Sibinjanin Janka, Zemun; ☎ 618 056
This restaurant, next door to the Millennium tower in Zemun, has a garden with a wonderful view over Zemun, the Danube River and Belgrade. *Open 10.00–02.00.*

Kod Kapitan Kej Oslobođenja, Zemun
This is another of several restaurants that specialise in serving fish along the Zemun waterfront, with a pleasant dining area right next to the Danube.

Perper Omladinskih brigada 18a, Novi Beograd; ☎ 606 046
Perper is considered by some aficionados to produce the best grilled meat in Belgrade. Try *leskovačka mučkalica* – spicy grilled pork with vegetables. *Open 12.00–01.00. Another branch in Zemun offers a 24-hour take-away service.*

Sent Andreja Kej Oslobođenja bb; ☎ 199 557
A Zemun restaurant that, as well as fish dishes, has the usual range of meat offerings to choose from.

Šaran Kej Oslobođenja 53, Zemun
Šaran (meaning Carp) is considered to be one of the best fish restaurants along the waterfront in Zemun.

Restaurants

Venecija Kej Oslobođenja 66, Zemun; ☎ 616 372

This is an unpretentious riverside *kafana* in Zemun, with a large terrace and very moderate prices.

BARS AND CAFÉS

Belgrade has a bewildering number of café-bars that range from extremely upmarket, with luxurious furniture and gleaming Italian espresso machines, to quite bohemian fly-by-night places that have been set up by enthusiasts in converted flats. These more marginal places tend to come and go quickly in equal measure so the best you can do is ask around and get local advice. As stated elsewhere, the boundary between what defines a place as a bar, a café, a restaurant or a nightclub is a blurred one – some institutions may serve as all four. By the same token, the notion of what constitutes a 'pub' is not exactly the same as one might expect in the UK.

Old Town

Ben Akiba Nušićeva 8: ☎ 3237 775 [4 G8]

This small, quirky bar, tucked away in a converted flat up an alleyway just off Nušićeva, gets very busy late at night. There are paintings by local artists hung on the wall and a large selection of unusual cocktails to choose from at around 200–300din each.

Bollywood Šafarikova 11; ☎ 3224 733 [4 J7]

This curious café lies at the end of a quiet street just off busy 29 Novembra. The bar is downstairs in the basement, with a large video screen for showing Bollywood movies; at street level is an enclosed area of comfortable seating with wicker-ware tables and shaded pavilions at the corners are ideal for sprawling. The atmosphere is very laid back, almost oasis-like; perhaps more Arabian Nights than Bollywood in spirit.

Caffe OK.no Obilićev venac 17; ☏ 629 072 [3 E7]
Next door to the Jazz Café, this establishment, one of several trendy cafés on this street, is a real curiosity with its mining-nostalgia theme. Even the doors on to the street have pick-axes for handles and, once inside, the extensiveness of the coal-mine theme becomes apparent, with faux ventilation ducts and pit props, miners' lamps hanging from the ceiling and tools suspended on the walls. Not surprisingly, everything is painted black to enhance the subterranean atmosphere. There is a sitting area outside too, although here the mining theme is much less apparent. There is a wide range of beers, juices, coffees and cocktails to choose from. *Open 09.00–02.00.*

Also on this street are **Identico Caffe**, **Irish pub**, **Caffe Hardy**, **Café Ulaz** and **Stress-Stress**.

Caffe Paleta Trg Republike 5; ☏ 633 027 [4 F7]
Located next door to the IPS bookshop in the Dom štampe (Press building), with comfortable armchairs and a stainless-steel bar in the corner, Caffe Paleta has a relaxed atmosphere, with a mixed crowd of young couples, weary shoppers and garrulous intellectuals.

Club of World Travellers (Udruženje svetskih putnika) 29 Novembra 7; ☎ 3242 303 [4 H6]

This curious place is down in a basement opposite the Optimist pub. The name is a wry joke as the club was set up during the hard years of the Milošević era when all most Belgraders could do was dream of travel. These days it attracts a slightly older crowd of artists and intellectuals.

Dorian Gray Kralja Petra I 87–89; ☎ 634 151 [I E2]

This is a posh café-restaurant at the upper end of Silicon Valley that seems quite popular with Belgrade's expat community.

Edison Inex Trg Republike 5; ☎ 621 940 [4 F7]

Edison Inex is just one of several cafés that look out on to Belgrade's most famous square. A large, two-storey place that is always busy with shoppers taking a break and young couples meeting on dates, this has a wide selection of sticky, sweet cakes to choose from, and a pizzeria upstairs. Most people come here for the ice creams, of which there is a wide selection. Located on the opposite side of the square, closer to the equestrian statue, is **Kod Spomenika Caffe/Poslastičarnica**, with a similar selection and prices.

Hot Spot Café Studentski trg 21; ☎ 639 205; www.hotspot.co.yu [I D4]

This light, airy café at the northwest end of Studentski trg has window stools with a view over the park, tables and chairs near the bar and a comfortable sofa area at the back. Plenty of coffees, teas, beers and cocktails to choose from but a very limited selection of food available, just pre-made sandwiches.

Inex Club Kneza Mihaila 39; ☎ 633 586 [3 D5]
A good place, about halfway along this popular *korso* route, to take a cool drink at one of the pavement tables. It is a little cheaper than most too.

Jazz Café Obilićev venac 19; ☎ 3282 380 [3 E7]
As the name says, the musical focus is jazz in this relaxed hangout, which has modern art on the walls and wooden benches to sit on. Occasionally, live music is staged here. *Open 10.00–02.00.*

Kandahar Strahinjića bana 48; ☎ 064 334 3970 [2 F2]
A café with an oriental theme along the upper reaches of Silicon Valley, Kandahar has carved wooden partitions, low tables and chairs and an Arabian tent ambience. There is a variety of flavoured teas to choose from, made with a mix of leaves, seeds and petals rather than teabags. There is proper Turkish coffee too, served with pieces of rose-flavoured *lokum*.

Kevin's Bar Kneza Mihaila 50; ☎ 635 706 [1 C4]
Formerly Snežana Pizzeria, this café-bar on the corner of Kneza Mihaila and Kralja Petra, next to Tribeca, serves a range of cakes, Mexican-style bar snacks, draught Jelen or Weifert beer and a wide range of lethal-sounding cocktails such as Burned Out Bitch (tequila, vodka, rum, triple sec, orange and grenadine).

La Revolucion Uskočka 66; ☎ 2698 888 [3 C5]
The iconic image of Che Guevara identifies this place: a Cuban/Mexican theme-bar with excellent Latin music. Inside, the bare brick walls are covered with black-and-white

photographs of Che, Castro, Zapata and other revolutionary leaders. The ceiling is vaulted and there is an upstairs gallery with additional seating. In keeping with the Cuban theme, the waiters all sport Che T-shirts and red 'pioneer' neckerchiefs. Coffees, beers, spirits and cocktails are available, all at reasonable prices, with draught beer going for 60din a glass. La Revolucion has occasional live (mostly Latin) music.

Living Room Café Makedonska 22; ℡ 3248 202 [4 G7]

Effectively, this has taken over half of the lobby of the Dom Omladine Centre, a venue for films, theatre and live music; the rest of the space is taken up by a book and record shop. This is a good meeting place, with large windows looking out on the street and real espresso coffee. Being in such a large space means that it is less smoky than average. There is also a cavernous pool hall downstairs and a noisy internet café above. *Open 09.00–01.00, Sun 17.00–01.00.*

Mamma's Biscuit House Strahinjića bana 72; ℡ 3284 776 [2 H4]

With two city branches: one on Terazije near the Hotel Moscow and the other along Strahinjića Bana. Not that many biscuits, despite the name, but a wide selection of absolutely delicious (and highly calorific) tortes and cakes as well as the usual coffees and teas.

Moloko Kneza Mihaila 25 [3 E6]

The entrance of this brightly (some might say startlingly) painted café-bar, almost directly opposite the Tourist Information Centre, is reached by going through the entrance off Kneza Mihaila and climbing the stairs at the right to the first floor to find the door. The seats to kill for are the ones at the window that overlook the pedestrian street below.

Optimist 29 Novembra 22; ☏ 3808 269 [4 H6]
One of the closest things Belgrade has to being a 'pub' in the British sense: usually packed; cheap draught beer, and a good atmosphere. *Open 08.00–04.00.*

Parlament Obilićev venac 27; ☏ 627 880 [3 E7]
Around the corner from the others on the Obilićev venac strip and next door to the Russian Tsar, Parlament offers a considerable range of coffees, cocktails and ice creams.

Plato Akademski plato 1; ☏ 2635 010 [3 E5]
On the square next to Belgrade University's philosophy faculty, hence the name, and located above an eponymous bookshop, this is one of Belgrade's most well-known institutions: a dark, trendy coffee-bar that attracts a mostly young crowd, not just university students. Plato is also very popular with foreign visitors and is usually crowded, despite being a little more expensive than most of the competition. A wide range of beers, cocktails, coffees, ice creams and pasta-based light meals is available, as well as a few vegetarian options. The music is a mixture of drum 'n' bass and Latin, with live jazz at weekends. Tables spread outside on to the square in summer.

Plum Inside the Millennium Shopping Centre, off Obilićev venac; ☏ 184 176 [3 E6]
This is a multi-levelled coffee bar that spirals upwards alongside the stairwell of a smart shopping mall mostly given over to designer clothing. Hermetically sealed off from the streets outside, you could be anywhere in the developed world; in fact, Belgrade seems an unlikely choice. Depending on your outlook, you might consider this either glamorous or pretentious. *Open, along with the shops, from 09.00 to 21.00.*

Bars and cafés

Republika Simina 22a; ✆ 3345 498 [4 H6]

This is a small bar, just off Skadarska, where the theme is that of the Tito-era communist republic. The walls are painted with maps of the former Yugloslavia, along with framed photographs of the republic's erstwhile leader and cases of medals. *Open 11.00–02.00.*

UNDERGROUND BARS

Matt Barr, www.acmwriting.com

They love a boozy night out, the Serbs, and as with many eastern European nations, it's such a part of the national psyche here that the waiter at one restaurant openly questioned my sexuality when I passed up the offer of a midday brandy. It's not unusual for locals to head out at midnight and return home ready for work in the daylight hours. But it's the other differences that make it so unique for the western visitor, with the city's 'underground' bars the real draw for the jaded Brit drinker tired of identikit bars and a formulaic drinking culture.

Hidden away in residential tower blocks and among unprepossessing office buildings, there are eight underground bars scattered around Belgrade and they are justly legendary. To the uninitiated visitor, even finding the bars is itself a bizarre experience, as you negotiate graffiti-covered stairways, labyrinthine corridors and, once you find the right door, unsmiling bouncers who look

Eating and drinking

Rio Bravo Kralja Petra I 54; ☏ 3284 050 [1 D3]
Named after a John Wayne film, this Western-style saloon bar has wooden swing doors and wall-mounted cartwheels. It serves a wide range of beers, whiskies and cocktails and is less popular with cowboys than you might imagine. *Open 11.00–02.00, Sun 17.00–02.00.*

ready to throw you back down the stairs. But once inside, the transformation is truly shocking, as you suddenly find yourself in the middle of a swanky bar that wouldn't be out of place in the middle of Soho – if drinks weren't a quarter of the price. Better yet, each of the bars – from the cocktail opulence of Ben Akiba (☏ 323 7775) to the slightly less hectic surroundings of the Tram (☏ 340 8269) – is a window on to the real Belgrade. This is where the locals come to socialise and relax.

   Nobody seems quite sure how the bars came into existence. Some think that, given the various level of subjugations they've had to endure over the years, the citizens learned to keep their leisure time, literally, underground. Others reckon that some enterprising and whimsical souls simply decided to turn their homes into bars. Whatever the reason, the whole thing has had one serendipitous consequence, with Belgrade's bar scene now just about the trendiest in Europe.

Ruski Car (Russian Tsar) Obilićev venac 28; ℡ 633 628 [3 E7]
Close to Trg Republike, this large, elegantly faded café is identified by its name in Cyrillic only, but it is hard to miss as the building dominates the corner of Kneza Mihaila and Obilićev venac. The interior is smoky, with dusty chandeliers, faded Regency pink décor and portraits of Russian tsars on the wall. Beer, coffees, juices, ice creams and a wide selection of fruit teas are available. In summer, the outside tables spread over a large carpeted area pleasantly shaded by trees.

Scottish Pub Strahinjića bana 52 [2 F3]
If you are keen on being served by handsome young Serbs wearing kilts then this is the place to be. This is about as far as the Scottish-pub theme goes though; Serbians who visit Glasgow on the basis of this experience might be in for a shock.

Sinatra's Jazz Bar Braće Jugović 3; ℡ 2622 146 [4 F5]
On the corner of Zmaj Jovina and Braće Jugović, close to Studentski trg, this is a stylish café-bar that plays all sorts of music, not just jazz, with live music on some nights. Not much evidence of the influence of 'Ol' Blue Eyes', though, apart from one of the waiters who wears a trilby, and the availability of 'Cheesecake Sinatra'. Food is served throughout the day and the dish of the day is offered at a special price between 12.00 and 17.00.

Sports Café Makedonska 4; ℡ 3243 177; www.sportscafe.co.yu [4 G7]
With numerous television screens showing a variety of sporting events, a large video screen for important football matches, and a monitor dedicated to Fashion TV 'for the ladies', it is easy to be distracted from your beer here. This place has a convivial atmosphere that, surprisingly, is

not just 'men only'; signed shirts of internationally famous footballers surround the bar area. As well as a variety of beers, coffees and other drinks, light meals are also available.

Triangle Kralja Petra 4a [3 B6]
A trendy café-bar next door to the '?' providing a considerable culture shock if you visit both establishments one after the other.

Tribeca Kneza Mihaila 50 [1 C4]
Next door to Kevin's Bar with its own terrace and a smart stylish interior that perhaps tries a bit too hard. *Open 09.00–02.00, Sun 10.00–02.00.*

Via del Gusto Kneza Mihaila 48; ☎ 187 321 [3 C5]
They have a pizza oven and a pancake ring in the front window but many people come here for a take-away pastry or to sit outside with a coffee. Light French, Italian and Greek dishes and good sweet and savoury pancakes.

Zu-Zu's Obilićev venac 21; ☎ 635 906 [3 E7]
Another of the designer cafés on this street, with dark-wood panelling inside.

City centre
Bukowski Bar Kičevski 6; ☎ 436 796
This small intimate bar is close to the Vuk monument.

Greenet Masarikova 5; ☎ 3618 533
Near the entrance to the 'Beograd anka' building, with an excellent choice of coffees, this

place is always busy with office workers. Cakes, pizzas and pasta dishes are also available. There is another branch of Greenet along the Nušićeva passage.

Jump Café Njegoševa 10; ☎ 3239 860
Jump is just one of several smart designer cafés along this street by the Park hotel. *Open 08.00–01.00, Sun 10.00–01.00.*

The Three Carrots Knez Miloša 16; ☎ 2683 748; www.threecarrots.co.yu
An Irish pub, and Belgrade's first Hibernian representative. Its name apparently derives from an error in translation, as it was originally intended to be something to do with shamrocks. The Three Carrots has a vaguely faux-Paddy décor, with musical instruments and old wireless sets on the bare brick walls, a nice marble floor, and an upstairs area directly above the bar. The interior is wooden and darkish: quite atmospheric, if not strictly Irish. The pub is frequented by the city's young crowd as well as by expatriates and embassy staff. A wide range of whiskies and liqueurs is available, as well, of course, as draught Guinness, which costs about the same as it does in central Dublin.

Elsewhere in the city
Square Žarka Zrenjanin 32
A café situated, as the name says, on a square. This particular square, just off Bulevar Aleksandra, is in a pleasant residential area between the Vračar and Zvezdara neighbourhoods of the city. The same square also hosts a bakery, a quality fast-food takeaway and a fashionable restaurant (see *Zaplet*, page 133). *Open 09.00–02.00.*

Sunset Ada Ciganlija bb
This large outdoor café is close to the beach on the eastern shore of the lake at Ada Ciganlija and is very busy on summer weekends.

SNACK BARS AND TAKEAWAYS

These are everywhere throughout the city with similar prices and quality. A few usefully located ones are indicated below.

Ruski Car (*corner of Obilićev venac and Kneza Mihaila* [3 E7]) is a café-bar institution. There is a busy take-away counter on the Kneza Mihaila side, selling excellent, freshly made snacks: *pljeskavica, gibanica, pita višne, pita krompir* and so on.

Near the top end of Kneza Mihaila, there is the handy **Sarajevska pite i burek** on the east side of Kralja Petra I at number 34, by the junction with Uzun Mirkova [1 C4]. Also on Kneza Mihaila at number 49 is the **Boom** non-stop sandwich shop.

Just down Balkanska from the Hotel Moscow is the **Leskovac** fast-food take-away, which is highly rated by locals and serves enormous *pljeskavica* for 90din.

On Kolarčeva at number 8 (✆ 636 343 [4 F7]), between the Albania tower and Trg Republike, is the **Toma** bakery. This Belgrade institution is open 24 hours a day and sells pizza slices, cakes, croissants and 20 different types of sandwich. There are a few stand-up tables to eat at outside but this is very much a place to grab something on the hoof. Next door is a pancake place that is also open 24 hours a day.

Around the corner from the Plato café and bookstore at Vase Čarapića 29 is the **Plato Giros** fast-food outlet, selling Greek-themed fast food like *gyros* and *souvlaki* for about 100din apiece. It is open Monday to Saturday 08.00–04.00; Sunday 12.00–04.00. Closer to the park and opposite the Košava restaurant on Kralja Petra 43 is the **Tweety** chicken-sandwich shop, while the **Košava** restaurant itself has a counter selling pizza slices to take away. Another place for pizza by the slice is **Pizza Poncho** on Terazije close to the Hotel Moscow. On Skadarska the **Buki** grill near the bottom of the street has good take-away food, beer from the fridge and a few tables outside to sit at, if you are not inclined to undergo the full Skadarlija experience and just prefer to watch the world go by.

Pancakes or *palačinke*, with both sweet and savoury fillings, are very much a Belgrade thing. Quite an elegant place to sample them is the floating raft **Keops** on Dunavski kej in New Belgrade, close to the Hotel Jugoslavija, which claims to have 150 different flavours.

Good ice cream is available everywhere throughout the city and especially along Kneza Mihaila, where it comes in a huge variety of flavours. There is usually a stall doing brisk business outside the Ruski Car, and another further towards the park near the Plato bookshop. Another very tempting place for take-away ice cream is the small outlet that is located between Kandahar and the Scotsman pub on Strahinjića bana.

For cakes, the pastry shop in the **Hotel Moscow** is highly recommended with its staggering range of cream-rich *torte*, as is the nearby branch of **Mamma's Biscuit House** that lies just to the south on Terazije.

In Zemun, the **Lido Pizzeria** on Karađorđev Square at Glavna 13 (↘ *3164 485*) next to McDonald's does good sandwiches and snacks. Take-away food is available 24 hours a day from the Zemun branch of **Perper**, while its counterpart in New Belgrade at Omladinskih brigade 18a has long been considered worthy of a special trip across town.

Neolithic artefact

Entertainment and nightlife

MUSIC

Belgrade has a dynamic and ever-changing music scene with something for everyone from classical string quartets to trance. Many pubs, clubs, café-bars, restaurants, and sometimes even bookshops, put on live music in the evenings. To witness live gypsy music, you can pretty much guarantee that you'll hear something in the 'national' restaurants along Skadarska, as some have their own resident musicians on hand to serenade customers. For pop music or jazz, try some of the more upmarket pubs and cafés; they often advertise what is coming up with fly-posters. The website of the Tourist Organisation of Belgrade (*www.tob.yu.co*) has a listing of some of the major musical events during any particular month, as does their *This month in Belgrade* flyer. A more comprehensive listing appears in the free monthly magazine *Yellowcab*.

Classical

For classical music, try to find out what is coming to **Guarnerius**, a beautifully restored recital hall at Džordža Vašingtona 12 (✆ 3346 807; e *guarneri@eunet.yu; www.guarnerius.co.yu*), or at the former national theatre, **Madlenianum**, now a private opera house, in Zemun.

Occasional concerts are also staged by the various cultural institutes, particularly the French Cultural Institute on Kneza Mihaila and the Spanish Cervantes Institute nearby. The Fresco Gallery has a small concert hall that occasionally puts on performances by classical musicians and vocal groups, as does the Ethnographic Museum.

BEMUS, the Belgrade Music Festival, is held annually in October, with many international artistes and orchestras performing at a range of venues throughout the city. Information on the performance schedule can be found at www.jugokoncert.co.yu/srpski/bemus.

Rock, pop and electronica

For rock music there are frequent live performances by solo artistes and groups at the Youth Cultural Centre Dom Omladine at Makedonska 22 (✆ *3248 202;* e *dobinfo@dob.co.yu; www.dob.co.yu* [4 G7]). These tend to span the wide range of genres from hip-hop to jazz, with rock guitar bands being perhaps the best represented. Dom Omladine also has a booking office that can inform on coming events in the city. Other venues include the Student Cultural Centre (SKC), Hala sportova in New Belgrade, the Barutuna underground club at Kalemegdan, Akademija (✆ *2627 846)* and the 'Pinki' sports centre in Zemun (✆ *193 971).* Bigger, internationally famous names tend to play at the Sava Centar (*www.savacentar.com*) in New Belgrade.

The **ECHO** music festival, Belgrade's own response to Novi Sad's increasingly successful EXIT festival, usually takes place annually in late July. Recent artistes have included Morcheeba and Sonic Youth. The festival takes place on the Lido, the beach on the uninhabited island in the middle of the Danube and Sava confluence. Access is across a pontoon bridge from the Novi Beograd–Zemun waterfront and special boat services are also laid on. The event lasts for five days and tickets are cheap, costing around €40. Four music stages present a mixture of musical styles – rock, reggae, techno – some with DJs, others with live bands performing. Being Belgrade, acts start late and finish even later, with many festival goers not bothering to arrive before midnight.

For various reasons the festival did not take place in 2005 and at the time of writing it was unclear whether or not it would be staged in subsequent years. For further information check the website at www.echofest.com.

Folk and Roma music

This is often much the same thing really, as Roma musicians are pragmatic and tend to play whatever is requested of them, be it regional Serbian folk tunes or popular film themes. This occasionally upsets folk purists of the ultra-traditionalist variety. Roma combos usually come in two forms: string bands with violins, guitars and accordions – the sort that entertain diners in Skadarlija – and brass bands that play at weddings and outdoor celebrations. In Belgrade, there are often brass musicians hanging around looking for work at the patio of St Mark's Church or at Kalenić market, which lies close to a nearby registry office. These bands have the endearing habit of sometimes rehearsing on the street close to tall buildings, like those near the railway station, that provide natural amplification for what is already pretty loud music – a magical sound cutting through the rumble and clatter of rush-hour traffic.

Apart from occasional residencies at restaurants, Roma musicians have little in the way of regular or advertised gigs. One Roma group that is more mainstream than most, and which promotes itself as playing 'new gypsy music', is Kal, a highly experienced group of musicians based in Valjevo who have toured abroad and play regularly in the city.

Jazz and Latin

Both jazz and Latin music are popular in Belgrade and there are several regular venues where sessions take place:

42 Klub Optimist Milševska 42; ☏ 4443 292. *Open Mon–Sat 10.00–02.00; Sun 18.00–02.00.*

Tramvaj Klub Ruzveltova 2; ☏ 3808 269. *Open Mon–Sat 08.00–04.00; Sun 14.00–04.00.*

Sinatra's Braće Jugovića 3; ☏ 2622 146 [4 F5] *Open 11.00–01.00.*

THEATRE

There are plenty of Serbian-language productions but very little in English. It may be worthwhile contacting the following to see if any English-language productions are coming up.

National Theatre (Narodno pozorište) Francuska 3; ☏ 3281 333; www.narodnopozoriste.co.yu [4 F6]

The National Theatre is the largest and oldest theatre in the city, opposite the National

Museum on Trg Republike. In addition to drama the National Theatre also stages performances of ballet and opera.

Atelje 212 Svetogorska 21; ☏ 3247 342 [4 K8]
This attractive theatre, opened in 1956, specialises in modern theatre and new works.

Belgrade Drama Theatre (Beogradsko dramsko pozorište) Mileševska 64a; ☏ 423 686

BITEF Theatre Skver Mire Trailović; ☏ 3220 643 [4 K5]
This utilises the unfinished Evangelist church at Bajloni market, which was adapted for theatrical use in 1988–89. It is the home stage of the BITEF (Belgrade International Theatre Festival) that is held in the city each September.

Madlenianum Opera House Glavna 32, Zemun; ☏ 3162 533
This is for opera mostly but also puts on some theatrical productions.

CULTURAL CENTRES

All of the following put on regular exhibitions featuring the visual arts as well as staging occasional musical and theatrical events.

Belgrade Culture Centre Kneza Mihaila 6; ☏ 2622 071; www.kcb.org.yu. Open daily 09.00–20.00.

Belgrade Youth Centre (Dom Omladine) Makedonska 22; ☏ 3248 202; www.dob.co.yu [4 G7]

British Council Terazije 8; ☏ 3023 800; www.britishcouncil.org/yugoslavia [4 F7]

Centre for Cultural Decontamination Birčaninova 21; ☏ 681 422
Cervantes Institute (Spain) Čika Ljubina 19; ☏ 3034 182/3; www.belgrado.cervantes.es
[3 E6]
French Cultural Centre Zmaj Jovina 11; ☏ 3023 600; www.ccf.org.yu [3 E6]
Italian Institute Njegoševa 47/III; ☏ 244 7217; www.italcultbg.org.yu
Rex Jevrejska 16; ☏ 3284 534; www.rex.b92.net
Russian Centre Narodnog fronta 33; ☏ 642 178; wwwrcnk.co.yu
Students' Cultural Centre (SKC) Kralja Milana 48; ☏ 659 277; www.skc.co.yu

CINEMA

Thankfully, Belgrade's cinemas show all English-language films with their original dialogue and Serbian subtitles. Those listed below show the same range of Hollywood movies that you might expect at home.

Akademija 28 Nemanjina 28; ☏ 3611 644
Dom Omladine Makedonska 22; ☏ 3248 202
Dom Sindikata Trg Nikole Pašića 5; ☏ 3234 849
Jadran Trg Republike 5; ☏ 624 057
Kosmaj Terazije 11; ☏ 3227 279
Kozara Terazije 25; ☏ 3235 648
Millennium Kneza Mihaila 19; ☏ 064 110 7304
Odeon Narodnog fronta 45; ☏ 643 355

Roda Intermezzo Cineplex Požeška 83a; ☎ 545 260
Sava Centre Milentija Popovića; ☎ 3114 851
Tuckwood Cineplex Kneza Miloša 7; ☎ 3236 517

During the summer months (May–October) the following have screenings outdoors.

Kafe Ada Ada Ciganlija 2; ☎ 544 601
Tašmajdan Ilije Garašanina 26; ☎ 3231 533, 432 616
Zvezda Terazije 40; ☎ 687 320

The **Muzej Kinoteke** at Kosovska 11 next to the Union Hotel (☎ 3248 250 [4 H8]) shows classic films. They print a monthly programme of what is coming up and have the same information available on their website at www.kinoteka.org.yu.

Each year in February and March, **FEST**, the Belgrade International Film Festival, takes place at a variety of venues throughout the city: Sava Centre, Belgrade Cultural Centre, Dom Omladine and the Yugoslav Archive. About 70 films are shown over a period of ten days. Catherine Deneuve was guest of honour at the 2005 festival. Details of the programme may be found at www.fest.org.yu.

NIGHTLIFE

Belgrade offers some of the best nightlife in southeastern Europe, with a constantly changing, finger-on-the-pulse club scene that is sufficiently hip to attract international (actually, mostly British) performers and DJs. Despite the privations of recent years and low wages that make clubbing expensive for locals, the Serbian capacity for nightlife remains legendary. Dispense with any notions of a dreary, retrograde city locked into a grey, post-Yugoslav recession, Belgrade is up there with the best of them.

The focus for nightlife is spread throughout the city: much of the activity takes place on boats and rafts (*splavovi*) moored along the Danube and Sava. There is also a dance club located on one of the beaches of Ratno Ostrvo ('War Island'), a short ferry ride from New Belgrade, where you have the opportunity to dance in the sand underneath the stars. Other pockets of nightlife lie closer to the Old Town, near the top of Kneza Mihaila, at the top end of Kneza Miloša and along Resava. Note that there is a certain amount of crossover between the listings for cafés, bars and clubs: some restaurants have live music and double as night-time hot spots and so there is not always a clear division, although the opening hours should give a clue as to how lively they become at night. With such a constantly evolving scene, venues come and go in terms of popularity. Make enquiries about which places are currently in vogue.

Clubs

Akademija Rajićeva 10; ☎ 627 846; www.akademija.net [1 C4]
A club near the north end of Kneza Mihaila that plays mostly guitar-based rock music but which also has different theme nights. This was originally a place for students of the art faculty and was the place where Serbia's post-communism music scene really kicked off in

the late 1980s. The club still retains something of an underground atmosphere. The best nights are said to be Thursdays and Saturdays.

Aunderground Pariska 1a, opposite the Swedish Embassy; ✆ 3282 524; www.aunderground.com [3 A5]
Romantically located in the 18th-century catacombs beneath Kalemegdan Fortress, this has long been one of the city's top clubs, with an enormous dance floor, famous DJs at weekends, deafening house music and strobe lighting. For the faint hearted, there are also quieter sitting areas away from the dance action. *Open 22.00–04.00.*

Bassment Rajićeva; ✆ 3282 959 [1 C4]
Formerly known as Zvezda, this small club near the top of Kneza Mihaila remains very popular, especially in summer.

Beggars Banquet Resavska 24; ✆ 3346 168
Taking its name from a Rolling Stones LP, and with décor that creates the impression of a shrine to the aforementioned wrinkled rockers, this is a club with live rock music that caters for a slightly older crowd.

Bitef Art Café Skver Mire Trailović1; ✆ 3223 533; www.bitef.co.yu/bitef [4 K5]
This is a club in the converted church near Bajloni market that has theme nights and a variety of live music that ranges from classical on Tuesdays to rock bands at weekends. The musical mix ensures a mixed crowd of all ages.

Blue Moon Zmaj Jovina 4; ℄ 626 619

This functions as a restaurant by day, a club at night. It has a wide selection of drinks but is fairly expensive.

Bus Aberdareva 1b; ℄ 3340 671

This place has grown up around a red London double-decker bus, which now serves as the DJ's station. Surprisingly, the music played is not necessarily 'garage'. Bus is usually crowded and at its most lively on weekend nights. Drinks are relatively cheap and it has discounted prices on Tuesdays.

Cabaret Rose Vase Pelagića 54; ℄ 648 036

A very popular nightspot in the suburb of Senjak.

Crazy Svetogorska 14; ℄ 3346 727

This club has live music virtually every night.

Cvijeta Mali Kalemgdan bb; ℄ 2622 355

Located in a basement by Kalemegdan Park this is a smarter-than-average place that attracts a well-dressed fashionable crowd.

Easy Ada Ciganlija; ℄ 3559 366

Easy is located at the far end of the island and best reached by taxi. It has live music on some nights.

Ellington's Milentija Popovića 5 (Hyatt Regency hotel); ℄ 3111 234

Ellington's is a smart club inside Belgrade's top hotel. It used to function as one of the

Nightlife

city's best jazz clubs but these days a much wider variety of music is played. *Open 21.30–02.30.*

Ghetto Nemanjina 4; ☎ 641 145

Ghetto was known as Incognito in a former life. The music is house and R & B and the club tends to attract a younger crowd. Moderate prices.

Havana Nikole Spasića 1; ☎ 3283 108

This is a café-club on weekdays, playing jazz and Latin music. On Fridays and Saturdays there is a resident DJ and the emphasis shifts towards techno and house.

Idiot Dalmatinska 13

Idiot is a popular club with moderate prices in a sweaty crowded basement.

KST (Klub studenata tehnike) Bulevar Kralja Aleksandra 76; ☎ 3229 212

As its name implies, this is a student club, with cheap drinks and a youthful clientele. The music is hard-edged metal and punk. Live bands perform here frequently.

Liquid Njegoševa 6; ☎ 3238 164

Liquid is a pleasant, modern bar during the daytime that becomes a drum 'n' bass venue on weekend nights. *Open 09.00–01.00.*

Mr Stefan Braun Nemanjina 4/9th floor; ☎ 065 5566 456

This fashionable place high up in a high-rise office block is highly rated for its atmosphere and its spirited, dancing barmen. Currently it is one of the city's most popular night-time venues.

Nana Koste Glavinića 1; ☏ 648 777
This club in Senjak does not get going until very late, but then it continues until dawn.

Oh! Cinema In winter, at Gračanička 18; ☏ 627 059, in summer, at Kalemegdanska Terasa; ☏ 3284 000
Note the two different locations: at Gračanička, it is in a hall decorated with cinema posters; at the fortress, on an outside terrace. Both venues have live music and tend to keep going later than many of the other clubs. *Open 21.00–05.00.*

Plastik Takovska 34; ☏ 3245 437
Formerly known as Mondo, this remains one of Belgrade's most prestigious clubs and you may need to queue to get in. It attracts a fairly youthful crowd, the atmosphere is hot and sweaty, and the music played is electronica in its various forms – house, techno, drum 'n' bass etc. There are guest appearances by well-known DJs most weekends.

Sargon Pariska 1a; ☏ 063 667 722
This is another well-established club located inside the Kalemegdan caves with a good atmosphere and music mostly from the 1980s and '90s. Open only Thu–Sat. Fridays and Saturdays are DJ nights, Thursdays usually have a performing rock band. The interior has an interesting décor with stone reliefs from the Assyrian and Babylonian civilisations.

Tramvaj Ruzveltova 2; ☏ 3408 269
Tramvaj can be found just down from Vukov Spomenik, towards Novo Groblije on Rustelova. It has good draught beer and live musicians perform most nights of the week.

Floating restaurants and clubs (*Splavovi*)

Acapulco Bulevar Nikole Tesle bb; ℩ 784 760

With Mexican associations that are rather tenuous, this raunchy raft close to Hotel Jugoslavija is a prime location for turbo-folk, with all of its comic and less savoury manifestations. A night here is an interesting spectacle, watching Belgrade's new money strut its stuff, but it is probably not for those of a nervous disposition. You will be pleased to hear that guns are not allowed inside. *Open 12.00–03.00.*

Amfora Bulevar Nikole Tesle bb; ℩ 699 789

This is possibly the smartest and most exclusive of all of the *splavovi* along here. A smart dress code is enforced.

Bibis Bulevar Nikole Tesle bb; ℩ 3192 150

Bibis is one of the most popular of the *splavovi* café-nightclubs along the riverfront, lying just south of the Hotel Jugoslavija. This one has photos of famous sportsmen on the walls and is patronised by good-looking athletic types. *Open 10.00–02.00.* Similar upmarket places close by are: **Amsterdam**, **Monza** and **Danus**.

Black Panther Ada Ciganlija; ℩ 557 737

Most taxi drivers should know the location of this *splav*. The Black Panther is a lively place and one of the best venues in the city to see and hear Roma music performed. Tables serve a dual purpose for both dining and dancing. The club was allegedly one of the favourite haunts of William Montgomery and his wife during his stint as US ambassador in the city.

Blaywatch Kej Oslobođenja, Novi Beograd; ☎ 3191 228
This is another expensive and trendy *splav* fairly close to the Hotel Jugoslavija. The name is a Serbian–English pun that combines *Baywatch* – Pamela Anderson's former dramatic vehicle – with bley, the Serbian equivalent of 'chilling out'.

Exile Savski kej bb; ☎ 063 819 0855
One of many nightclubs on the Sava River, this one is close to Gazela most (Gazelle Bridge). Exile has techno and house music, a lively atmosphere and a resident DJ.

Sound Savski kej
Sound is another very popular club along the Sava riverside in New Belgrade, close to and similar in style to Exile, with its own local DJ and house music. Drinks tend to be on the expensive side. *Open in summer only.*

Gay Belgrade
Belgrade's gay scene, if indeed such a scene exists, is low key to say the least. A little discretion is in order as open displays of affection between those of the same sex are likely to provoke hostility in some quarters.

Club X Nušićeva 27
Next to the Politika building; the best night is said to be Saturday. *Open 23.00–07.00 Wed and Fri–Sun.*

Nightlife

BEACHES

In summer you can do what the locals do and swim from the beaches on the shoreline of Ada Ciganlija in the middle of the Sava River. There is also a discreet nudist beach here. Another beach is at the Lido opposite Zemun on Ratno (War) Island in the middle of the confluence of the Sava and Danube rivers. This can generally be reached by walking across the seasonal pontoon bridge that is set up in July and August.

Swimming pools

11 April Novi Beograd, Autoput 2; ℆ 672 939, 671 547
25 May Tadeuša Košćuška 63; ℆ 622 866
Košutnjak Kneza Višeslava 72; ℆ 559 745
Tašmajdan Ilije Garašanina 26; ℆ 3240 901

Shopping

Because it does not swarm with foreign visitors – for the time being at least – traditional souvenir items like T-shirts, handicrafts and the like can be fairly hard to find in Belgrade. However, if you look hard enough you will eventually come across that doll in traditional Serbian costume that you have been searching for. Belgrade is actually a good place to buy souvenirs as, with a little judicious searching, you should be able to find plenty of genuine handicrafts that are well worth buying: embroidery, wickerwork, knitted garments and crochet work, in addition to copperware products and Serbian crystal. Leather products are also a real bargain, and the city is full of shoe shops selling high-quality footwear at bargain prices. In addition to shoes, there are also leather suitcases, handbags and jackets worthy of consideration too.

OPENING HOURS

Shops in Belgrade are normally open Monday–Friday 08.00–20.00, Saturday 08.00–15.00 and closed on Sundays. There is often a long lunch break from noon until mid afternoon. Grocery stores keep longer hours: usually Monday–Friday 06.30–20.00, Saturday 06.30–18.00, and Sunday 07.00–11.00. Many supermarkets stay open longer than this, until late in the evening.

In keeping with Belgrade's tendency to go out and stay out late, most of the smart shops along Kneza Mihaila, as well as the music shops and bookshops like **Plato**, stay open until late in the evening – to midnight in some cases.

HANDICRAFTS, GIFTS AND SOUVENIRS

Artefakt Trg Nikole Pašića 8; ` 3345 979; f 3346 811; e wtwn@eunet.yu; www.wtwn.org.yu. *Open Mon–Fri 09.30–20.00; Sat 11.00–18.00.*

This, the showroom of the **Women's Textile Workshops Network**, offers a wide range of handmade textiles that include skirts, shirts, bags, cushions, hats, *čilims* and tablecloths. The WTWN is a non-governmental organisation of women that encourages self-sufficiency and economic empowerment for its members. WTWN membership includes over 300 disadvantaged women from all over the former Yugoslavia: refugees, single mothers, low-income and unemployed women. The quality of the goods on sale is extremely good and prices are reasonable. All proceeds go to the artisans who make the goods on display.

Maska Vlajkovićeva 7; ` 3241 905 (another branch at Skadarska 22; ` 3243 412). *Open Mon–Fri 10.00–21.00; Sat 10.00–17.00.*

This shop close to Trg Nikole Pašića sells a range of hand-crafted and ethnic art items, mostly imported from Africa and Asia.

Other shops selling handmade goods and souvenirs include:

Ethno Center Ariljska 12; ` 409 181
Ethno Boutique Gral Zetska 13; ` 3246 583
IPS Gifthouse Balkanska 14; ` 688 933
Singidunum Kneza Mihaila 42; ` 185 323
Zdravo Živo Terazijski prolaz, in the underpass by the Balkan hotel

Beogradski Izlog (Belgrade Window) at Kneza Mihaila 6/Trg Republike 5 (✆ *631 721* [3 F7]) has a wide range of specialised calendars, notebooks, posters, postcards, T-shirts, glassware and tea mugs, all with a Belgrade theme. It is open 09.00–20.00 Monday–Saturday and 10.00–20.00 on Sundays.

At the top end of Kneza Mihaila by the City Library is a line of **craft stalls** that sell handmade novelty and pottery items. Additionally, there are usually women selling embroidery and crochet work near the main entrance to Kalemegdan Park; they sometimes also sell their goods from small stalls along the middle section of Kneza Mihaila.

A reasonable range of **postcards** is available throughout the city, both at pavement stalls and in bookshops, but the ones showing bomb-damaged Belgrade with typically Serbian, sardonic humour ('The children's playground, designed by NATO' captioning a shot of boys frolicking in twisted wreckage; and, 'Sorry, we didn't know it was invisible – Greetings from Serbia' on a card showing a downed 'undetectable' F-117A spy plane) are becoming increasingly hard to find.

COMMUNIST MEMORABILIA

The **Kalemegdan Information Centre**, by the Outer Stambol Gate that leads into the Belgrade Fortress, has all sorts of curiosities on sale for those nostalgic for the former Yugoslavia. This Aladdin's Cave of communist kitsch, open Monday–Saturday 10.00–16.00 and Sunday 10.00–20.00, has a fascinating dog-eared collection of Tito photographs and plaques, postcards, long-out-of-date guidebooks, inflationary, multi-zeroed banknotes and what must be the national collection of communist lapel pins. The House of Flowers memorial centre also has a few lapel badges and T-shirts for sale.

In contrast to the above, and for those whose sense of irony is truly deep, there are sometimes stalls along Kneza Mihaila or in Kalemegdan Park that sell nationalist items like *četnik* flags and Radovan Karadžić T-shirts and calendars. It is probably best to keep a straight face if you decide to buy any of these.

ART

Many of the **art galleries** have copies of their work for sale, together with Serbian-language catalogues of the works on display. The **Ethnographic Museum** at Studentski trg 13 (❧ *3281 888* [2 D4]) also has a good gift shop.

Art sales galleries

107 Glavna 53, Zemun; ❧ 611 485

12+ Vuka Karadžića 12; ❧ 632 450

Artmedija Studentski trg 13; ❧ 3282 060

Beograd Kosančićev venac 19; ❧ 626 088

D/B Bulevar kralja Aleksandra 140; ❧ 451 847

Dada Čumićeva 54; ❧ 3242 091

Fabris Milentija Popovića 23; ❧ 3112 866

Magica Milentija Popovića 9; ❧ 3114 322

Mala Gallery Singidunum Uzun-Mirkova 12; ℩ 622 582
Oda Milentija Popovića 9; ℩ 3114 322
Paleta Bulevar Mihajla Pupina 10; ℩ 135 150
Pero Milentija Popovića 1; ℩ 3113 311
Radionica Duše Milentija Popovića 9; ℩ 3114 322
Remont Makedonska 5 II/2; ℩ 3344 171
Sebastijan Art Rajićeva 12; ℩ 185 653
Singidunum Kneza Mihaila 42; ℩ 185 323

For fans of naïve art, a wide range of paintings is available at **Naïve art – atelier Davidović**, Mihaila Pupina Bulevar 161/17, II floor, New Belgrade; ℩/f 3119 453.

FASHION AND ACCESSORIES

Kneza Mihaila has almost the same range of modern clothes shops that you might expect of any major Italian city. Prices are not cheap but you get what you pay for.

For smart, designer boutiques and a privileged, chi-chi atmosphere, there is the **Millennium Centre** shopping mall (*open 09.00–20.00* [3 E6]) at Obilićev venac 16, just off Kneza Mihaila, while **City Passage**, Obilićev venac 20, which leads through to the Millennium Centre, has much of the same sort of thing. In New Belgrade, there is a similar range of exclusive boutiques in the cavernous **Sava Centre** building (*Milentija Popovića 9*). There is also a shopping centre at **Piramida**, Jurija Gagarina, Blok 44 in Novi Beograd.

For original Serbian-designed clothes there are the following:

Uppa Druppa Višnićeva 2
A small boutique that has an original range of quaint designer clothes, hats, shoes and bags as well as some distinctive jewellery.

Kjara Višnićeva 7
Directly opposite Uppa Druppa.

For jewellery:

Marjanović Makedonska 5; ℩ 627 676
New York Fine Jewellery Hyatt Hotel, Miletija Popovića 5; ℩ 3011 204
Zepter Jewellery Kralja Petra I 32; ℩ 3281 414

MARKETS
Much of Belgrade's commerce is carried out in far less refined surroundings than the places mentioned above – either at the **street stalls** that line some of the main roads or at outdoor markets. Although they have tightened up recently, copyright laws in Serbia are lax, to say the least, and so 'genuine' Versace clothing, Cartier shoes, computer software and recent-release CDs and DVDs are often available at knockdown prices. The clothes packaging may look suspect, and the cover art on the CDs may be slightly blurry, but the chances are that if you cannot tell the difference then it is unlikely that anyone else will be able to do so

either. Whether or not such facsimile items infringe copyright outside of Serbia is a moot point, of course.

Belgrade's largest open-air market is at **Kalenić pijaca** at the bottom end of Njegoševa, within sight of the enormous dome of St Sava's Church. It is a dense warren of activity that is open every day but at its busiest on Friday and Saturday mornings. Every imaginable type of food produce is sold here: vast piles of seasonal fruit, heaving mounds of greens and onions, sheets of pastry dough, plastic bags of handmade pasta, strings of peppers, rounds of cheese, hams, wooden tubs of *kajmak*, and enough garlic to dispatch any vampire straight back to Transylvania. With most of the stalls run by unhurried, cheerful women in headscarves, Kalenić is the spirit of the Serbian countryside transposed to the city. As well as food produce, and an adjoining area devoted solely to flowers, the market also has a section where chain-smoking Roma men sell a range of quite bizarre antiques – perhaps 'bric-a-brac' is a better term for the items on display here. Search amongst the broken 1940s' wireless sets, World War II Partisan medals and broken watches for your own bargain. Haggling is quite acceptable.

Closer to Stari Grad, just below McDonald's and the city bus stops on Brankova, is **pijaca 'Zeleni venac'** [3 D8], which has less in the way of fresh produce but more cheap clothing and other items. The market is housed in the area beneath the Chinese-looking, chequerboard towers; buildings which raised some controversy when they were first erected as they were considered by some to have some influence of the Croatian coat of arms in their design.

At the bottom of Skadarlija is **Bajlonova pijaca** [4 K5], named after the brewery near by that has a number of stalls selling fruit, vegetables and dairy produce as well as clothes and bric-a-brac.

In New Belgrade there is a large open-air market at **Buvlja pijaca** on Proleterske solidarnoste near the railway bridge at Blok 43. The market extends outside as those individuals who cannot afford to rent a stall sell their goods from pitches on the pavement beneath the railway bridge. It is a colourful and noisy place, with the odd beggar and wandering Roma accordionist. Seeing the limited goods that some of these people have to sell is a reminder that this is a rather poor part of the city.

Just down the road from Buvlja pijaca at Blok 70 on Bulevar Jurija Gagarina is the so-called **Chinese market**, which as the name implies is central to New Belgrade's sizeable Chinese community.

FOOD AND DRINK

Vinoteka Makedonska 24; ☏ 3224 047
This has a good selection of wines from various Serbian vine-growing regions.

Čokolada TC Milenium local 67, also Njegoševa 90
This is a great place to buy handmade chocolates. There is also an excellent shop on Kneza Mihaila, close to and opposite the Tourist Information Centre, that sells boxes of chocolates and fruit liqueurs at bargain prices.

MUSIC

There are several CD shops on Kneza Mihaila that stay open until late at night, and which, along with the buskers, are responsible for providing the soundtrack for a walk along that street. The best selection of all is in the basement of the **IPS** shop at Kneza Mihaila 6/Trg Republike 5 [4 F7], which has a good range of folk, jazz, world and pop releases, as well as music DVDs. Serbian CDs cost around 500din, while those of foreign artistes, 800–1,000din. The trade in bootleg CDs is not what it was but there are still street and market stalls that sell good-quality copies of popular titles for 150–200din.

On Sunday mornings there is an excellent **record market** held in front of the Student Cultural Centre building on Kralja Milana. This is a great place to buy cheap vinyl, especially if you are a devotee of jazz and 1970s' Yugoslav rock. These days bootleg CDs and DVDs compete for attention with the 12"s on sale. This unofficial market was closed by the police for a while because of a clampdown on copyright infringement but it appears to be up and running once more.

BOOKS

Foreign-language books are available at **IPS**, Kneza Mihaila 6/Trg Republike 5 (✆ 3281 859 [4 F7]), at the **Oxford Centre**, Dobračina 27 (✆ 631 021), and also at the **Plato** bookshops. The branch of Plato at Kneza Mihaila 48 (✆ 625 834 [1 C4]) has a much better selection of foreign-language books than the one beneath the café on Akademski plato. The **IPS** shop, downstairs in the basement of the

Belgrade Window gift shop, has by far the greatest range overall, especially art and history books, and magazines.

Another excellent bookshop, also owned by IPS, is **Akademija** at 35 Kneza Mihaila (✆ 636 514 [3 D5]), a two-storey bookshop in a beautiful neo-Baroque building that has a fairly wide selection of English-language books. The **Prospeta** bookshop on the same street has a secondhand section downstairs that includes some English-language books.

Other bookshops

Antikvarijat Kneza Mihaila 36; ✆ 638 087
Beopolis Makedonska 22; ✆ 3229 922
Geca Kon Kneza Mihaila 12; ✆ 2622 073
Plato Akademski plato 1; ✆ 3034 808
SKC Kralja Milana 19; ✆ 3231 593
Zepter Kralja Petra 32; ✆ 3281 414

Shopping

Walking tours

Many of Belgrade's most appealing landmarks lie within the comparatively small area of Stari Grad – the Old Town. This may be defined as being the part of the city that lies southwest of Dunavska, with its western boundary circumscribed by Karađorđeva and Kalemegdan Park, and its southern limit set by Brankova. Stari Grad's southeastern boundary is vaguer, but undoubtedly it extends as least as far as Skadarska, a leafy, cobbled street of restaurants serving up national cuisine. This haystack-shaped concentration of Belgrade's older buildings is bisected by Vase Čarapića, an important artery that connects Trg Republike, the spiritual heart of the city, with Kalemegdan Park by way of Studentski trg. The pedestrian thoroughfare of Kneza Mihaila runs parallel to this.

The two walks listed below can be done in either direction, or by reversing one of them can be combined together for a longer, slightly meandering, circular walk. It depends on the time of day to some extent, as it is always pleasant to complete a wander around Old Belgrade with some time in the park. Walk One should take two to three hours; Walk Two, around two hours; but it really depends on how often you stop to take photographs and how many coffee breaks are included.

THE OLD TOWN: WALK ONE

Trg Republike (Republic Square [4 F6]) is a good place to begin any walk around the Old Town. This large, elongated square is flanked by the imposing neo-Classical edifice of Narodni Musej – the **National Museum** (see page 218) – at its north side, with the **National Theatre** (built 1869) just across Vase Čarapića to the east. Dominating the part of the square that stretches up to link with Kneza Mihaila is **Dom Štampe** (The House of the Press), a glass and concrete example of 1950s' Socialist architecture and a window cleaner's nightmare. The square has been renamed recently as Trg Slobode – Freedom Square – but most Belgraders simply refer to it as 'Trg'. A set of fountains divides the square at this side, stretching down to reach the **equestrian statue of Prince Mihailo Obrenović**, who reigned from 1839 to 1868 and was widely hailed as a great liberator of Serbia from the Turks. The prince points steadily south, towards the lands that were still under Ottoman rule during his reign and which were yet to be liberated in the name of the motherland. The base of the statue has relief work which depicts episodes from the struggle against Turkish domination. This famous landmark is at the heart of the city and the statue has become an important meeting place for young Belgraders who simply say *'Kod konja'* ('Meet you at the horse') to each other.

With the equestrian statue and museum to your left, cross the road to the steps of the National Theatre then go round the corner to walk down Francuska. Take the second street on the right – Simina – and this will bring you to the top end of Skadarska.

Skadarska is the principal street of the tiny bohemian enclave of **Skadarlija** [4 H6]. This corner of the city was first settled by Roma in the 1830s who occupied the abandoned trenches in front of Belgrade's defensive walls. Their flimsy gypsy huts were replaced by more solid buildings in the middle of the century as the area became home to craftsmen and lower-rank bureaucrats. The street received its current name in 1872 in honour of the Albanian city of Shkoder and, by the turn of the 20th century, Skadarska had become a focus for the city's bohemian life and a haunt of Belgrade's artists, actors, writers and musicians. The writer Đura Jakšić lived here and his former home is still used as a poetry venue for occasional 'Skadarlija nights'. Belgraders like to compare Skadarlija with Montmartre in Paris but this is probably pushing things a bit. Effectively, the area consists of just one main cobbled street, Skadarska, together with a couple of lanes that lead off it such as Cetinjska. Skadarlija does its level best to conjure up the atmosphere of bygone times in the city, albeit in a slightly self-conscious fashion. The street itself is certainly picturesque – narrow, cobbled and leafy with plane trees – but its main attraction, particularly in summer, is the concentration of 'national' restaurants that are squeezed in along here. Running all the way down the street is a chain of old-time restaurants, all of which compete with each other to be the oldest, the most authentic, have the oddest name – My Hat, the Three Hats, the Two Deer, There Are Days etc – and host the best musicians. The appeal is there for both locals and visitors. Large groups of friends and extended families gather here to drink, eat and celebrate, while foreign tourists, especially those on a flying visit to the city, come to absorb the bohemian atmosphere. The food is Serbian with frills: plentiful grease, grilled meat and *kajmak*. The formula is similar whichever restaurant you decide to patronise: slick waiters circulate with endless plates of meat as gypsy bands surround diners at their tables and play for tips. The whole experience should not be taken too seriously: how much fun you have is really a matter of attitude. Skadarlija is certainly the 'real' Serbia, but it is also the closest that Belgrade comes to having any sort of tourist trap (see also under *Restaurants*, pages 126–8). Walking down the street past restaurants on both sides you will come to a bronze statue of **Đura Jakšić**, the work of Jovan Soldatović, which was erected in 1990. A little further down on the left, outside **Tri šešira**, the street's oldest restaurant, is another statue; this one is the work of Jova Petijević and represents the 'ageless travelling actor'. Continuing down the street, the premises of the **Bajloni Brewery** are on the right; the large chimney that dominates the neighbourhood belongs to it. The brewery was established at the end of the 19th century by a Czech, Ignjat Bajloni, who decided to bring his family here as opposed to migrating to the USA. The brewery had its own freshwater source and Bajloni developed the existing small, hand-operated brewery into a much larger one that was very much state of the art and the first in the city to use electrical power. The walls of the brewery that face on to Skadarska now bear large murals in a *trompe l'oeil* style. Standing at the bottom of Skadarska, at the junction with the busy thoroughfare of Džordža Vašingtona, is an Ottoman-style public fountain [4 K5], which is an exact copy of the **Sebilj Fountain** from the Baščaršija district of Sarajevo, a gift from that city to Belgrade in 1989 and a reflection of friendlier times. Opposite is a green market, **Bajlonova pijaca**, which takes its name from the Skadarska brewery, and a line of florists facing the tramlines of Džordža Vašingtona. Two churches lie nearby:

to the right of the market, just off Džordža Vašingtona on Knez Miletina, is the unfinished **Evangelical Church** [4 K5], which has been a theatre since 1989; to the left, a little way along Cara Dušana, the continuation of Džordža Vašingtona, is the church of **Svetog Aleksandar Nevski** (St Alexander Nevsky, see page 230 [2 J4]) built in 1928–29 in memory of the mobile military chapel, dedicated to the same Russian saint, that stood here in the late 19th century.

Walk back up Skadarska just a little way to the first junction by the bakery then turn right on to **Strahinjića bana** (see box: *Belgrade's 'Silicon Valley'*, page 183). Walk along Strahinjića bana for five or six blocks until you reach the junction with Višnjićeva where there is a supermarket on the corner.

This is pretty much at the heart of the city neighbourhood known as **Dorćol**, its name coming from the Turkish *dört yol*, meaning 'four roads'. The four roads in this case originally referred to the crossroads where Cara Dušana crosses Kralja Petra I but now the name is used to describe the whole of the quarter that stretches northwards from Skadarlija to Kalemegdan, and eastwards from Studentski trg to the Danube riverbank. Formerly, Dorćol was host to a cosmopolitan community of Turks, Austrians, Greeks, Jews, Vlachs and Serbs. The 19th-century Jewish community occupied the area delineated by the streets of Tadeuša Košćuška, Visokog Stevana, Braće Baruh and Dunavska (one of Belgrade's first synagogues was built here, at the corner of Solunska and Jevrejska), while the neighbouring Turkish quarter of Zerek lay in the streets that surrounded the intersection of Kralja Petra and Cara Dušana – the *dört yol* crossroads itself.

Nowadays, Dorćol is a largely working-class residential area with a far more homogeneous population. Dorćol has its share of high-density housing and can seem a little down at heel in places, particularly in its northern reaches approaching the river. At its northern edge on the Danube, near the May 25 Sports Centre, there is a popular promenade that follows the river east towards the Danube quay and west to Kalemegdan Lower Town; a route which is busy in summer evenings with cyclists, courting couples, dog walkers and locals enjoying the fresh river air.

Turn left here on to Višnjićeva [2 F2], which climbs quite steeply uphill. The second road to bisect Višnjićeva is Gospodar Jevremova and on the corner to the right here stands the mid-18th century, Turkish–Balkan-style building that serves as the premises for the **Museum of Vuk and Dositej** (see pages 222–3 [1 E3]). During the First National Uprising (1804–13) the building housed the Grand School, which had Dositej Obradović as its principal teacher and Vuk Karadžić as a promising pupil. Documentary evidence of their highly productive lives can now be seen on the ground and first floors respectively. Continue uphill to reach Studentski trg, a walled park. Opposite, at the corner of Braće Jugović and Višnjićeva, is the **Türbe of Sheik Mustapha** [1 E4], a Muslim holy man. This is one of the few Turkish monuments that still survive in Belgrade. It was built in 1784 as a mausoleum, and originally stood in the courtyard of a Dervish monastery that has now completely vanished. The sheik is still venerated in some quarters and you may see Roma women kissing the locked doorway, posting dried flowers through the window, tying scraps of cloth to the metal grille and collecting plants from the grass outside. Observing the young Roma

Walking tours

men helping motorists to park in the spaces along Braće Jugović in the hope of receiving a tip, it would seem that their sons have less spiritual concerns. **Studenski trg** was originally a Turkish graveyard, which was later cleared to make way for a marketplace. When the Serbs took over the administration of the city the market area was transformed into a public park. The building facing the square at Studentski trg 1 is the former **Residence of Captain Miša Anastesijević**, an important 19th-century city merchant and business associate of Prince Miloš. The building, with a light-coloured fascia and red ornamentation, was constructed in 1863 in a combination of Gothic, Roman and Renaissance styles. Today it is the seat of the rector's office of Belgrade University. The **Ethnographic Museum** (see pages 209–10 [1 D4]) stands on the square's northern side in a 1930s' building that originally housed the Belgrade Stock Exchange.

Continue along Braće Jugović to reach Kralja Petra I. A brief detour to the right here will take you downhill past the **Hotel Royal** [1 D3] which, surprisingly, is Belgrade's oldest hotel. Just beyond here to the left, at Gospodar Jevremova 11, is the city's only surviving mosque (at one time there were 30 in the city). The **Bayrakli Mosque** (see pages 232–3 [1 D2]), which dates from the Turkish re-conquest of the city in 1690 and was built as a memorial to Sultan Suleiman II, has clearly seen better days. Somehow, this solitary remnant of the Muslim faith gives the impression of deliberately hiding itself away in predominantly Orthodox Belgrade. With good reason perhaps; it was recently damaged during the riots that were the backlash of the anti-Serb pogrom in Kosovo of March 2004. It has since been repaired and at the time of writing was under the supervision of two, occasionally snoozing, policemen. The spirit of Orthodoxy is actually very close, just around the corner at the **Fresco Gallery** (see pages 211–12 [1 D3]) on Cara Uroša. The area's Jewish history can be discovered at the Jewish History Museum back on Kralja Petra I almost opposite the Royal Hotel. Such a close co-existence of Islam, Judaism and Orthodoxy gives a clear indication of Dorćol's multi-ethnic past.

Kralja Petra has a number of other sights. Heading back uphill to cross Uzun Mirkova you come to a pair of fine Art Nouveau buildings on the right-hand side just before the junction with pedestrianised Kneza Mihaila. The building at number 41 with the green-tiled façade dates from 1907 and was the house of a city merchant called Stamenković. Next door at number 39 is another fine **secessionist-style building** [1 C4] that has a motif of a female face flanked by two doves above its upper balcony. This was built in the same year as its neighbour for Aron Levi, a wealthy Belgrade Jew. In great contrast, facing them, next to a *burek* take-away on the opposite side, is the 1997 Zepter building, designed by the architects Branislav Mitrović and Vasilije Milutinović, a post-modern steel-and-glass edifice that looks as if it has been slickly shoe-horned into the limited available space. It is worth going round the back of this interesting building to take a look at the semi-circular rear entrance that faces on to the narrow alleyway off Uzun Mirkova.

Turn right at Kneza Mihaila. On the left you will pass the **Grčka kralja** restaurant, originally an inn dating from 1867. On the same side, on the corner with Rajićeva, is the neo-Renaissance **School of Fine Arts of Belgrade University**,

BELGRADE'S 'SILICON VALLEY'

Strahinjića bana in Dorćol has transformed itself over the past few years to become one of the trendiest areas for nightlife in the city. The street is lined with a series of smart cafés and restaurants and it is an excellent place to stop for a drink or a snack day or night. Like many Belgrade streets it is pleasantly shady, and highly fragrant with lime blossom in early summer.

The street is affectionately known as 'Silicon Valley' to locals, which is something of a misnomer but refers to the supposed cosmetic surgery utilised by the glamorous women who haunt its pavements. In reality, the truly glamorous hardly touch the pavement at all but rather arrive by car and park directly outside their chosen venue.

It is said that many of the young women who come here are on the lookout for what they call 'sponsors', and a worthy sponsor requires a worthy car. Recently there has been talk of making the street pedestrian-only, which would make sitting outside at one of its many café terraces even more enjoyable, although this would mean there would be far less opportunity for Belgrade's well-heeled males to display their four-wheeled wealth. As things stand, the street is often lined with an impressive display of German automotive design at night.

which originally served as the private home of the influential lawyer, Marko Stojanović, and went on to become the Austrian Consulate at the beginning of the 20th century. From here you will pass a line of stalls selling all manner of souvenir porcelain to reach the **Library of the City of Belgrade**, which, like the Grčka kralja, was originally conceived as a hotel when it was constructed in 1869.

Kalemegdan Park (see pages 240–3 [1 B4]) lies across the road: a leafy, green refuge from the city, busy with strolling couples at any time of year and situated on a bluff overlooking the confluence of the Sava and Danube rivers. Depending on the time of day you may wish to linger here awhile or, if you have the energy, explore the fortress and the military museum. The very best time to be here, with no particular agenda or urgency to see the sights, is around sunset. You will certainly not be alone as it is a popular place – understandable when the view is so good and the general atmosphere so pleasant. This is where our first walk ends.

THE OLD TOWN: WALK TWO

This one also begins at Trg Republike [3 F6], unless you choose to make your way to Kalemegdan Park first and do it in reverse – just as good.

With the Prince Mihailo statue and National Museum behind you, head south up Kolarćeva. On the opposite side of the road is the old Yugoexport building with its figures of globe-carrying giants. Soon you will come to the junction of the south end of Kneza Mihaila and the beginning of Terazije. The tall building towering above the video screen showing advertisements on the corner is known as **'Albania'**

Tower [3 F7]. This building, dating back to just before World War II, was Belgrade's first skyscraper. Somehow, it managed to avoid the attentions of German bombers in 1941. This is more or less the southern limit of Stari Grad, the Old City, and the traffic here, an unholy alliance of cars, taxis, buses and streetcars, is such that it is a relief to turn the corner and enter the bottom end of the pedestrian-only street of Kneza Mihaila.

The urban terrain covered by Kneza Mihaila dates back to the original Roman settlement of Singidunum, later developed during the Turkish period to become an area of houses, drinking fountains and mosques. The street itself was laid out in 1867 by Emilijan Josimović, the same city planner responsible for Kalemegdan Park, and it was immediately occupied by the great and the good of Belgrade society. In 1870, the street was given the name it still bears today.

Walking northwestwards towards the park, you soon come to the IPS building and the fountains that lead the way down to Trg Republike on your right. On the left-hand side of the street, wrapped around the corner of pedestrianised Obilićev venac, is the Russian Tsar coffee house [3 E7], once an elegant hotel, now a café-bar and casino. Heading down here away from Kneza Mihaila, the street turns a corner at the Hotel Majestic to reveal a clutch of a dozen or so trendy café-bars. Just off the street are two modern shopping malls with very up-to-date, if somewhat expensive, shops: City Passage and Millennium.

Continuing along Kneza Mihaila to where Zmaj Jovina crosses the street, the **Progress Palace** [3 E6] lies at the corner on the left-hand side. Built in 1994 by the architect Miodrag Mirković, the design, which has a rounded corner façade of reflective glass, is a post-modernist combination of styles from different epochs. Immediately opposite, on the other corner of Zmaj Jovina, is the French Cultural Centre, a popular location for art exhibitions. A little further on, in the middle of the street, is the **Soldiers Fountain** (Delijska Česma [3 D5]), a large drinking fountain that as well as providing cool drinking water seems to provide a focus for street musicians too. This is actually the third fountain of the same name and was built during the reconstruction of Kneza Mihaila in 1987, close to the site of an earlier Turkish fountain destroyed by the Austrians. To the right, steps lead down to the University of Belgrade's philosophy faculty, the Plato bookshop and café, and Studentski trg. To the left, on the corner with Đure Jakšića, is the beautiful late secessionist-style building of the **Serbian Academy of Sciences and Arts**, built in 1923–24, part of which has now become the Akademija bookstore [3 D5]. At the next junction – that with Vuka Karadžića – is the neo-Renaissance building of the **Nikola Spasić Foundation**, one of several late 19th-century buildings at this end of Kneza Mihaila. Its lower floor provides exhibition space for the Gallery of the Society of Serbian painters (ULUS). Continuing further along the street, you pass several grand buildings, all dating from around the 1870s, constructed in a transitional style that lies somewhere between Renaissance and Romantic.

On reaching the junction with Kralja Petra I turn left to head downhill. The **National Bank of Serbia** (Narodna banka Srbije) is on your left at number 12.

National Bank of Serbia

This Renaissance-inspired building was built in 1889 and it is this same branch that still serves as the National Bank's headquarters today. It is claimed that the bank was built upon the site of a Roman *thermae* that stood here during the 1st or 2nd century AD. Further down, on the opposite side at number 7, is the **Kralja Petra Elementary School**, another neo-Renaissance building constructed in 1905–06 and designed by Serbia's first woman architect, Jelisaveta Načić. This was built on the site of an earlier school where Vuk Karadžić used to teach. His image, along with that of his teacher, Dositej Obradović, can be seen on the façade.

Continuing downhill from here you arrive at the **Orthodox Cathedral** (Saborna Crkva, see page 227 [3 A5]), constructed between 1837 and 1840 on the orders of Prince Miloš Obrenović, who is buried here. Its main entrance, with gilded panels above it, is round the corner facing the steps of the Museum of the Serbian Orthodox Patriarchy. Directly across Kraja Petra I just before the corner is a low, wooden-framed 19th-century building, the **'?' café**. This café – a traditional Serbian *kafana* – was built for Prince Miloš Obrenović in 1823 by a man called Naum Ižko. The prince made a present of it to his personal healer, Ećim Toma, who decided to open it as a *kafana*. The property changed hands several times, as did its name, being known at first as 'Toma's kafana', then 'Shepherd's Inn' and then, in 1892, as 'By the

Cathedral'. There were objections by the ecclesiastical authorities to this last name and so a temporary sign showing a question mark was put up, which ended up becoming its name. Setting its individual history to one side, the '?' is a rare Belgrade example of a wooden-framed, Turkish–Balkan building, as well as being a fine location for a drink or a meal (see also under *Restaurants*, page 125).

Just beyond the '?' café turn left on to Kneza Sime Markovića. Just beyond the junction, standing away from the road to the right is **Princess Ljubica's Konak** (see pages 220–1 [3 B6]), a fine example of civil architecture from the first half of the 19th century. This was a palace built to be the official residence of Prince Miloš in 1829–30. Because of the proximity to the Turkish garrison, the prince rarely stayed here, so Princess Ljubica, along with her sons Milan and Mihailo, moved in instead, while Prince Miloš took up residence at Topčider.

Cross back over Kralja Petra I, passing the **Museum of the Serbian Orthodox Patriarchy** (see page 222 [3 A6]) to your left. This will bring you out at the bottom of Pariska, the street that fringes Kalemegdan Park. Turn right up Pariska and, instead of crossing the street to enter the park by way of the steps opposite, continue uphill towards Kneza Mihaila. The aforementioned stone steps were built during the early years of the 20th century as part of a revitalisation programme and echo the spirit of Italian Renaissance gardens; they are the work of Serbia's first female architect, Jeslisaveta Načić (1878–1955), who also designed the Elementary School on Kralja Petra I. Immediately opposite the steps, at Pariska 11, and best viewed from the park itself, is the French Embassy built in 1930 with Art Deco influences. Its clean white façade is topped with three female figures that represent the French republican symbols of Freedom, Equality and Brotherhood. At the top of the hill, where Pariska is joined by the top end of Kneza Mihaila, cross the road to enter the park, being careful to avoid being flattened by a number 2 (or 11 or 13) tram.

The main path leading into the park is usually lined with a variety of improvised stalls selling anything from lapel badges and old banknotes to Chetnik paraphernalia. Old women put out displays of handmade lace for sale and popcorn sellers do a roaring trade. Following the main path into the park you soon reach the first of two major sculptures by the Yugoslav artist Ivan Meštrović. This is the **Monument to France** (see page 242 [1 A3]), which depicts a figure bathing and dates from 1930. The second Meštrović monument is reached by taking the path to the left of the Monument to France, which leads through trees to reach the promenade that runs above the river Sava. This leads down a staircase to enter through the 18th-century **King Gate** by means of a drawbridge. This emerges at the base of Meštrović's **Messenger to Victory Monument** (see pages 241–2), erected in 1928 to commemorate the anniversary of the breach of the Salonika front. The nude male figure faces across to New Belgrade, its buttocks facing the sunbathers and canoodling couples in the park. On the plateau just above the monument is the elegant Balkan-style building of the **Belgrade Landmarks Preservation Bureau**. Sitting on the wall here, or on the grassy mound above the Messenger to Victory Monument, is the perfect place to watch the sun set and take in the view across the confluence to New Belgrade and Zemun beyond.

CITY CENTRE WALK

The sights of modern Belgrade are fewer and farther between than those of Stari Grad but they are interesting nevertheless, especially when considering the city's more recent history. This tour of the city centre begins and ends at the Albania Tower at the bottom end of Kneza Mihaila.

A short walk along **Terazije** from its junction with Kneza Mihaila soon brings you to the imposing and attractive façade of the **Hotel Moscow**. This building, built in Art Nouveau style in 1906 for the 'Russia' insurance company, is one of Belgrade's more notable landmarks but the view across to the neon signs of Terazije, with a gaudy McDonald's concession wedged into a dull row of traffic-grimed buildings, is less pleasing. Sitting opposite the Hotel Moscow is the rather less grandiose Hotel Balkan, while directly in front of it is the **Terazije Fountain**. The fountain was constructed in honour of Prince Miloš's return to power in 1860. It was moved twice in the 20th century: to Topčider when Terazije was reconstructed in 1911, and once again in 1975 when it was returned to its present position. On Ascension Day, Belgrade's *slava* (saint's day) that takes place 40 days after Orthodox Easter, the large procession that marches between the Orthodox Cathedral and the Church of the Ascension stops here to dedicate prayers to the city's good health.

A detour down Prizrenska from here will soon bring you to Zeleni venac, an important terminus for the city's bus network and the prized location of a McDonald's branch. From the terrace above the bus park you can see the chequerboard-patterned roofs of **Pijaca 'Zeleni venac'** [3 D8], condemned by some nationalists for echoing the Croatian coat of arms in its design. In the street behind, hidden away at Maršala Birjuzova 19, is the city's only currently active **synagogue**, built in 1924–25 on a piece of land donated by the Belgrade Municipality. The gate leading into it appears to be locked nearly all of the time. Steps lead up from this rather woebegone street to Obilićev venac and its parade of designer cafés.

From the Hotel Moscow continue south along Terazije, which soon morphs into traffic-crazed **Kralja Milana** (formerly called Marshal Tito and also known as Srpskih vladara). On the left-hand side at Terazije 39 is the **Smederevo Bank** building, built in the secessionist style in 1912 as an office and residence for a prominent Belgrade merchant. On the right opposite are two impressive buildings. The first, at number 34, is the **Krsmanović House**, built in 1885 in a neo-Baroque style as a family dwelling for a city merchant. The house served as a temporary royal palace between 1918 and 1922 and it was here that the Kingdom of Serbs, Croats and Slovenes was declared in December 1918. Another secessionist building, the **Photography Studio of Milan Jovanović**, is at number 40, with a relief showing two cupid figures with a camera above the entrance. These days the entrance to the studio leads into the Zvezda cinema. Opposite at Terazije 41 is the building of the **Ministry of Justice**, constructed in 1883, with a mural by Ibrahim Ljubović of a hot-air balloon on the gable above it. Just beyond this on the right-hand side is the **Ministry of Education**, which was originally built in 1870–71 but had its façade altered considerably in 1912 to the secessionist style. The ornamentation above the door shows two female heads and the Serbian coat of arms, along with interwoven motifs that reflect the influence of the Morava School.

A little further on, just off the street on the edge of Pionirski Park to the left, stands the **City Hall**, built in 1882 as the royal palace of the Obrenović dynasty in an Italian Renaissance style. The building now houses the mayor's offices and is the premises of the Belgrade city assembly; it was also used by Tito for a while in the early days of the post-war Yugoslav republic. Sadly, the stained-glass windows that represent scenes of Partisan struggle during World War II are not on view to the general public. Walk past the gardens and newly restored fountain next to the City Hall to reach the **New Palace**, which was built between 1913 and 1918 for Petar I Karađorđević. This was restored after being badly damaged during World War I and reoccupied in 1922 when it became the official residence of the Serbian royal family until 1934 when King Aleksandar was assassinated. Today the building serves as the seat for the Serbian State Assembly. It is interesting to note how the residencies of the two rival dynasties have now been usurped to serve the somewhat gentler rivalries of city and state.

Turning left down Andrićev venac, the **Ivo Andrić Memorial Museum** (see page 214) at number 8 makes use of the former residence of the writer and Nobel Prize winner. There is also a monument to him at the street corner facing **Pionirski Park**, which also has a number of other statues that include a monument to the painter Nadežda Petrović; a seated bronze of a girl with a jug, and a bronze figure of a boy to commemorate the founding of the Association of Scouts in Yugoslavia.

Returning to the main road and continuing a little further along Kralja Milana, **Kneza Miloša** leads off downhill to the right. It was this part of the city that took the brunt of some of the most damaging of the 1999 NATO attacks, with cruise missiles homing in on the government buildings of the Federal and Republican Ministries of Internal Affairs (see box: *The NATO campaign of 1999*, page 197). The building of the Republican Ministry of Justice on nearby Nemanjina Street was also hit shortly after, and the twin towers of the Yugoslav Ministry of Defence, which stood on the corner of Kneza Miloša and Nemanjina, were bombed twice, on 29 April and 7 May of that same year. The US Embassy complex at Kneza Miloša 50 was abandoned just before these raids took place, to be lightly vandalised in the weeks that followed. The crumpled remnants of the buildings remain in place, for the time being at least: their contorted concrete and exposed girders a chilling testament to precision bombing; indeed, they look as if they have suffered from freakishly localised earthquakes.

From Kneza Miloša turn left on to Masarikova (or right if you have to retrace your steps uphill once more, having chosen to venture further down Kneza Miloša). The large, dark obelisk-like edifice towering above you is the Belgrade Palace building, perhaps better known as **'Belgrade Girl'** (*Beograd anka*). This was the tallest building in the city for six years, until it was trumped by the building of the West Gate in New Belgrade. There is a memorial fountain in front of the building, to the memory of the victims of the bombing of 6 April 1941. On the other side of the road is the Student Cultural Centre, better known as the SKC, in front of which a vinyl, CD and DVD market takes place every Sunday.

With the Belgrade Girl building behind you and to the left, cross Kralja Milana to head up Resavska (Generala Ždanova). This will soon bring you to Bulevar kralja Aleksandra, formerly known as Bulevar Revolucije (Revolution Boulevard) and the terminus for trams 3 and 7. Cross the road and head straight towards **St Mark's Church** (*Sveta Marka*, see pages 227–8) that looms up in front of you in striking yellow and red, as a larger-scale copy of the Gračanica Monastery in Kosovo. St Mark's is a popular place for grand weddings and there is quite often a number of Roma musicians hanging around outside in the hope that they may be hired to perform.

Just to the east of St Mark's, in the shadow of the larger church, is the much smaller **Church of the Holy Trinity**, which is part of the Moscow Patriarchate and also known as the **Russian Church**. This low, white church was built in 1924 for Russians who had fled the October Revolution. On Aberdareva, directly behind the church, stands the **RTS Serbian State TV Headquarters**. The technician's wing of this building was hit by a NATO missile on the night of 22–23 April 1999, killing 16 RTS workers and wounding 18 others. The damage wreaked is still plain to see. Apparently the management were fully aware that the building was going to be targeted but had decreed that any employee leaving the building during working hours, even in the event of an air raid, would be threatened with a martial court.

A monument to the victims stands overlooking the site at the edge of **Tašmajdan Park** and asks the simple question, *Zašto?* – 'Why?'. Walking into the park along the central path, with the east door of St Mark's Church behind you, you will come to another war monument that commemorates the children killed by the

Tašmajdan Park

1999 NATO bombings. This one was erected by one of Serbia's leading daily newspapers – *Večernje novosti* – and expresses anger at NATO in Serbian and English, simply stating: 'We were just children'. A poignant note is added when you notice just how popular this park is with small children.

Return to Bulevar kralja Aleksandra and turn right in the direction of the Hotel Moscow. On the corner with Takovsa is the imposing but rather drab edifice of the **Main Post Office** built in 1938. An altogether more pleasing structure is just around the corner on Kosovska, where the white and red **Old Telephone Building** at number 47 is a fine example of Serbian–Byzantine style dating from 1908 that displays a fusion of Art Nouveau and Morava School influences.

Crossing Takovska to continue along Bulevar kralja Aleksandra, the Classical-style **Federal Parliament Building** is on your right. The building of this started

City centre walk

in 1906 but it was not fully completed until 1936. The original design was by architect Jovan Ilkić although the work was completed under the supervision of his son, Pavle Iklić. In front of the main entrance stand two groups of prancing horses in bronze, erected in 1939, the work of sculptor Toma Rosandić. It was in front of here that many of the opposition rallies against the Milošević regime took place in October 2000. The building remains at the centre of national politics as the meeting place for the **State Union Parliament of Serbia and Montenegro**.

Trg Nikole Pašića lies directly ahead. This is the youngest of the city's squares, built in 1953 along with its central fountain and originally known as Marx and Engels Square. It was turned into a pedestrian zone in 1976 and a fountain was added ten years later during reconstruction. The monument to statesman and politician Nikola Pašića at the square's centre is a very recent (1998) addition. Swooping around in an arch along the square's western side is the imposing 1952 social-realist structure of **Dom Sindikata** (Trade Unions Centre), which now houses a number of banks, cinemas and shops. Leaving the square with Dom Sindikata to your right, you arrive back at Terazije just to the south of the Hotel Moscow and Albania Tower where this walk ends.

ZEMUN WALK

Zemun is now a Belgrade municipality but it used to be a separate town. The town is, in fact, much older than Belgrade. With such a favourable position on the banks of the Danube, some sort of settlement existed here even in Neolithic times. Later,

THE NATO CAMPAIGN OF 1999

To get an idea of the devastation wreaked by NATO bombing in spring 1999 you might wish to take a look at the following. This is not to encourage 'war tourism' but simply to learn what it might be like to be on the receiving end of 'humanitarian action'. Taking photographs of any of these might be considered insensitive and ill-advised.

Yugoslav Ministry of Defense buildings Corner of Nemanjina and Kneza Miloša. These were hit on 7 May 1999. Although this was targeted very precisely, all the windows within two blocks broke.

Yugoslav Ministry of Interior at Kneza Miloša 75 and the **Serbian Ministry of Interior** across the street.

RTS TV Station Aberdareva. On 23 April 1999 a missile hit the technician's wing killing 16 employees.

Chinese Embassy Bulevar Nikole Tesle, Novi Beograd. The story goes that this was accidentally hit because of 'out-of-date' maps. The building was half-destroyed and four employees killed, causing a diplomatic crisis.

Avala TV Tower On the same hill as Meštrović's Unknown Soldier Monument, this was taken out by NATO on the night of 30 April 1999, putting a halt to TV broadcasts for ten hours.

ZEMUN

SIBINJANIN JANKA

Groblje

SINĐELIĆEVA

Šaran

St Nicholas

Millennium Tower

Kod Kapitan

GLAVNA

Hotel Zlatnik

GROBLJANSKA

NJEGOŠEVA

KARAMATINA

Sent Andreja

DOBANOVAČKA

Trg Radičevića

Perper

ZMAJ JOVINA

Omladinskih Trg

Stari Kapitanija

Gospodska

Venecija

Sundial building

GLAVNA

Market

Danube

Skala

Central

BEŽANIJSKA

SVETOSAVSKA

DUBROVAČKA

Zemun Museum, Spirta's House

Air Forces headquarters

VRTLARSKA

NEMANJINA

Gradski Park

Chapel of St Archangel Gabriel

Đ ĐAKOVIĆA

KEJ OSLOBOĐENJA

Dunav

0 ————— 400m
0 ————— 400yds

© Bradt Travel Guides Ltd

KARAĐORĐEVA

Marinero

ŽARKA MILADINOVIĆA

BULEVAR MIHAILA PUPINA

DŽONA KENEDIJA

DŽONA KENEDIJA

BULEVAR NIKOLE TESLE

Bombardier

GOCE DELČEVA

Hotel Jugoslavija

GOCE DELČEVA

Acapulco Nightclub, Bahus

Bradt

N

in the 3rd century BC, the area was settled by a Celtic tribe, the Scordisci, who named the town Taurunum. The current name probably came about with the arrival of the Slavs, with the name derived from the Slavic term for the dugouts – *zemnica* – that housed the original inhabitants. With the arrival of the Austrians in 1717 the town came under Habsburg control and it was developed as an important fortification along the border with the Ottoman Empire. The town's importance as a trade centre on the border of two conflicting empires helped to boost its standing as a cultural centre, with handicrafts and industry becoming central to the town's economy. By the start of the 20th century Zemun had become one of the most economically developed regions of Serbia and this wealth is still plain to see, with an abundance of fine buildings from the 18th and 19th centuries. Until quite recently, Zemun had something of a reputation as a mafia centre, largely because of the existence of the so-called 'Zemun Clan'. Such gangsterism is not at all apparent on the ground; indeed, if anything, Zemun has a rather staid, sleepy provincial feel to it.

A sightseeing walk here could be combined with a visit to the Museum of Contemporary Art in New Belgrade, dinner at one of the floating restaurants on the Danube shore – or both. The walk outlined below begins at the edge of Zemun in New Belgrade and takes in a good number of Zemun's most impressive buildings and landmarks. You should allow the best part of half a day.

The walk begins at the edge of New Belgrade at the Hotel Jugoslavija. This can be reached from the city centre by taking a number 84 bus from Zeleni venac. After crossing the Brankova Bridge the bus turns right along Bulevar Nikole Tesle. The recently rebuilt Ušće Business Centre is on your left. Get off at the first stop if you wish to visit the Museum of Contemporary Art; otherwise, continue for another couple of stops past Park Prijateljstva on your right and the Federation Palace (also known as SIV) on your left until you see an enormous concrete edifice with a large car park on your right – the Hotel Jugoslavija.

Walk down to the river. At the shore stands the monument commemorating the pilots who defended Belgrade from attack in 1941. This part of the Danube shore is crammed with nightclub rafts (*splavovi*) and boat restaurants that stretch along the Danube shore here almost aft to stern. Those that front the Hotel Jugoslavija, particularly those a little way to the right along the shore, are the most exclusive and expensive ones in the city – Bahus, Bibis, Monza, Amfora. Turn left and walk along the promenade towards Zemun, passing many other boats and rafts along the way. There are usually lots of ice cream and popcorn sellers along here and you will probably come across the groups of men who gather here to play chess. After ten minutes or so you will enter a riverbank area shaded by trees with some high-rise blocks off to the left – this is the beginning of Zemun.

Turn down the first major street that you come to leading away from the river to the left – Đure Đakovića; this will bring you out at Trg JNA on the main road, Glavna. Turn right and immediately left on to V Bubnja. The building on your right facing the square is the **Air Forces Headquarters**, an interesting modernist building designed by Dragiša Brašovan that dates from 1935. There are Art Deco touches to the building's design that relate to its function, such as round windows that bring to mind the business end of a jet engine; the architect's concept was that the building resemble a fighter jet although, as a whole, the building tends to look like a ship more than anything else. Another aerial theme can be seen on the façade that faces on to Glavna where there is a large figure of Icarus, the work of sculptor Zlata Markov. The building was bombed in the 1999 NATO campaign and has only been partially repaired since; a plaque outside lists the names of the victims.

Continue along V Bubnja to Nemanjina at the other side of the square. To the left, backing on to Trg JNA at number 25, is the **Boy's Primary School** dating from 1913, that displays a mixture of neo-Classical and secessionist styles. Turning right along Nemanjina you pass the Pinki Sports Centre to come to the **Zemun Grammar School** on the left, a neo-Renaissance building from 1879. This is at the north end of **Gradski Park**, Zemun's largest green space. The park was built on the former site of the quarantine area of Kontumac, the largest of several quarantine complexes that used to sit on the border of the Austrian and Turkish domains and functioned in the 18th and early 19th centuries. All that remains of the complex today are two chapels: the **Quarantine Chapel of St Rocco**, built in 1836 as a Roman Catholic chapel, and the **Quarantine Chapel of St Archangel Gabriel**, a Baroque-style Orthodox chapel of 1786. Of the two, the former appears to be sadly neglected while the latter now serves as a women's monastery.

On the corner of Svetosavska and Štrosmajerova opposite the park is a Franciscan monastery with a church dedicated to St John the Baptist. The Franciscans arrived in

Zemun in 1739, having abandoned Belgrade when the Turks repossessed it. The monastery dates from around this time although it was later restored following lightning damage. Turn right down Štrosmajerova back on to Glavna and turn right. At the next corner, on the left at number 6, is a single-storey late 18th-century dwelling in a Classical style, the birthplace of Prince Miloš Obrenović's secretary, Dimitrije Davidović, statesman, diplomat and the founder of Serbian journalism.

Turning around to head in the opposite direction, at Glavna 9 on the left-hand side you come to **Spirta's House**, a residence built for a Vlach family in the mid 19th century in a neo-Gothic style. It now serves as the premises for the **Museum of Zemun** (see pages 224–5). Opposite, next door to the Hotel Central is a handsome secessionist-style building with a fine wrought-iron balcony. Continue along Glavna, passing the square with McDonald's on your left. At the corner with Dubrovačka is the so-called **Sundial House**, built at the beginning of the 19th century in a mixed Classical and Baroque style. The famous Serbian writer Jovan Subotić spent his last years at this house. Turn left down Dubrovačka and turn right on to Svetosavska where, at the next corner, you come to Srpski Dom, a large single-storey building in neo-Romantic style. Just to the right of this, on Rajanićeva, is the **Church of the Holy Mother of God**, built in 1775–83 in late Baroque style. Continuing along Svetosavska to the next corner you arrive at **Petar Ičko's House**, a merchant's house dating from 1793 that reflects a style transitional between Classical and Baroque. The building was restored in 1991. Turn right here at Bežanijska to return to Glavna where you will see the **Madlenianum Opera**

House virtually opposite. Turn right along Glavna and take the second left. This is Gospodska, a pedestrian street with several outdoor cafés, shops and fine old houses that leads down to the Danube. Halfway down at Trg Pobede is the **Oath Cross**, erected by a rich merchant in 1863 to atone for his sinful life. Facing it is the elegant early 19th-century **Treščik Pharmacy**. A little further down Gospodska you come to the **Church of the Blessed Virgin Mary** at Omladinski trg, a Catholic church built between 1784 and 1795 on the same site as an earlier Turkish mosque. There is a lively outdoor market just to the right of here at the square that you may wish to investigate; otherwise continue to Kej Oslobođenja and turn left. Pass Kapitanija, the harbour building to your right. A short detour to the left along Karamatina will bring you to the **House of the Karamata Family** at number 17, built in 1764 for a wealthy merchant and bought in 1772 by Dimitrije Karamata whose descendants still live in it. The house has a well-preserved 18th- and 19th-century interior. Continue past a clutch of fish restaurants and turn left on to Veslarska. The **Church of St Nicholas** (see page 231) lies at the next corner, a Baroque-style church built between 1721 and 1731 that lies on the same site as an earlier church. Turn right here to climb up Sinđelićeva then left on to Grobljanska, which will bring you to the **Sibinjanin Janko Tower** atop Gardoš Hill. The tower, which is alternatively known as the Millennium Tower, was built in 1896 to commemorate 1,000 years of Hungarian statehood.

Because of its vantage point on top of the hill, the Millennium Tower is a landmark from even as far away as Kalemegdan Park in Old Belgrade. The tower is a curious hotchpotch of styles and although it seems to be permanently closed it affords wonderful views across the rooftops of Zemun towards Belgrade. The tower itself is looking a little neglected these days, covered in graffiti and surrounded by broken glass and discarded beer cans. Just across the road is the distinctively yellow, neo-Byzantine **Church of St Dimitrije** that has an iconostasis by Pavle Simić. The large and lovingly tended graveyard by the church is an interesting and peaceful place to wander in for a while. Next door is a restaurant with an outdoor terrace and a great view, a good choice for a drink or a meal. Alternatively it is only a five-minute walk downhill to the cafés and fish restaurants of the Zemun waterfront.

Museums and sightseeing

10

MUSEUMS

Belgrade has many top-quality museums. Rather than trying to see too many in too little time you should pick and choose to follow your own particular interests. That said, there are some that have great appeal even though their subject matter may not seem immediately enticing. For example, the Military Museum at Kalemegdan tells a fascinating story of Serbia's history, even for those not normally interested in military matters, while the Nikola Tesla Museum provides an affectionate testimony to an eccentric genius and is not solely of interest to scientists. Unfortunately, at the time of writing (summer 2005) the National Museum remains closed, awaiting structural repairs, as numerous artefacts normally stored in the basement have had to be moved to higher floors because of flooding. Most but not all museums are closed on Mondays.

Museum of African Art Andre Nikolića 14; ℻ 651 654
This museum, located in the suburb of Senjak, features the private collection of Yugoslav diplomats, Veda and Dr Zdravko Pečar. Most of the exhibits are from West Africa, with particular emphasis on masks and magical objects. *Open Tue–Sat 10.00–18.00, Sun 10.00–14.00; closed Mon.*

Museum of Automobiles Majke Jevrosime 30; ℻ 3342 625 [1 D2]
This houses the collection of Bratislav Petković and includes about 50 historically important automobiles together with motor accessories and archives relating to

the development of motor sport. The building, designed by Russian architect Valeriy Stashevsky, was constructed as the first public garage in the city centre. *Open Tue–Sun 10.00–12.00 and 18.00–21.00 except Mon and holidays.*

Banjica Concentration Camp Museum Velkja Lukića-Kurjaka 33; ☏ 669 690
This is located just south of the Red Star Belgrade FC stadium, on the same site as the World War II concentration camp that was set up here in June 1941 and saw the deaths of thousands of Slavs, Jews and Roma. *Open Tue–Fri 10.00–16.00, Sat and Sun 10.00–14.00; closed Mon.*

Belgrade Fortress Museum Kalemegdan; ☏ 631 766 [1 A3]
Not to be confused with the more martial collection of the Military Museum, this small museum has a permanent display of models showing the development of the complex, plans and texts relating to the evolution of the fortress, and some of the tools used by the builders. *Open summer 10.00–19.00, closed Mon; winter Sun 11.00–14.00.*

Museum of the City of Belgrade Zmaj Jovina 1; ☏ 638 744; www.mgb.org.yu [3 D6]
This is the headquarters of a collection of over 130,000 artefacts. It is divided into three departments: art, archaeology and history. There is no permanent exhibition due to lack of space and exhibitions are staged elsewhere. Enquiries may be made about the whereabouts of exhibitions during normal office hours.

Museum of Contemporary Art Ušće bb, Novi Beograd; ☎ 3115 713;
www.msub.org.yu

This purpose-built gallery is in New Belgrade in parkland by the banks of the Danube. The museum, established in 1958, houses a large collection of Yugoslav painting and sculpture of the 20th century. The permanent exhibition is divided into three periods: 1900–18, which includes the impressionistic work of Nadežda Petrović and Richard Jakopič; 1918–41, with a wider range of styles – Constructivism, Expressionism, Surrealism and Critical Realism – and featuring artists such as Petar Dobrović, Milan Konjović and Marin Tartalja, to name just a few; and 1945–present day, the era with the widest variety of styles – neo-Surrealism, action painting etc – and the largest number of artists. Of special interest is the Serb and Croatian art of the 1920s and 1930s, which was clearly influenced by the Paris School, but overall it is an impressive collection and you will have to take time to pursue your own tastes and inclinations. My own recommendation is to seek out *The Frenzied Marble* by Serbia's leading surrealist Marko Ristić, and look for the scandalous but playful portrayal of lascivious monks and nuns in *Bacchanal* by Vilim Svečnjak. Modern art is bound to reflect a parallel history, and Frano Šimunović's *Column of Partisans* captures the defiant spirit of armed resistance against the Nazis perfectly. With a brooding sky, dark wintry light and soldiers with tough, worn faces marching wearily across a snowfield, the painting just radiates cold and engenders a mood of grim resignation. Another timely work features a wall covered in a play of symbols that surround a portrait of a pink-faced Tito. Above the portrait is a kitschy floral heart crowned by communist banners. This 1969 piece is entitled, *Comrade Tito – The White Violet – The Whole World Loves You*. It reflects a time when it was considered necessary that art be political, although there is undoubtedly a degree of irony in its message.

As well as a permanent exhibition there is a gallery that stages the work of foreign artists in addition to occasionally putting on retrospective exhibitions of acknowledged Serbian artists. There is also a separate collection of sculptures that begins in 1900 and extends to the 1970s.

The best way to reach the museum is take bus number 15, 84, 704E or 706 from the Zeleni venac terminus by McDonald's in the city centre. Once the bus has crossed the bridge over the Sava River, and has turned right on to Bulevar Nikole Tesle, get off at the next stop. You can walk through the park along a concrete path to reach the museum from here. The entrance facing the park, away from the river, is actually the main entrance; not the one at the side that confusingly says, 'Official entrance'. The museum is unusual in being open on Mondays. *Open daily 10.00–17.00, except Thu 12.00–20.00 and Sun 10.00–14.00; closed Tue. Admission is 80din.*

Museum of FC Crvena Zvezda ('Red Star') Above the home ground stadium at Ljutice Bogdana 1A; ↘ 3224 412; www.fc-redstar.net/musej/musej.html
This is where you can see Red Star Belgrade's impressive collection of trophies including the UEFA Champions Cup of 1991. As well as the silverware, there are

photographs and newspaper cuttings relating to the club's illustrious history. The museum entrance is located to the right of the main doors, just beyond the souvenir shop. Go through the glass door and climb the stairs; the museum is located next to the directors' boardroom on the first floor at the end. *Open Mon–Sat 10.00–14.00; closed Sun. Admission free.*

Ethnographic Museum Studentski trg 13; ☏ 3281 888; www.etnomuzej.co.yu [1 D4]
This well-maintained museum has a fascinating range of ethnographic artefacts from all over Serbia, Kosovo and Vojvodina with the emphasis on regional dress and village economy. The ground floor is given over mostly to costumes, the first floor to textiles, and the second floor to agriculture and traditional economy. Of particular interest are the bridal costumes formerly worn by the women in parts of Serbia like Šumadija, with their elaborate caps incorporating coins, dried flowers and peacock feathers. There is a detailed exhibit on *čilim* manufacture that shows all aspects of the weaving and dyeing of the cloth, as well as demonstrating the important role the monasteries had in promulgating these skills. Old photographs show the unusual sight of village men spinning, and it is interesting to note how the distaff is of great spiritual importance to Serbs, associated as it is with many folk beliefs and customs. Elsewhere on the second floor, scattered amongst the displays, are strange Bosnian Bogomil gravestones with ghoulish, cartoon-like faces. The museum has a shop selling a range of books, craftwork and postcards, and a special exhibition area. Occasionally, musical

Museums

A GIANT, WHETHER SLEEPING OR AWAKE

Manchester United enthusiast Paul Stott offers his take on the Red Star Museum

For much of the 20th century, Red Star Belgrade stood unquestionably as one of the giants of European football. Yugoslav champions 23 times, Red Star were European champions with a multi-ethnic team as recently as 1991, an achievement made all the more remarkable by the fact that Yugoslavia was breaking up all around them.

That team's three greatest players were a Macedonian, Darko Pančev, a Montenegrin, Dejan Savićević, and a Croat, Robert Prosinečki. With the break-up of Yugoslavia, and the considerably better wages offered by clubs in Italy, Spain and England, such a success will be difficult, if not impossible, to repeat.

The club museum is a treat for any football supporter. Accessed by walking past the boardroom, the museum contains an enormous collection of trophies, photographs, sculptures, plaques, press cuttings and souvenirs from the club's history. On my visit some of these trophies, incredibly, were not even in display

and other cultural events are put on in the museum's large lecture hall. *Open Tue, Wed and Fri 10.00–17.00, Thu 10.00–19.00, Sat 09.00–17.00, Sun 09.00–13.00; closed Mon. Entrance is 60din, students 30din.*

cabinets but were placed openly on tables. A section of the museum is used for press conferences, and it is possible to walk right up to the table where new players are introduced to the world's media.

Some items in the museum concentrate on Red Star's matches against European rivals. The greatest ever Manchester United team, the Busby Babes, played their final match in Belgrade in 1958. Busby's team held Red Star 3–3 in a thrilling European Cup quarter-final. After refuelling in Munich their plane crashed on take off, killing eight players and 15 other travellers, mostly journalists and club officials. A poignant picture of the United players taken immediately before kick off, along with a priceless card autographed by each player, can be viewed.

Given Red Star's central place in Belgrade, and indeed Serbian life, it would be foolish to say that the club will not return to its former glories.

The Red Star Belgrade website has an English-language section that can be viewed at www.fc-redstar.net/index.php?change_lang=en.

Fresco Gallery Cara Uroša 20; ☏ 621 491 [1 D3]
This is actually a branch of the National Museum that is filled with quality replicas of some of Serbia's most important religious art. It is a good idea to familiarise

yourself with the contents of this gallery first if you plan on venturing into the Serbian back-country to see the real thing. Although the spiritual atmosphere of a city museum cannot compare to that of a half-hidden monastery in a remote valley, at least the copies on show here can be viewed with greater ease than many of the originals, being far more conveniently positioned and better lit. Concerts of classical music, particularly religious choral works, are sometimes staged in the main hall. Admission is free but a voluntary donation can be made as you see fit. *Open Mon, Tue, Wed, Fri and Sat 10.00–17.00, Thu 12.00–20.00, Sun 10.00–14.00.*

Museum of Yugoslav History – Josip Broz Tito Memorial Complex: Museum of '25 May' Bulevar Mira 92; ☏ 661 290 (management) and the **'House of Flowers'** (Kući cveća) Botićeva 6; ☏ 661 290
The memorial complex in Dedinje can be reached by taking a number 41 trolleybus from Studentski trg or a number 40 running down Kneza Miloša. Get off at the second stop after turning into Bulevar Mira. The museums are reached by following the path uphill from the road.

There are three main buildings in the complex. The large building seen from the road is what used to be known as the 'Museum of the 25 May', taking its name from the former Yugoslav leader's birthday. This used to house a large collection of Tito memorabilia but these days it serves as the administrative centre for the Museum of Yugoslav History and as an exhibition space for artworks. It is open 11.00–19.00 Tue–Sun; closed Mon. In the foyer downstairs are two of Tito's state vehicles, a Rolls

Royce and a Mercedes, both highly polished and redolent of fine leather. Upstairs is a large gallery space for art exhibitions.

To visit Tito's mausoleum at the House of Flowers head to the gatehouse that lies above and to the left of the 25 May Museum. A footpath, marked with arrows to avoid pedestrian congestion, a precaution from the days when large numbers of pilgrims used to visit the site, takes you up past lawns and trees to the building that contains his tomb. These days the House of Flowers receives just a fraction of the visitors it used to get. There is a quiet renaissance though, and Slovenes in particular are starting to make the pilgrimage once more; indeed, a large group of Slovene Hell's Angels have been paying an annual visit for the past few years.

The mausoleum has an opening roof that covers a centre court landscaped with cheese plants. Tito's grave lies centre stage under a large marble slab that bears the simple inscription: 'Josip Broz Tito 1892–1980'. A corridor around the tomb leads to several rooms. The Chinese room is filled with ornate lacquer-work furniture and a carpet showing hunters on horseback, with angels around the edge (Tito was a keen hunter although the angel motif does not sit so well with his communist proclivities). The state room next door has a heavy wooden desk and bookcase, and a dark broody portrait of a weary Tito sat at his desk, beleaguered by the weight of state. Another room to the left is filled with the ceremonial batons (*štafeta mladosti*) that, each year on the occasion of his birthday, were relayed 9,000km around the federation by Yugoslav youth before being presented to the president in the JNA stadium (now the home of Partisan FC). The tradition survived him but the very last baton made its final journey in 1987 (see box: *Passing the baton for Comrade Tito*, opposite).

Walking back down the path to the entrance with the House of Flowers to your rear there is a building to the right that houses a large collection of gifts given to Tito during the course of his presidency. This is quite an extraordinary collection and probably just a fraction of the gifts he received during the long years of his rule. There are numerous folk costumes from the states of the former Yugoslavia and beyond (Tito apparently enjoyed dressing up) as well as musical instruments, swords, pistols and other assorted weaponry. There are a few curiosities too, like a varnished turtle shell and a one-string violin that appears to have been carved out of a single piece of limestone. The gifts came from all over the world, although it is apparent that political fellow travellers – China, some African states and the revolutionary movement in Bolivia – were often those most lavish with their donations. The most touching exhibits though are the personal gifts made by ordinary Yugoslav women: cushions, scarves, waistcoats and even woolly socks, embroidered with '*Drugu Titu*' and red-star motifs. The shop here is the place to purchase your very collectable Tito lapel badge if they still have any left, a bargain at 100din for a set of three.

Ivo Andrić Museum Andrićev venac 8; ☎ 3238 397
Located at the home of the diplomat, writer and Nobel Prize winner, born in 1892, four rooms of his former home have been converted into a museum to show the life and work of the writer. *Open Tue, Thu and Fri 11.00–17.00, Sat and Sun 09.00–14.00; closed Mon and Wed.*

PASSING THE BATON FOR COMRADE TITO

The tradition began on the eve of Tito's 53rd birthday when the first mass relay of Yugoslav youth was organised. The runners were to carry batons containing written birthday messages, which they would relay to their leader in Belgrade.

The first relay baton set off from Kumrovec in Croatia, Tito's birthplace, but in following years the journey started from different places throughout Yugoslavia, marking anniversaries of events from the history of Yugoslav nations and celebrating its various ethnic groups. The batons were carried over a period of months along predefined routes. They were carried underwater by divers, to mountain tops by climbers, by parachutists jumping from airplanes; lightweight miniature ones were even transported by carrier pigeons. The public was informed daily about the progress of the baton by radio and television reports.

More than 20,000 relay batons were made during the first 12 years of the tradition. They were made by artisans and were usually of wood or metal, with decorative features such as a five-pointed star or a torch on the top. The culmination of the relay was always on 25 May, Tito's official birthday, when the baton would be handed over to Tito at the Yugoslav People's Army Stadium (now the home ground of Partisan FC).

Jewish History Museum Kralja Petra I 71a; ↘ 622 634; f 626 674; www.jim-bg.org [1 D3]

As much a research centre as anything else, this museum has a fascinating display that charts the history of the Jewish community in the former Yugoslavia from first arrivals until the present day. Much of the focus is on the persecution and privations suffered by the Jewish community during World War II and their participation in the National Liberation War. One particularly chilling panel indicates how the Jewish population was decimated (quite literally – it was reduced to a tenth of its former number) during the Holocaust. The museum is more or less opposite the Hotel Royal. Enter the doorway and take the stairs to the first floor where you will see the entrance and can ring the bell. *Open Mon–Fri 08.00–15.00; closed weekends and holidays. Admission is free.*

Jovan Cvijić Museum Jelene Ćetkovića 5; ↘ 3223 126

A museum set up in the former home of the internationally renowned geographer, scientist and academic, Jovan Cvijić (1865–1927). *Open Mon, Tue, Thu and Fri 09.00–16.00; Wed and Sun 10.00–17.00; closed Sat.*

Manak's House Gavrila Principa 5; ↘ 633 335

This houses a collection of objects, costumes and jewellery relating to the peoples of southern Serbia that was accumulated by the painter Hristofor Crinilović. *Open Tue–Sun 10.00–17.00; closed Mon. Entrance is free.*

Military Museum Belgrade Fortress; ☎ 3343 441 [1 A3] Here you'll find a huge collection of military hardware and associated paraphernalia from all periods of Serbian history, including an enormous range of weaponry, paintings, engravings, uniforms and flags, as well as items of specific interest like a Turkish suit of armour that dates back to the 1389 Serbian defeat at the Battle of Kosovo. Virtually all of the labelling is in Cyrillic but the significance of much of what is on display is self-evident enough. The collection is as much a history of Serbia itself as it is a mere display of military effects: a turbulent and violent history that can be charted as a relentless succession of invasions and conflicts. Perhaps the most moving of all of the rooms is the very last one, which deals with Serbia's most recent conflicts and inspires the visitor to reflect on the cyclical nature of human conflict in the Balkans. *Open Tue–Sun 10.00–17.00; closed Mon.*

Natural History Museum Njegoševa 51; ☎ 3442 147
The museum is not just natural history but geology as well. The material is organised into four sections: mineralogy, palaeontology, zoology and botany. *Open Mon–Fri 08.00–16.00.*

Gallery of Natural History Museum Mali Kalemegdan 5; ☎ 3284 317 [1 A2]
Located in a former Turkish guardhouse at the fortress, on the way to the Upper Town, the museum presents its exhibits thematically and, as well as interesting displays of Serbian fauna, there is also a large collection of mineral samples and fossils on show.

Museums

Open winter Tue–Sun 10.00–17.00, closed Mon; summer daily 10.00–21.00. Admission is free.

National Museum Trg Republike 1a; ✆ 624 322 [4 F6]
Founded in 1844, the National Museum possesses a priceless collection of artefacts from all periods of Serbian history – prehistoric (including findings from Lepenski Vir), Roman, Graeco-Illyrian, medieval and Ottoman – as well as an impressively wide range of classical and modern art, both Serbian and foreign, including a few by Rubens and Tintoretto, a number of 19th-century French masters – Renoir, Manet – some works by Picasso, and English artists like Sickert and Nash. The museum's greatest treasure is Miroslav's Gospel which, dating from around 1190, is the earliest example of a Cyrillic manuscript in existence. The National Museum is without doubt one of the best collections in Europe, having over 200,000 exhibits in total, but the tragedy for the visitor is that the museum is currently closed for an indefinite period while structural repairs are underway. (Not for the first time: J A Cuddon in his 1968 *Companion Guide to Jugoslavia* remarks that during his research the museum was closed for a whole 18 months while roof repairs were carried out.) Some items from the collection may be farmed out to other museums in the city in the meantime but nothing seems very certain. *The museum is currently closed but it is normally open Tue, Wed, Fri and Sat 10.00–17.00, Thu 12.00–20.00, Sun 10.00–14.00; closed Mon.*

Nikola Tesla Museum Krunska 51 (on the corner with Prote Mateja); ☏ 3258 945; www.tesla-museum.org
Nikola Tesla was a great Serbian physicist and inventor who almost, but not quite, became an international household name. Many say that if it were not for occasional stubbornness and a poor sense of financial management, Tesla might have ended up as famous as Edison or Einstein. Despite a lack of international recognition, he remains a Serbian national hero, and it is his face that currently decorates the 100din note. You may note that Tesla bears an uncanny resemblance to the young Frank Zappa, another famous eccentric. The museum has captions in English and a guidebook is available in Serbian and English. Regular tours in English are given by the enthusiastic and knowledgeable staff members who work here. Some of the rooms relate to Tesla's scientific work and have a number of hands-on displays and dynamic working models that are fun for children and adults alike. There is also a wonderful poster that shows Tesla nonchalantly reading a book while surrounded by enormous arcs of electrical discharge. You somehow wonder if he had PR representation trying to cultivate the image of 'mad scientist'. Two more rooms are dedicated to the personal life of the physicist. The urn containing his ashes is housed here too, as well as his death mask. *Open Tue–Fri 10.00–18.00, Sat and Sun 10.00–13.00; closed Mon. Admission 100din.*

Pedagogy Museum Uzun Mirkova 14 (close to Kalemegdan Park); ☏ 627 538
[1 C3]

This small museum was established in 1896 by the Association of Teachers in Serbia with a view to preserving the various school books, teaching aids and other artefacts used in elementary education over the centuries. The museum documents the Serbian history of education from the 9th century until the beginning of the 20th. There is also a reconstruction of a typical 19th-century classroom as part of its permanent exhibition. Although there are no captions or illustrative material in languages other than Serbian, it is easy enough to make sense of most of what is on view. *Open Tue–Fri 10.00–17.00, Sat and Sun 10.00–15.00; closed Mon. Admission free.*

Prince Miloš Mansion (Konak kneza Miloša) Rakovički put 2 in Topčider; ✆ 660 422

This houses the exhibition of the Historical Museum of Serbia. The permanent display is entitled 'Serbian Revolution 1804' and is dedicated to the 1804 uprising. The display includes documents, arms, flags and personal possessions of Prince Miloš and Karađorđe that relate to the insurrection against Turkish rule. In front of the museum grows one of the oldest and most beautiful plane trees in Europe. *Open Tue–Sun 10.00–17.00; closed Mon.*

Princess Ljubica's Konak (Konak Kneginje Ljubice) Sime Markovića 3; ✆ 638 264 [3 B5]

This *konak* is an early 19th-century mansion demonstrating the architecture, furniture and interior design of that period. This luxurious dwelling was an inspiration of Prince Miloš Obrenović, who had the mansion designed by architect Nikola Živković. The prince's wife and two sons moved into this Turkish-style residence in 1831, just after its completion, and lived here for the next ten years. After restoration in 1970 it was turned into a museum. The *konak* gives a good insight into the luxurious living conditions that royalty and the upper classes of the period enjoyed. There are several beautifully reconstructed rooms, all in the so-called Serbian–Turkish style that blends Ottoman spaciousness with a more formal, Western rigidity. The rooms are filled with exquisitely carved furniture collected from a number of Belgrade houses. Some are very Turkish in style, with exquisite *čilim* carpets, carved wooden *mashrabiyya* screens and low seating around a central area, while others reflect a central European influence that would have been considered very modern for the time. There is also a Turkish-style *hammam* with a raised marble slab and a ceiling punctuated with cut-out stars but this was closed for technical reasons in summer 2005. Downstairs in the cellar is a large exhibition space that is given over to temporary exhibitions. *Open Tue–Fri 10.00–17.00, Sat and Sun 10.00–16.00; closed Mon. Admission 150din.*

PTT Museum Majke Jevrosime 13; ⟍ 3210 325
This one, which chronicles the history of the Serbian post office, might be of interest to philatelists and holidaying postmen. Admission is free. *Open Mon–Fri 09.00–15.00; closed weekends.*

Museums

Railway Museum Close to the station at Nemanjina 6; ℃ 3610 334, ext 5079
This has a permanent exhibition that traces the history of Serbian railways since
1849. *Open Mon–Fri 09.00–14.00, Sat and Sun scheduled group visits only. Admission free.*

Museum of Science and Technology Ðure Jakšička 9; ℃ 187 360
This museum has a collection showing Serbia's scientific and technological heritage.
Occasionally exhibitions are staged at the gallery of the Serbian Academy of Arts
and Sciences at Kneza Mihaila 35. *Open Mon–Fri 09.00–15.00; closed Sat and Sun.*

Museum of the Serbian Orthodox Church Kralja Petra 5; ℃ 3282 596 ext
36; www.spc.yu [3 A6]
This collection, housed in the Serbian Patriarchate next to the Orthodox
Cathedral, illustrates the development of the Serbian Orthodox Church, with
manuscripts, icons and a variety of religious objects. *Open Mon–Fri 08.00–14.00, Sat
08.00–12.00, Sun 11.00–13.00. Entrance is free.*

Museum of Vuk and Dositej Gospodar Jevremova 21; ℃ 625 161 [1 E3]
The Vuk and Dositej museum is dedicated to the work of two great scholars and
national heroes. Vuk Stefanović Karadžić (1787–1864) was a self-taught linguist who
devised the first Serbian dictionary and single-handedly reformed the Serbian
language. Dositej Obradović (1742–1811) was a great writer, philosopher and
educator. The museum is housed in the Turkish residence in which Obradović

founded the first Serb high school in 1808; Vuk Karadžić was one of the first pupils here. The part of the museum dedicated to Dositej Obradović is on the ground floor, while the first floor deals with the life and work of Vuk Karadžić. Exhibits include a copy of the plaque that commemorates Obradović's 1784 residency in London at St Clement's Court EC4, and a copy of John Bowring's English translation of Vuk Karadžić's poetry from 1827. The bust of Vuk Karadžić on display, like the monument at Vračar, confirms that he sported a quite splendid moustache in his later years. Virtually all of the captions are in Cyrillic but there may be a guidebook in Serbian and English available. To enter, go through the gate to the back of the building and ring the bell. *Open Tue–Sat 10.00–17.00, Thu 12.00–20.00, Sun 10.00–14.00; closed Mon. Admission 50din.*

Theatre Art Museum Gospodar Jevremova 19; ☏ 2626 630; www.theatremuseum.org.yu [1 E3]
This is tucked away on the same street as the Museum of Vuk and Dositej and presents the historical development of the theatrical arts in Serbia. *Open Mon–Fri 09.00–15.00, Sat 09.00–14.00; closed Sun. Admission free.*

Tome Rosandić Memorial Museum Vasilija Gaćeše 3; ☏ 651 434
A museum dedicated to the work of one of Yugoslavia's greatest sculptors, Tome Rosandić (1878–1958). *Open Tue, Thu and Fri 11.00–17.00, Sat and Sun 08.00–14.00; closed Mon and Wed.*

Yugoslav Aeronautic Museum Belgrade Surčin Airport; ↘ 670 992, 601 555 ext 3582

Housed in a modernist purpose-built structure that looks like an enormous glass tyre, this collection of nearly 50 exhibits includes World War II aircraft like Spitfire, Hurricane and Messerschmidt, together with Russian MiG fighters, helicopters and gliders. There are also parts of the downed American stealth fighter that Serbians are so fond of displaying. Outside the museum lie the battered remains of numerous other decommissioned planes that did not make it into the collection. *Open summer Tue–Sun 09.00–19.00, winter 09.00–15.00; closed Mon. Entry is 300din.*

Yugoslav Cinematic Museum Kosovska 11; ↘ 3248 250 [4 H8]

This is located on the same street as the Hotel Union. Admission is free. *Open daily 15.00–23.00.*

Yugoslav History Museum Trg Nikole Pašića 11; ↘ 3340 731

This museum has a permanent display that illustrates the history of Yugoslavia from 1918 to the present day. *Open Tue–Sun 10.00–17.00; closed Mon.*

Zemun Museum Glavna 9, Zemun; ↘ 617 752.

The material on display here illustrates the development of Zemun, once a completely separate town from Belgrade, from prehistory through to the present day. *Open Tue–Fri 09.00–16.00, Sat and Sun 08.00–15.00; closed Mon.*

GALLERIES

Art Pavilion 'Cvijeta Zuzorić' Mali Kalemegdan 1; ᐩt/f 621 585, 622 281; e ulus@tehnicom.net; www.ulus.org.yu

The exhibition space of the Association of Fine Artists of Serbia (ULUS), this gallery is a showcase for the work of its members and for renowned foreign artists. Special exhibitions are staged twice annually in spring and autumn. *Open Tue–Sat 10.00–20.00, Sun 10.00–14.00; closed Mon.*

Đura Jakšić House Skadarska 34; ᐩ 324 734 [4 H6]. *Open daily 08.00–15.00 and 19.00–23.00.*

Gallery 'Andrićev venac' Andrićev venac 12; ᐩ 3238 789. *Open Mon–Fri 10.00–14.00 and 17.00–20.00, Sat 10.00–15.00; closed Sun.*

Gallery of Fine Arts Faculty Kneza Mihaila 53; ᐩ 630 635. *Open Mon–Fri 10.00–20.00, Sat and Sun 10.00–14.00.*

Gallery of the Serbian Academy of Arts and Sciences Kneza Mihaila 35; ᐩ 334 2400 ext 242. *Open Tue, Wed and Fri 10.00–20.00, Mon and Thu 10.00–18.00; closed Sat and Sun.*

Gallery of Students' Culture Centre Kralja Milana 48; ᐩ 688 468. *Open Mon–Fri 11.00–19.00, Sat 11.00–15.00; closed Sun.*

Gallery of the SULUJ Terazije 26/II; ↘ 685 780; www.galerijasuluj.org.yu
The SULUJ (the Union of Yugoslav Artistic Associations) gallery puts on a wide range of exhibitions of work of Serbian and foreign artists. *Open Mon–Fri 10.00–17.00, Sat 10.00–14.00; closed Sun.*

Gallery of the ULUS Kneza Mihaila 37; ↘ 621 954; www.ulus.org.yu
This, the other gallery of the Association of Fine Artists of Serbia, has put on a themed autumn exhibition since 1928. *Open Mon–Fri 10.00–20.00, Sat 09.00–16.00; closed Sun.*

Graphic Art Gallery Obilićev venac 27; ↘ 627 785. *Open Mon–Sat 10.00–14.00 and 18.00–21.00; closed Sun.*

Ilija M Kolarac Foundation Studentski trg 5; ↘ 185 794. *Open Tue–Sun 10.00–20.00; closed Mon.*

Youth Hall Gallery (Dom Omladine) Makedonska 22; ↘ 3225 453 [4 G7]
Open Tue–Sun 11.00–20.00; closed Mon.

CHURCHES

Orthodox Cathedral (Saborna crkva Sv Arhangela Mihaila) Kneza Sime Markovića 3; ☎ 636 684 [3 A5]

The Holy Archangel Michael Church, better known as the 'Gathering Church', was constructed between 1837 and 1840 on the orders of Prince Miloš Obrenović, who is buried here in the crypt together with his two sons, Mihailo and Milan. The church, a mixture of Classical and Baroque styles, was designed by the Pančevo architect Kvarfeld and occupies the site of an earlier church that dates back to 1728. The interior contains a finely carved iconostasis by Dimitrije Petrović and icons by Dimitrije Avramović. During World War II, the relics of Prince Lazar were brought here for safekeeping, away from the hands of the Ustaše who had already stolen the prince's rings from his corpse in its resting place at a monastery in the Fruška Gora. This conferred considerable importance to the cathedral as a pilgrimage centre, until 1987 when Lazar's remains were sent on a nationwide tour prior to being deposited in their final resting place at Ravanica Monastery. Prince Lazar was not the only revered Serbian to be interred here: Vuk Stefanović Karadžić, the scholar responsible for phoneticising Serbian and producing a definitive dictionary of the language is also buried in the church's graveyard, together with Dositej Obradović, another great Serbian educator and writer.

St Mark's Church (Sveta Marka) Bulevar kralja Aleksandra 17; ☎ 3231 984

This Serbian–Byzantine-style church in yellow and red was built between 1931 and

1936 and occupies the site of an older church from 1835. St Mark's has been constructed as a larger-scale copy of the Gračanica Monastery in troubled Kosovo, one of the most hallowed religious monuments of the Serbian psyche. The hall interior is quite bare and dominated by four massive pillars supporting the roof, but the church contains a rich collection of icons from the 18th and 19th centuries, as well as the sarcophagus that contains the remains of the Serbian Emperor Dušan who died in 1355, which were moved here from the Saint Archangel's Monastery in Prizren. The church also contains the tomb of Patriarch German Ćorić.

St Sava's Church (Hram Svetog Save) Krušedolska 2; ␆ 432 585
This lies quite close to Slavija Square in the Vračar district of the city. The church is built in Serbian–Byzantine style and St Sava's enormous dome can be seen from all over the city, gleaming through Belgrade's haze in all directions like a beacon. The time taken over St Sava's construction must surpass that of cathedral building in medieval times: even today, the church remains unfinished although with the relative peace that reigns in Serbia these days there is at least an end in sight. Given the country's history over the past century, there have been very good reasons for the snail's pace of its construction. Preparations began as far back as 1894. The site at Vračar was chosen as the place where the Ottoman ruler, Sinan Pasha, had the holy relics of St Sava burned in 1594, having taken them from Mileševa Monastery in Raška. The design was sought by public competition and the winning plan, by architects Bogdan Nestorović and Aleksandar Deroko, was finally approved in 1926.

Construction work began in 1935 but was seriously interrupted in 1941 by Nazi bombing, and in the immediate post-war period there were the far more pressing needs of civil reconstruction. Work was continued in 1985, only to be halted once more when Serbia became embroiled in the civil war that accompanied the break-up of Yugoslavia. Following the comparative frenzy of construction that has taken place in the post-Milošević period, it was hoped that all building work would be finished by the end of 2004. However, although the construction of the external shell has now ended, along with the landscaping of the plateau outside, the church's interior remains incomplete. Now, it seems, the work may finally be completed in the not too distant future. Unless the feat is trumped by an even more grandiose project elsewhere, which seems unlikely, St Sava's will then be the world's third-largest Orthodox building. Whatever the final outcome, it is already a very impressive structure: a neo-Byzantine colossus with echoes of St Sophia in Istanbul.

A large landscaped area fronts the church to the west leading down to Bulevar JNA. On the south side of this stands the **National Library of Serbia**, constructed in 1970 to replace the earlier one that was burned to the ground in the Nazi bombing raids of 6 April 1941. On the west side, on a small mound facing Bulevar JNA, is a **monument to Karađorđe**, erected in 1979 on the 175th anniversary of the First Serbian Uprising.

The Rose Church of Our Lady (Crkva Ružica) Kalemegdan 6; ☏ 624 604
An older church, built during the reign of Stefan Lazarević, is said to have stood on

the same spot but this was razed by the Turks during their invasion of 1521. The current building was originally built as an arsenal during the 18th century but was later converted into an army chapel between 1867 and 1889. The building was restored in 1925. The icons represent several contemporary prominent figures from this time: King Petar, Prince Aleksandar, Tsar Nicholas II and politician Nikola Pašić.

Immediately above this church at Kalemegdan is the **Church of St Petka** (Sv Paraskeva), built on the site of a sacred spring of the same name. The spring was considered to have miraculous powers for barren women and Belgrade's women still come here in large numbers on 27 October, the *slava* of the church's patron. The current church was built in 1937 to the design of Momir Korunović.

St Alexander Nevsky Church (Svetog Aleksandar Nevski) Cara Dušana 63; 629 274 [2 J4]

The proposal for a church in the Dorćol area first came from Russian volunteer troops stationed in Belgrade at the end of the 19th century. It was arranged that a mobile military chapel consecrated to the Russian saint be brought to Belgrade, and half a century later, in 1928–29, a church dedicated to the same saint was constructed at this location. The church is in the style of the Morava School and it has a white marble iconostasis that contrasts nicely with its smoke-blackened interior. The iconostasis was originally intended for the Karađorđević mausoleum at Oplenac but was bequeathed to the church by King Aleksandar. The northern choir has a monument to the soldiers killed in conflicts of 1876–78, 1912–13 and

1914–18. In the southern choir is a monument to Tsar Nikolai II of Russia and King Aleksandar I.

Church of St Vasilje of Ostrog Partizanske avijacije 21A, Novi Beograd
This New Belgrade church is interesting on two counts: its age and its design. It is the newest Orthodox church in Belgrade, begun in 1996 and completed in 2001, and was constructed by donations made by devotees of St Vasilje of Ostrog, a reputed miracle worker. The church is of unusual design, with large round windows and a detached belltower.

The Church of the Holy Father Nicholas Njegoševa 43, Zemun
This Zemun landmark is the oldest Orthodox church in the Belgrade area. It was constructed in Baroque style between 1725 and 1731 on the same site as an earlier church of the pre-Turkish period. Many icons in the church are the work of the 19th-century Zemun artist Živko Petrović; the fine iconostasis was painted by Dimitrije Bačević. The belltower was reconstructed in 1870.

Church of the Holy Mother of God Rajačičeva 4, Zemun
This, the biggest church in Zemun, was built in Baroque style between 1775 and 1783. Like the church above it also contains many icons and paintings by local artist Živko Petrović. The iconostasis is the work of Aksentije Markovića and Arsenije Teodorović.

Churches

MONASTERIES
Rakovica Monastery
This monastery, located 12km south of the centre in wooded hills on the edge of the city, was first founded in the late 14th century by Radul I the Black who married Prince Lazar's daughter. The monastery was destroyed by the Turks in the 16th century but was restored in 1861–62 after coming under the patronage of the Obrenović dynasty. The existing buildings consist of a mid-16th-century monastery church and a mid-19th-century residence. The church is in the style of the Morava School and has a collection of icons from the 18th and 19th centuries and an iconostasis that dates from 1862, a donation of Prince Mihailo. The monastery is the resting place of two influential figures from the First Serbian Uprising: Vasa Čarapić, who died in the siege of Belgrade in 1806, and Naum Ičko who signed a deal with the Turks in that same year.

The monastery can be reached from the city centre by taking a number 37 bus from the stop on Francuska (or on Kneza Miloša near the junction with Birčaninova) and travelling all the way to the terminus. The monastery lies just beyond to the south.

MOSQUES
Bajrakli Mosque Gospodar Jevremova 11; ✆ 2622 428 [1 D2]
This is Belgrade's only remaining mosque, built in 1690 by Sultan Suleiman II. It received its current name during the 18th century after the flag (*bajrak* in Turkish)

it used to display to indicate the call to prayer for all of the mosques stretched across the city. The mosque lost its original minaret during the second period of Austrian rule in the city when it was converted into a Jesuit church for a while. When the Turks left the city for good it was abandoned but it was eventually reopened in 1893 to serve those Muslims that remained in the city. It was badly damaged by fire during the riots of 2004. It has since been restored and continues to be used by the city's Muslim community.

SITES AND MONUMENTS

Belgrade Fortress Kalemegdan [1 A1]

Admission to the complex is free. The Roman Well and the Clock Tower can be visited from 09.00–21.00 for 50din, or 80din for both. Admission to these is free on the last weekend of the month. The Military Museum is open Tuesday–Sunday 10.00–17.00, closed Monday.

The plateau on which the Belgrade Fortress sits, Kalemegdan, which takes its name from a combination of two Turkish words, *kale*, meaning field and *megdan*, battle, is such an obviously strategic site – high above the surrounding plain, with clear views in all directions overlooking the confluence of two great rivers – that it seems no wonder that it was occupied and defended at the first opportunity. The first military defences here were built by the Celts, later to be expanded by the Romans during their tenancy of the site. Later, in the medieval period, the fortress was rebuilt, and ramparts constructed around the lower town by the Serbian leader Despot Stefan

Lazarević who managed to cling on to power here despite rapid Turkish expansion to the south. When the Turks finally arrived, the fortress fell into neglect and it was not until the arrival of the Austrians at the beginning of the 18th century that it was reconstructed in its present form. A good idea of the development of the fortress can be had by studying the models on display at the Belgrade Fortress Museum next door to the Clock Tower. This also clearly indicates how the small manmade harbour on the Danube below was created and defended, as well as how it subsequently vanished from sight.

Clock Tower

There are remnants of the earlier structures still in existence, like some of the medieval fortifications, but much has been re-used as building materials or as a foundation for subsequent rebuilding. Some deep wells remain that are of Roman origin: the 60m-deep so-called **Roman Well** by the **King Gate** below the Victory Monument was rebuilt by the Austrians in 1731 to ensure a safe water supply to the fortress. A double spiral staircase leads 35m down 208 steps to the water level. It was here at the site of the Roman well that Stefan Lazarević used to hold court in the 15th century and, of the surviving medieval fortifications, the most impressive date from the period of his rule. Most notable is the **Despot's Gate** (Despotova Kapija) at the northeast corner of the complex, which is named after Stefan Lazarević himself, the best preserved of the fortifications from that period. This gate formed the main entrance to the upper town in medieval times; above the gate stands the **Dizdar Tower** that is now used as an astronomical observatory. Beyond this lies the **Zindan** or **Prison Gate**, constructed in the middle of the 15th century a few years before the Despot's Gate to provide a heavily fortified entrance to the fortress. The Zindan Gate consists of two low round towers that could be defended with cannons, with a bridge crossing the ditch to the entrance between them. A dungeon was installed in the cellars underneath, hence the name. Across the drawbridge in front of the Zindan Gate is the late 17th-century **Leopold Gate**, which was built to honour the Austrian emperor of the same name; the initials LP (Leopoldus Primus) that have been carved into it are evidence of this. A short distance to the north is **Jakšić Tower**, a late 15th-century tower that was removed by the Austrians in the early 18th century and reconstructed in 1938. This looks down over two churches: the **Rose Church of Our Lady** (Crkva Ružica), built in 1730 and restored in 1925, and the smaller, later church of **St Petka**, built at the site of a holy spring.

Elsewhere within the fortress complex, features of interest of a later construction include Sahat-kula, the **Clock Tower Gate**, built in the second half of the 18th century above the south entrance to the Upper Town and used by the Turks as a lookout, and **Karađorđe's Gate**, reached by taking the path to the right of Meštrović's Monument to France. This last gate was constructed in the mid-18th century and so-named because the eponymous leader of the First National

Uprising passed through it to enter the city in 1806. The **Outer Stambol (Istanbul) Gate** directly opposite dates from the same period. The paths from both gates converge in front of the **Gallery of the Museum of Natural History** [1 A2] built in 1835 by the Turks as a guardhouse and which, rather surprisingly, is of Classical design. In front of this, the **Inner Stambol Gate**, constructed in the late 18th century with fine stone blocks, leads into the fortress.

Standing near the centre of the Upper Town is one of Belgrade's three surviving Turkish religious monuments, the **Tomb** (or in Turkish, *türbe*) **of Damad-Ali Paša**, which dates from 1783 and was built to commemorate a vizier who was killed at Petrovaradin in 1716. The focal point of the Upper Town, the **Military Museum** [1 A3], is situated in a building that used to house the Military Geographical Institute and, dating from 1923–24, is not as old as it might appear to be on first glance. The museum is easy to find; just look for the neat ranks of World War I and II tanks and anti-aircraft guns that fill the ditches surrounding it.

All of the above are to be found in the **Upper Town** sector of Kalemegdan but the **Lower Town**, the riverbank zone of the fortress, has a few sights of its own, although far more has been destroyed here. The Baroque **Charles VI Gate** (Kapija Karla VI) was built in 1736 as a ceremonial entrance to the city and bears a coat of arms that shows a boar's head being pierced by an arrow. A late 18th-century cannon foundry stands next to the gate, later to become an army kitchen. Nearby stand a **hammam**, built around 1870 for the Serbian army, which these days serves as a planetarium for an astronomical society, and a building from around 1820 that was originally the **kitchen** for the Turkish garrison. In addition to that of Charles VI, three more gates lead into the Lower Town: the **Vidin Gate**, built by the Turks in the mid-18th century, and two earlier 15th-century **Eastern gates** that lead into the Lower Town from the Vidin Gate. The latter were damaged by Allied bombing in 1944. The most prominent feature in the whole Lower Town area is the 15th-century **Nebojša Tower**, which stands near the river on Bulevar Vojvode Bojovića and was originally constructed around 1460 to protect the harbour with cannons. There was great resistance here during the 1521 siege of the city by the Turks: only after setting fire to the tower was the Lower Town successfully taken. Later, during Ottoman rule, it became a dungeon and torture chamber.

The Royal Compound

The Royal Compound is located to the south of the city on the highest point of Dedinje Hill. It consists of two palaces, a church, and other buildings in a parkland setting of 135ha.

Group visits to the Royal Compound may be made from 1 April and 31 October on Saturdays and Sundays between 10.30 and 12.30. The maximum group size is 50 and. prior registration is mandatory. Tickets may be booked at the Tourist Organisation of Belgrade office in the underpass beneath Albania Tower (✆ 635 622 or 064 8181 016) or by contacting Ms Anđelka Vuković (e dvor@belgradetourism.org.yu). Bus departure is from outside Nikola Pašića 12. No food and drink, bulky luggage or smoking is allowed within the compound and shorts should not be worn.

Sites and monuments

The **Old Court** (Stari Dvor), sometimes referred to as the Royal Palace, was built between 1924 and 1929 for King Aleksandar I. It was designed in the Serbian–Byzantine style by the architects Zivojin Nikolić and Nikolai Krassnoff, both members of the Royal Academy. The entrance hall is decorated with copies of medieval frescoes from Dečani and Sopoćani monasteries while the drawing-rooms, the Blue and Gold salons, with carved wooden ceilings and brass chandeliers, are in Baroque and Renaissance styles respectively. Along with Beli Dvor, the Royal Court is also home to a valuable collection of paintings mostly of the Renaissance school. The basement, which has a wine cellar, a billiards room and a projection room, is decorated in the style of the Kremlin's Terem Palace in Moscow with motifs of the Russian firebird legend and scenes from Serbian national epics.

The **White Court** (Beli Dvor) was built as a summer residence for King Aleksandar I between 1934 and 1937. The king was assassinated the year construction began and it became the home of the prince regent, Paul, instead. The house, by architect Aleksandar Đorđević, is in Palladian style, similar in design to the English country house Ditchley Park. The interior, in the styles of Louis XV and Louis XVI, was by the French firm Jansen who were also responsible for the White House in Washington. After World War II Beli Dvor became the official residence of President Tito although he tended to use it mainly for official functions, as did Slobodan Milošević during his presidency later on. The house has since been returned to the Serbian royal family and has been the residence of Crown Prince Alexander II since his return to Serbia in 2002.

The **Palace Church of St Andrew the First-called**, which lies to the south of the Royal Court and was built at the same time, is based upon the model for King Milutin's church at Studenica. It is also influenced by the Church of St Andrew on the Treska River in Macedonia. The frescoes inside are copies of those found in Serbian medieval monasteries and were painted by a team of Russian painters under the supervision of the exile Nikolai Krassnoff.

OTHER PLACES OF INTEREST

The **Belgrade Fair** complex, Beogradski Sajam, Bulevar Vojvode Mišića 14; ↘ 655 555; e info@sajam.co.yu

The Belgrade Fair is a trade and convention centre that puts on a variety of trade shows throughout the year as well as the occasional concert. The complex consists of about 20 separate buildings covering an area of around 40ha next to the Sava River just to the north of Ada Ciganlija. Regular events and shows are staged here throughout the year: February, March and October see a number of fashion events, April is car show month and May the time of a technology fair. In October the Belgrade Book Fair takes over (and rooms in Belgrade's cheaper hotels become hard to find). A furniture fair follows this in November and the year ends with the by now traditional New Year's Fair. In spring 2005 the country's first Erotic Fair was staged here, which raised quite a few eyebrows in the city. For more information about events here see www.begfair.com/indexe1.htm.

Sava Centre Milentija Popovića 9, Novi Beograd; ⟩ 3114 322/3; f 2605 578; www.savacentar.com

The Sava Centre is a multi-functional congress, cultural and business centre close to the Hyatt and Inter-Continental hotels in New Belgrade. Covering a site of 10ha there is a 4,000-seat theatre and 15 conference halls. As well as business conventions, international movie premieres are regularly held here as well as concerts by international artistes that range from the Moscow Philharmonic to Jethro Tull.

PARKS AND ESCAPES
Kalemegdan Park

Although Kalemegdan gets its name from a combination of two Turkish words, *kale* (field) and *megdan* (battle), the Turks also referred to the site as '*Fitchir-bayir*' ('Hill for Meditating'). The park still fulfils much the same function for many of Belgrade's citizens today and is probably the city's favourite outdoor space for most Belgraders. The park covers a total of 52ha and is divided into two halves: Kalemegdan, the main part with the Meštrović monuments, and Mali (Little) Kalemegdan, the area east of the Outer Stambol Gate that has the Cvijeta Zuzorić Art Pavilion and the zoo.

From the park's higher reaches, marvellous views may be had of the Sava and Danube rivers below, the high-rise buildings of New Belgrade on the opposite bank, and the wooded countryside of the pancake-flat Pannonian Plain that lies north of the city limits, and which draws the eye to a hazy vanishing point far upstream. The view is best in the morning – or better still, in the early evening, when the *bloks* of Novi Beograd are silhouetted with the setting sun and the river gives off a silvery glow. Looking south, beyond the urban sprawl of the city, low hills stretch away towards central Serbia. It is at this time of day that Belgraders are most likely to linger here; strolling, talking, playing chess and sometimes singing and dancing in impromptu groups. It is also a favourite spot for courting couples and rightly so: it is without doubt the city's most romantic spot.

The park was created in 1867 by Prince Mihailo Obrenović on the occasion of the fortress being handed back to the Serbs. The project was put in the hands of Emilijan Josivović, Belgrade's first urban planner. Originally, it only extended as far as the stone stairway leading up to the lower terrace but after 1931 the park was extended to include the upper city. The horse chestnut trees that were planted at this time have now reached full maturity and are a splendid sight when in flower in late spring.

Walking along the western pathway above the Sava River you soon come to the **Messenger of Victory** (Pobednik) **Monument**, a landmark that was inaugurated in 1928 to commemorate the tenth anniversary of the breach of the Salonica front. This defiant and proud statue by Ivan Meštrović was originally intended to stand in the city centre but had to be relocated here because of prudish complaints about its full-frontal nudity and quite obvious masculine attributes. Now it stands looking west over the Sava River, facing unashamedly towards New Belgrade and to Austria and Hungary beyond. As well as its more obvious manly charms, Meštrović's warrior figure has two symbols of Serbian nationhood incorporated in its design: in his left hand, the warrior holds a falcon to symbolise Slavic freedom, and in the right, a sword representing the defence of peace. Belgrade has been required to take up this sword of peace many times, usually at great cost to its citizens, but at no time was the city's freedom more threatened than during the Nazi bombings and subsequent occupation of World War II. As a reminder of this, four graves of more recent heroes lie nearby, to the right of the main path just before entering the King Gate from below. Among these are those of Tito's right-hand man in the Partisan struggle, Ive Lole Ribar, and the Marxist, Moše Pijade, one of the theoreticians that helped to give Tito an ideological framework for his reconstruction of post-war Yugoslavia.

Meštrović has another work located in the gardens nearby: his **Monument to France** [1 A3], which was erected in 1930 and depicts a figure bathing. It is dedicated to the French who perished in Yugoslavia whilst fighting in the Great War. Symbolically, the statue is meant to represent the soldiers as bathing in the waters of courage. It is an altogether different monument to the Messenger of Victory, and being of a softer, more feminine nature, has never aroused the same degree of controversy. Close to this monument, behind the bouncy castle and kids' electric trucks and beneath the shade of trees, is a fountain that depicts a figure wrestling heroically with a snake, a 1906 work of sculptor Simeon Roksandić that is entitled 'The Struggle'. The walks and pathways in this part of the park contain several more busts and statues; they are mostly dedicated to famous Belgrade poets and writers.

Being such an obviously strategic site, high above the surrounding plain, with clear views in all directions overlooking the confluence of two great rivers, it seems no wonder that it was occupied and defended at the first opportunity.

Belgrade Zoo To the north of the fortress at Mali Kalemegdan 8; ⅄/f 624 526 Belgrade Zoo, which Rebecca West described as 'a charming zoo of the Whipsnade sort', spreads across the Kalemegdan plateau's northern slope. When Nazi Stuka dive-bombers attacked the fortress in 1941 they hit the zoo too, damaging many of the cages and allowing some of its more dangerous inmates to wander freely through Belgrade's ruined streets. It has a café and gift shop as well as 200 different species of fauna. *Open every day from sunrise to sunset. Admission is 100din for children, 200din for adults.*

Tašmajdan Park
The park is a pleasant, leafy space that hosts an annual Honey Fair each October when over 100 beekeepers gather to provide a wide range of different honeys and associated bee-produce from every part of Serbia. Being the park that is closest to the city centre it is a popular place with Belgraders, especially families with young children. Tašmajdan is named after the former quarry that was located at the site of the park. Much of the stone for Belgrade's older buildings came from here. As a

Parks and escapes

consequence the ground underneath the present-day park is riddled with galleries and tunnels. During the First Uprising in 1806 some of the rebels had their camp here. Before it served as a quarry, the Romans constructed catacombs here; this funereal tradition continued until the 19th century when the graves from the cemetery were transferred to Novi Groblje.

Jevremovac Botanical Garden (*Botanička bašta*) Takovska 43; ℡ 768 857, 767 988
The garden is actually a unit of the University of Belgrade's Biology faculty, and was formerly an estate owned by Prince Milan Obrenović. It was donated to the university in 1889 on condition that it was named after the prince's grandfather, Jeverem, from whom he had inherited the estate.

There is only one entrance, at the corner on Takovska. The gardens cover 5ha and have about 250 species of tree and shrub, both native and exotic. Some of these are labelled with their names in Serbian, English and Latin together with a distribution map. There is also a hothouse, constructed in 1892, and the offices of the Institute of Botany. The hothouse, which was once one of the very best in eastern Europe but now looks a little careworn, is jam-packed with exotics but only the central section was open during my visit. Signs from the hothouse indicate the direction of the Japanese Garden (Japanski Vrt), which has all the ingredients you might expect: a pool, a shallow stream, sensitively placed rocks, a wooden footbridge, stone pagodas and a pavilion. Rather than ornamental carp, the pool has a tame terrapin that seems a bit lonely. *Open between 1 May and 1 November from 09.00–19.00; weekends from 11.00–18.00. Admission is 100din. Free guided tours are given on Saturdays at 12.00 starting from the main gate.*

Ćirilo and Metodije Park

This small park lies just southeast of Tašmajdan Park and is probably better known for the monument it contains – the **Vuk Memorial** statue (Vukov spomenik). This statue by Đorđe Jovanović, which stands at the park's western edge, was unveiled in 1937 to celebrate the 150th anniversary of Vuk Karadžić, the famous Serbian linguist and ethnographer. The statue depicts the great educator seated with book in hand, sporting a moustache so large that soup would have been out of the question.

The park is also the location of Belgrade's only **underground station**, a state-of-the-art white elephant that is well worth a look (see box, *The Underground that never was*, page 90). Across Ruzvetola west of the park is Belgrade University's Faculty of Technical Sciences, in front of which is a large seated statue of Nikola Tesla.

Topčider Park

This park is a vast green space to the south of the city, close to the residential enclaves of Dedinje and Senjak. Topčider was the first of the city parks to be created. It sprang up around the residence of Prince Miloš with the wide-scale planting of plane trees in the 1830s. The name derives from Turkish, meaning 'Valley of Cannons', as it was here that the Turks set up makeshift foundries to produce the cannons used for the 1521 attack on the city. Later, the area was used for vineyards and the summer residences of the wealthy but in 1831, after having had a *konak* built for his wife and children in town, Prince Miloš Obrenović gave instructions for the setting up of a park and settlement here. He ordered the construction of a church, a *kafana* and an army barracks, in addition to a mansion for himself that was to be designed by the same architect, Hadži-Nikola Živković, who had been responsible for his wife's residence near to the cathedral (see Princess Ljubica's *konak*, pages 220–1). The building, now housing the permanent collection of the **Historical Museum of Serbia**, is in Serbian–Balkan style, with some elements of central European influence. The prince stayed here only occasionally during his first reign, which ended in 1839, but this became his permanent home throughout his short, second reign that began in 1859. He died here on 14 September 1860.

There is a number of monuments that lie close to Prince Miloš's residence: an **obelisk** erected in 1859 to celebrate Prince Miloš' re-establishment of the Obrenović dynasty; the **Monument to Archibald Reiss**, a Swiss who accompanied the Serbs through Albania in 1915; and the **Monument to the Woman Harvester**, dating from 1852 and one of the oldest-surviving monuments in the city.

Košutnjak Hill

Košutnjak Hill ('Doe Hill') is a 330ha expanse of mixed forest and open areas that is criss-crossed by numerous walking trails. It owes its name to the deer that once roamed here, as it was a royal hunting reserve until 1903 when it was opened to

TUNNELS UNDER TOPČIDER

According to a report in the Serbian newspaper *Večernje Novosti*, there is a secret underground world hidden away in the leafy suburb of Topčider. It has recently come to light that what has been dubbed a 'concrete underground city' exists deep beneath the ground in this residential area. The complex, which is said to extend over an area of 3km^2, was constructed in the 1960s on the orders of Tito and until recently its existence was known only to government and senior military officers. Tito had it built as a wartime command centre, apparently because of his fear of nuclear attack by the Russians from whom he had distanced himself after his 1948 split with Stalin. Unconfirmed sources have stated that a 60m elevator shaft leads down to the six-storey complex, where lengthy tunnels connect a complex of rooms, offices and bunkers.

Slobodan Milošević is said to have used the base as his command centre during the 78-day NATO bombing campaign of 1999. Since their discovery there has been much speculation that the tunnels have been more recently used as a hideout for other internationally famous fugitives from justice but currently there is no real evidence to support this.

the public. Despite the fact that this park witnessed the murder of Prince Mihailo Obrenović in 1868, Košutnjak has become a favoured picnic spot for many of Belgrade's citizens. Horse-drawn carriages are available for hire for trips around the park, and it is worth seeking out the enormous 200-year-old plane tree that has branches so massive it require braces to keep them up. The park area contains two specialised facilities: Pionirski Grad ('Pioneer's Town') with its sports and recreational centre, and Filmski Grad ('Film Town') with studios and buildings to service the film industry. The Košutnjak Sports and Recreational Centre lies further down the hillside with football pitches, tennis, volleyball and basketball courts, athletics tracks and several swimming pools. There is also a ski practice slope open all year. Lying at the foot of the hill is a spring called **Hajdučka česma** that is reputed to have been favoured as a resting spot for members of the Obrenović dynasty when they went on their hunting forays; the name translates as 'Brigand's Fountain'. This lies close to the spot where Prince Mihailo was killed.

Ada Ciganlija

This long, flat island near the mouth of the Sava River, between the suburb of Čukarica and New Belgrade, is the preferred leisure spot of many Belgraders, especially in summer when tens or even hundreds of thousands migrate to its beaches at weekends. Like Zemun, its name is supposed to have a Celtic origin, coming from a combination of *singa* ('island') and *lia*, a word for submerged ground. Much of the island is covered in deciduous forest but there are extensive beaches that face on to the artificial 4km-long lake that was created by damming both ends of the island in 1967. These beaches have water for bathing that is cleaner and warmer than the Sava River itself and are very popular with bathers in summer. In addition to swimming, the lake provides an ideal environment for a whole range of watersports including rowing, sailing and water polo, and national and international championships are frequently held here; there is also a discreet nude-bathing beach 1km upstream of the main beach area. In addition to the beaches there are other distractions in the form of open-air cafés and floating restaurants, as well as shops, picnic areas, bicycle hire, pony rides, mini-golf courses, and even bungee jumping. There is a marina in the Čukarica channel for boats, yachts and smaller ships. In summer, outdoor musical events are sometimes staged here.

Coming from the city to the north, Ada Ciganlija announces itself with the sight of a large jet of water spurting from the lake, Lake Geneva-style, and a curious set of concrete monuments that locals call 'Stonehenge' for very obvious reasons. On a summer's weekend at least, you will also be greeted by the sight of an awful lot of exposed flesh. The main entrance to the island is by way of the causeway, the road across the northern end of the lake. Bike hire is available on the other side of the causeway – an ideal way of getting around, especially if you would like to circuit the lake.

Ada Ciganlija can be reached from Stari Grad or the city centre by taking one of the A1 buses that run from Zeleni venac. The bus calls in every 20 minutes or so in summer and drops off and picks up near the barrier by the entrance to the island. Other buses stop fairly near to the entrance – 92, 55 and 56. If you are driving be aware that there is quite restricted parking available on the island and cars must pay 150din to go beyond the barrier. Many locals avoid this by driving down the narrow road that runs parallel to the south side of the lake and finding a place to park here.

The north shore of the island can be reached by ferry from New Belgrade. Crossing the island past the sports centre you will soon come to the north shore. The shore here is very different from that around the lake itself: instead of an open beach, the trees at the water's edge give the impression of being a mangrove swamp. There are hundreds of rafts along the shore here, half-hidden by the trees, often reached by rickety wooden walkways. A few of them serve as cafés or restaurants but most are privately owned, the pride and joy of Belgraders who come here to potter about at weekends. It is an atmospheric place and surprisingly peaceful once out of sight and earshot of the hordes that crowd around the lake beach.

Just to the left of the volleyball courts and the Baobab and JAT airline restaurants, and next to raft café 'Ljubica', are the piers for ferries across to Blok 70 in New Belgrade. There are two or three boats that ply this route, leaving regularly between 08.00 and 21.00 and charging 30din single, 50din return. The journey takes about five minutes or so and provides a good view of the smaller island, Ada Medjica, and the picturesque line of brightly coloured rafts stretching westwards along Ada Ciganlija's northern shore. Once you reach the Sava's north shore turn left then follow the wide path that soon appears to the right – this will lead you through the tower blocks of Blok 70 and bring you out at the Chinese market on Jurija Gagarina, an interesting place in its own right. A number 11 tram from here will take you back over the Sava past the bus station to Kalemegdan Park and Dorćol.

Novo Groblje (New Cemetery)

The New Cemetery is actually the oldest existing cemetery in Belgrade. New Cemetery was founded in 1886 and, after the cemetery at Tašmajdan closed, remains of the great and the good were moved here shortly after. The cemetery is large, with several different sections and over 1,500 sculptural monuments. Just before the entrance, on Ruzeltova to the south, is the French Military Cemetery, with neat straight rows of white crosses of the French soldiers killed during World War I. At the cemetery's far northern edge, next to the Italian military graveyard, is the British equivalent, in this case dating from World War II.

The New Cemetery is a fascinating place to wander at will, examining monuments and enjoying the dense shade of the lime trees and respite from the heavy traffic outside. Many of the graves, in typical Orthodox fashion, have little fenced compounds around them and a bench for visitors. There are several grand memorial monuments scattered throughout the cemetery. At the far north is the memorial that stands above the cemetery of the victims of the 1941 and 1944 bombings. South of this, just off the main driveway, stands the Serb ossuary from World War I that contains the remains of around 4,000 Serb soldiers; nearby is the memorial of the Russian soldiers and officers who lost their lives during World War I, which has a splendid sword-wielding winged angel towering above it. The mundane is equally moving: most Orthodox graves have an engraving of the face of the deceased, or a life-sized statue. Some of them allow fashion to give clues as to the time of their demise, like the statue of a young woman wearing a miniskirt, cut off in her prime in the early 1970s.

On the other side of Ruzeltova is the **Jewish Cemetery**. At the bottom of it is a slightly forlorn 1952 monument to the Jewish victims of fascist terror, the work of architect Bogdan Bogdanović, with rusting hands and Star of David. Unlike the cemetery over the road, which is usually busy with mourners attending the graves of their loved ones, this is more likely to be deserted. Despite this, it is still actively in use. Next door to the Jewish Cemetery is the **Memorial Cemetery of the 1944 Liberators of Belgrade** that holds the graves of over 2,000 Partisan and Red Army soldiers. This was opened in 1954 on the tenth anniversary of the liberation of Belgrade.

Veliko Ratno Ostrvo (Great War Island)

This flat, heavily wooded island was formed by deposition at the confluence of the Danube and Sava rivers. It got its current name during the Austrian occupation of Belgrade in 1717 and, because of its strategic position between both Zemun and Belgrade, it was a constant source of friction between the Turks and the Austrians. They divided the island between them in 1741 but during the next conflict in the latter part of the 18th century the Turks took it over once more and used it as a base from which to bombard their enemy in Zemun. Karađorđe's rebels reconquered it during the First National Uprising in 1806 but abandoned it soon after.

These days it serves as a refuge for wildlife, especially birds, and a place of relaxation for Belgrade's masses. The northern tip of the island has the Lido beach which can be reached by ferry and, in summer, by pontoon bridge from Zemun. The Lido beach is also the setting for the Echo Music Festival that takes place in July.

Dedinje
Much of this suburb is quite self-consciously exclusive, with luxurious mansions glimpsed behind thick, protective hedges and expensive German cars swishing the tarmac; a natural abode for foreign ambassadors, film stars, politicians and Belgrade's new money. With the anonymity desired by some of its residents, it is perhaps not surprising that the neighbourhood, while pleasant enough, is rather lacking in real character. But Dedinje also has the common touch, and plays host to the home grounds of two of Belgrade's most well-known football teams – **FC Crvena Zvezda** (aka Red Star Belgrade) and **FC Partizan**. The aggressive and tribalistic graffiti that decorate the exterior walls of both of these grounds injects a tougher and grittier element into what is primarily an upper-middle-class neighbourhood. This is perfect if you are both wealthy *and* a football fan. The turbo-folk star Ceca still lives in the 'wedding cake' villa that her husband Arkan had built overlooking the Red Star ground. Her villa is not at all difficult to spot, on the corner opposite the western gates to the stadium, although you might be approached by several burly, shaven-headed men if you spend much time hanging around her front door.

Parks and escapes

Vinča

Vinča is a prehistoric site on the bank of the Danube, 14km from the centre of Belgrade on the Smederevo road. The site is home to the remains of a large Neolithic settlement that covered an area of 10ha on the banks of the river Danube. Excavations that took place in 1908 uncovered evidence of several turf houses and the remnants of a considerably developed material culture. Artefacts found included a variety of stone and bone implements and weapons as well as earthenware vessels for everyday and ritual use. In addition a large number of anthropomorphic and zoomorphic figurines were also found, along with jewellery made of semi-precious stones. The collection is shared between the National Museum, the Belgrade City Museum and the Vinča collection at the Faculty of Philosophy at the University of Belgrade.

Evidence suggests that the Vinča culture of around 4000BC extended further than any other Neolithic territory in Europe at the time. It appeared to reach a peak around 3800BC before being surpassed by the Bronze-Age cultures that had been developing around the same time.

The Vinča archaeological site is best visited by taking one of the guided tours provided by the Tourist Organisation of Belgrade. A bus leaves from Trg Nikola Pašića 12 every Saturday at 11.00. The tour lasts for three hours and costs 280din.

Beyond the city

11

If you are visiting Belgrade for just a couple of days then there is probably enough to keep you busy in the city to consider any trips away from it. With a slightly longer stay you might want to consider a half-day excursion to see a little more of the country. Belgrade is centrally situated in the northern part of Serbia and so most places in central Serbia and Vojvodina can be reached within a few hours. The places suggested below are all perfectly feasible as day trips although Novi Sad has so much to see in its own right that it would be better to spend at least one night there.

MOUNT AVALA

Mount Avala lies 18km south of the capital and is a popular summer day trip for many of Belgrade's citizens. The 511m peak stands out dramatically from the flat, agricultural terrain of the Danube and Sava valleys, and Avala serves as a natural plinth for the **Unknown Soldier Monument** that has pride of place on top of it.

The monument, a striking work by the sculptor Ivan Meštrović, was constructed in 1938 as a tribute to Serbian soldiers killed in World War I. Nearby is another monument dedicated to Soviet war veterans who died in an air crash in 1964 while on their way to Belgrade to celebrate the 20th anniversary of the liberation of the capital. At the foot of the mountain, in the village of Jajinci, is a **Memorial Garden** that pays tribute to the 80,000 Yugoslavs executed by the Nazis during World War II.

The mountain itself is covered in a mixture of coniferous and deciduous forest and has been under state protection since 1859. The town of Žmov dominated the mountain top in the medieval period, serving an important role in controlling the access roads to Belgrade. Later, in the 15th century, the town was seized by the Turks who built a fortress on the summit. The most recent reminders of war are the severely damaged buildings and rubble that remain from when the 195m tower of the RTS state television network was targeted in the 1999 NATO bombing raids. Some of the black marble blocks of the Meštrović monument were also slightly damaged – chipped by flying shrapnel.

There are a few restaurants and hotels at the mountain for those who wish to stay the night, although most people just come here for the day, having lunch and a stroll in the woods before returning to the capital.

To reach Mount Avala from Belgrade without your own transport the best bet is to take a bus bound for Mladenovac from the main bus station. This will drop you off at the junction by the main road from where you can walk up to the summit. It is a stiff climb but you may be able to find a taxi here that could take you up, from where you could return back down from the monument on foot.

PANČEVO

Pančevo is an industrial town of around 100,000 situated on the river Tamiš, a tributary of the Danube. Although the town existed as an important centre of Serbian culture during the Turkish occupation, Pančevo expanded during the early

18th century when it received migrations of Serbs from Romania and German colonists from the Upper Rhine region. The modern town has grown up around its post-World War II petrochemical industry.

On the night of 15 April 1999, NATO attacked the city, bombing the HIP chemical complex that produced petrochemicals and fertilisers. Fires and explosions at the factories caused huge quantities of toxic chlorine compounds to be released into the air and river, and large tracts of land were polluted with oil derivatives, mercury, ammonia and acids. The effects of this widespread ecological catastrophe are still being felt in the area and the Pančevo district remains one of the most ecologically damaged regions in all Serbia.

Despite its troubled recent history, Pančevo has a quiet, relaxed town centre with a number of attractive 19th-century buildings, which makes a good half-day trip from the capital. Interesting walks may be had down by the Tamiš River and there are some pleasant places to eat and drink down at the waterfront.

Pančevo can easily be reached from Belgrade by taking one of the Beovoz trains that run more or less hourly from Zemun by way of Beograd Centar, Karađorđev Park and Vukov Spomenik. Fairly regular buses also run to and from Belgrade, although some of the Belgrade buses go only as far as the Dunav bus station in the north of the city by Dunavska Bridge. The railway station and the bus station are some distance from each other in the town. The railway station is a 20-minute walk south of the city centre, while the bus station is more central, to the east of the river. Next to the main railway station of Pančevo Glavna is a large open-air market,

Pančevo

known locally as the **Chinese Market**, which is well known for the cheap smuggled goods from Romania that it has on sale.

There is just one place to stay in Pančevo, the **Hotel Tamiš** at Mose Pijade (℡ 013 342 622/345 840), which has singles for around €15 and doubles for around €25. For food, there is the **Citadela** restaurant (℡ 013 515 286) close to the Byzantine-style church on Dimitrija Tucovića, the main street that leads from the railway station to the centre. Down by the Tamiš River there is an old railway carriage that serves both as a café-bar and unofficial railway museum. There a couple of restaurants by the river down here: **Kakadu**, on a boat on a river, and also the **Kafana Stari Tamiš**.

Information on events in the town can be had from the **Tourist Organisation of Pančevo**, Sokače 2 (℡ 013 351 366).

SMEDEREVO

Smederevo is a port and industrial town of about 40,000 inhabitants that is of interest to visitors mainly because of its outstanding **fortress**. The fortress is remarkable for the sheer scale of its defences and for its state of preservation, which is impressive considering that it has languished in cheerful neglect for centuries.

Smederevo began life as a Roman settlement on the route from Singidunum to Viminacium. In 1427, it became the new Serbian capital, when the Serbs were ousted from Belgrade by the Hungarians. The castle's construction was by order of

Đurađ Branković, son of Vuk, who was despot at the time. The notion was to provide an impenetrable barrier to the Turkish advance that was taking place during this period. One legend states that the impoverished peasants who built the castle were obliged to provide thousands of eggs to mix with the mortar in order to firmly secure the stones, while another asserts that it was Branković's tyrannical wife, Jerina, who gave the order for the castle's construction. Either way, it is undeniable that a great deal of forced labour had to be recruited to build such an extensive and imposing structure in such a short time.

The Turks eventually arrived to subdue the fortress but it took them more than 20 years to do so. Smederevo Fortress was finally surrendered in 1459 to Sultan Mehmet I, which marked the final victory of the Ottoman Turks over Serbian territory. Immediately, the Turks made the castle the headquarters of their *pašalik* in the region and it remained in Turkish occupation, with the exception of a brief period of Austrian control, until 1805 when Karađorđe formally received its keys following his initial successes with the First National Uprising. Having survived the medieval period more or less intact, the fortress suffered considerable damage in far more recent times when an ammunition dump blew up part of it in 1941, and then later in 1944 when it was bombed by Allied forces.

The castle is triangular in shape, with five gates, 25 large towers, double ramparts and a moat. At one end of the complex is a smaller stronghold that consists of a palace and a citadel, which has its own moat and four bastions. On one of the bastions is the date of the building, 6938, the number of years reckoned by the

Orthodox Church to have elapsed since the world was first created, which corresponds to the date 1430 in the Roman calendar. Considering that the castle was erected very quickly, within a year from 1429–30, its dimensions are hugely impressive: the walls of the keep at the north of the inner fortress are about 15ft thick, and the total distance around the perimeter is not far short of a mile.

Also in Smederevo is an early 15th-century **monastic church** that dates from around the same time as the fortress. The church is built in the style of the Morava School, in brick and stone with three apses and a central dome, and contains some 17th-century frescoes that illustrate the life of Christ and the Psalms. The town's other main church, the **Church of St George**, is located in the central square and dates from 1854. This church, designed by the Czech architect Jan Nevola, is built in the Romantic style and blends Serbian medieval heritage with Baroque influences. The interior and the iconostasis were painted by the Russian artist, Andrea Vasilevich Bicenko.

Smederevo can be reached from Belgrade by taking one of several buses that run each day from the Lasta bus station, most of which continue on to Bela Crkva. The fare is around 200din. The bus station in Smederevo is close to the castle, as is the railway station, although there are no normal train services to Belgrade apart from occasional services of the *Romantika* tourist train on certain summer weekends, which leave Belgrade at 08.15 and arrive at Smederevo at 10.45, where a pre-booked tour of the town and its museums can be made before the train returns to Belgrade at 18.30, arriving at 20.15. Enquire at any TOB office for details and dates.

Smederevo's close proximity to Belgrade makes it highly suitable for a day trip but should you wish to stay there is the perfectly adequate **Hotel Smederevo** in the central square at Izletnicka bb (✎ *026 222 511/221 432*), which has doubles for around € 20 and singles for € 13. For eating, there are a number of restaurants, cafés and bakeries situated around this same square.

SREMSKI KARLOVCI

This small historic town, 11km southeast of Novi Sad on the banks of the Danube, is possibly one of the most attractive in all Serbia. The tree-shaded central square, Trg Branka Radičevića, named after the Romantic poet Branko Radičević, a native of the town, has a 1770 marble fountain with four lion figures as its centrepiece. Surrounding this is an array of buildings from the 18th and early 19th centuries: a neo-Classical **Town Hall** built between 1806 and 1811, a Baroque Orthodox **Cathedral** constructed between 1758 and 1762, with a 19th-century façade, and a considerable number of 18th-century houses. The cathedral has a splendid carved iconostasis by Teodor Kračun and Jakov Orfelin, with icons by other renowned 18th-century Serbian artists. Several of the wall paintings are by Paja Jovanović.

Another building of note is the **High School**, which as an institution in the town dates from 1791. The current building is a striking combination of traditional Serbian and secessionist styles. The neo-Byzantine patriarchate nearby is now home to the town's **Museum**, which provides an archaeological, historical and ethnographical account of the town and surrounding area, in addition to having a gallery of work by local artists from the 18th century to the present.

The **Upper church** in the northern part of the town was originally founded at the end of the 15th century as a nunnery, a property of the monastery at Hilandar in Greece. It was rebuilt in 1737. The **Lower church** south of the main square dates from the first quarter of the 18th century and has a very old and beautiful plane tree in its churchyard.

Historically, the most important building is the so-called **Peace Chapel**, which stands on a hill at the south end of the town. This curious, circular building commemorates the signing of the Treaty of Karlowitz in 1699 that brought peace between the Turks and the Austrians in the region. The current chapel was built in 1817 and mimics the shape of a Turkish military tent with four entrances to enable all of the participating parties to enter the room at the same time, thus putting them on equal terms. The chapel's windows are said to be patterned on the Union Jack flag – a nod of recognition to Britain, which was a co-signatory of the treaty.

The **Tourist Office** on the main square at Branka Radičevića 7 (✆ *021 882 127;* f *021 881 026;* e *info@karlovci.org.yu*) is very helpful and well resourced, with plenty of information about the history of the town as well as more general detail about the Fruška Gora area. They sell a detailed map of the town for 120din.

The **Hotel Boem** (✆ *021 881 038;* f *021 27 124;* e *hboem@eunet.yu*), opposite the cathedral at Trg Branka Radičevića 5 can provide accommodation for around €13 per person per night, although it tends to get booked up well in advance. For dining, there is the **Kućerak i Sremu** restaurant by the High School and the **Netirn** (☏ *021 881 987*) at Stražilovska 20. Fish meals may be had at **Riblji Restoran Dunav** (☏ *021 881 666*) or **Restoran Sremski Kutak** (☏ *021 882 343*), both on Dunavska, the road that leads under the railway line to reach the river Danube. There is also a bakery that sells good *burek* just around the corner from the Hotel Boem, and a few simple restaurants and a bank on the strip where the bus stops near the main road.

Sremski Karlovci can be reached by direct bus from Belgrade although there are far more services via Novi Sad. This, however, requires a change of bus stations in Novi Sad and would mean a long day out. Buses to Novi Sad's main bus station from Belgrade are very frequent and buses 61 or 62 run from Novi Sad's fish market bus station to Sremski Karlovci more or less half hourly between 06.00 and 21.00.

Perhaps the most satisfactory way to visit the town on a day trip is to take the *Romantika* tourist train that runs from Belgrade on specific days on summer weekends. The *Romantika* departs from Belgrade at 08.45 and takes about an hour and a half to reach Sremski Karlovci; the return service arrives back in Belgrade at 19.55. The Magelan Corporation Tourist Agency of Novi Sad arranges tours that can be pre-booked to meet the train at Sremski Karlovci. For the precise dates of these weekend excursions enquire at a TOB office. The tours can also be booked at several travel agents, including branches of Putnik and KSR, as well as at the main railway station itself at desk 10.

NOVI SAD

Capital of the Vojvodina region and, with a population of more than a quarter of a million, Serbia's second-largest city, Novi Sad is a relatively prosperous commercial, industrial and university town on the north shore of the Danube.

The city's most striking feature, the **Petrovaradin Fortress**, is not in Novi Sad itself but across the Danube in the separate town of Petrovaradin. Three bridges used to link the two sides of the river but all were destroyed during the hostilities of 1999. Two of these have since been replaced: one has been rebuilt, while the other is a temporary structure on pontoons. The city centre has a number of noteworthy buildings, mostly in the Baroque style, together with some excellent museums and art galleries. It is quite feasible to visit the city as a day trip from Belgrade if time is short but a longer stay here will repay dividends. Not only are there various sights in the city to enjoy, Novi Sad also serves as an excellent base for trips to other parts of Vojvodina, as well as excursions into the **Fruška Gora** hills that lie just to the south.

Transport

There are over 30 buses a day that link Novi Sad with Belgrade; some of these are express buses that use the motorway, while others are slower and stop more frequently along the way. Fares are between 150 and 250din depending on the speed of the service. All of the trains that link Belgrade with Budapest and the north stop in Novi Sad and so there are relatively good rail connections too.

Most of what you will want to see in Novi Sad is close enough to visit on foot but a couple of the city bus services are useful, in particular those that link the city centre with the long-distance bus and railway stations. To reach the city centre from the bus or train station take the 11b bus that passes right to left along Bulevar Jaše Tomića in front of the stations on the opposite side of the road. The bus stop is at the corner of Bulevar Oslobođenja, the main road into the centre. To reach the long-distance bus or train station, take the 11a bus from Riblja pijaca bus station. This will drop you off immediately in front of the stations, opposite the Hotel Park. The fare is 15din and you pay the driver.

Tourist information

Novi Sad is fortunate in having an excellent tourist information centre with an efficient and dedicated staff (9 Mihajla Pupina Bulevar; \f 421 811, 421 812, 451 481; e ticns@ptt.yu; www.novisadtourism.com and www.novisadtourism.org.yu). The helpful, English-speaking staff can provide visitors with city maps, museum information and details of current events, as well as advising on accommodation and transport. They have numerous brochures available detailing the city's museums and galleries, as well as booklets on aspects of Novi Sad's diverse ethnic make-up and history.

Accommodation

Novi Sad has a wide range of accommodation that includes some recently opened, privately owned pensions. Below is just a small selection. The telephone code for Novi Sad is 021.

Pansion (or **Boardinghouse**) **Rimski** Jovana Cvijića 25; ℣/f 443 231, 443 237, 333 587; e rimski@eunet.yu; www.rimski.co.yu
This is a privately run hotel, first opened in 2001, that is located in a quiet street fairly close to the bus and railway stations. There are 23 rooms and 3 luxury apartments, all complete with bathroom, central heating, cable TV, telephone and minibar. The hotel has a restaurant with a no-smoking section and a conference room. Sgl occupancy is €48; dbl €64.

Pansion (or **Boardinghouse**) **Zenit** Zmaj Jovina 8; ℣ 621 444; f 621 327; e office@pansionzenit.co.yu; www.pansionzenit.co.yu
This cosy, well-run private hotel is right in the heart of the city centre just off Trg Slobode. Sgl rooms are 4,100din, dbls 4,700din, inner-facing rooms 3,500din.

Hotel Vojvodina*** Trg Slobode 2; ℣ 622 122; f 615 445
This establishment, built in 1854, is the city's oldest hotel and has a very convenient central location right next to the Catholic Cathedral and the City Hall. The rooms are light and spacious, and some of them look out over Trg Slobode. Sgl rooms cost from 1,800–2,400din depending on whether or not you choose to have a TV set and a king-size bed; dbl rooms range from 2,600–3,200din; triples go for 3,300din; apartments, 3,600–5,000din.

Hotel Putnik*** Ilije Ognjanovića 24; ℣ 615 555; f 622 561
This is another state-run hotel just around the corner from the Hotel Vojvodina, with its own casino, 63 dbl rooms and 22 sgls. Prices are slightly more expensive than the Hotel Vojvodina.

Hotel Novi Sad*** Bulevar Jaše Tomića bb; ℡ 442 511; f 443 072
With 78 dbls and 24 sgl rooms, this large, traditional hotel is very convenient for the bus and train stations but at some distance from the city centre. It has a 250-seat restaurant, conference hall, cocktail bar, discotheque and bar. Sgl rooms cost 2,300din; dbls 3,200din.

Pansion Fontana Pašićeva 27; ℡ 621 779
The Fontana Restaurant, close to the city centre, has a few rooms to rent above its dining area. The rooms are simply furnished but clean and pleasant. Breakfast is served in the courtyard below. Twin rooms go for 1,500din for sgl occupancy, 2,000din for dbl.

The city's only hostel is the recently opened **Hostel Brankovo kolo** at Episkopa Visariona 3; ℡ 528 263, 422 784, 622 160; e office@hostelns.com; www.hostelns.com.

Eating and drinking
Novi Sad is well provided with restaurants of every type. The squares and pedestrian areas around Trg Slobode, Modene and Zmaj Jovina are full of bars, cafés and pizzerias with plentiful outdoor seating in the warmer months of the year.

Alla Lanterna Dunavska 27; ℡ 622 022
This is a very popular pasta and pizza place at the end of the pedestrian stretch of Dunavska.

Bela Lađa Kišacka 21; ☏ 616 594

A traditional restaurant that offers local dishes and a wide selection of Vojvodina wines at very reasonable prices. There is traditional music to accompany your meal most nights.

Beli Lav Zmaj Jovina 28; ☏ 452 788

This four-star restaurant is considered one of the best in Novi Sad. The food is mostly Italian, with *antipasti* from 250din, pasta dishes from 300din and meat dishes starting at 500din. The fish dishes are good, but expensive. *Open Mon–Fri 10.00–23.00, Sat 10.00–midnight; closed Sun.*

Bistro Café Modene 4

This excellent establishment serves good coffee and draught beer in a plain, no-nonsense bar with a convivial atmosphere. The prices are perhaps the cheapest in the city centre, with cappuccino for 30din and half-litres of *točeno pivo* (draught beer) for 50din. In summer, there is also outdoor seating on a terrace outside.

Cezar Modene 2; ☏ 623 538

This is a central pizzeria that has seating inside and out, and which sells pizza by the slice, either to eat on the premises or to take away. It also sells several varieties of *burek* and *pita*, like mushroom and potato – all excellent – as well as sandwiches.

Dukat Đorđa Rakovića 12; ☏ 525 190; www.dukat.co.yu

Dukat is a smart four-star family restaurant that serves traditional dishes in an elegant setting. It has live music on some nights.

Fontana Pašićeva 17; ☏ 621 779

Fontana is a Serbian restaurant, located just off Zmaj Jovina, that has several wooden-panelled rooms inside, and a pleasant courtyard with secluded seating around a fountain outside. There is live folk music here some nights.

Sečuan Dunavska 16; ☏ 529 693

This is a reasonable three-star Chinese restaurant close to the bottom of the pedestrian part of Dunavaska. As well as Sichuan cuisine and *dim sum*, it also serves Serbian dishes.

Surabaja Primorska 26; ☏ 413 400; f 414 130

This is a rare thing in Serbia – an Indonesian restaurant. Surabaja is located next to the Apollo business and shopping centre, close to the National Theatre. It also serves Chinese food. *Open Mon–Sat 09.00–midnight.*

For **fast food**, as well as the places on Modene mentioned above, there is a concentration of food kiosks on Gimnazijska at the side of the Bishop's Palace and at the fish market bus station.

Sightseeing

Most of the city's sights are within a small area of the centre. The hub is spacious **Trg Slobode**, with the neo-Gothic brick-clad **Roman Catholic Cathedral** on one side of the square and the neo-Renaissance **City Hall** facing it on the other. The pedestrian area of the square continues along café-lined **Zmaj Jovina** to the

Bačka Bishop's Palace at its eastern end and the **Orthodox Cathedral** just beyond this. The **Bačka Bishop's Palace** (Vladicanski Dvor) is the residential palace of the Serbian Orthodox Bishop in Novi Sad. It was constructed in 1901 on the site of a former palace that dated from 1741. The building style is curiously eclectic: a mix of secessionist and Serbian Romanticism, with pseudo-Moorish plasterwork decoration on red brick. In front of the palace stands a statue of **Zmaj Jovana Jovanović**, the city's famous doctor and poet.

Leading off from here is the pedestrian street of **Dunavska**, one of the city's most attractive thoroughfares with many 18th- and 19th-century buildings. The **City Library** (1895) is on the corner with Gimnazijska and further down, close to the junction with Ignatja Pavlasa, is the **Gallery of Foreign Art** at number 29. Beyond here, the street runs along the edge of a pleasant park with a small lake – **Dunavska Park** – a leafy escape from the city bustle.

Returning to the Orthodox Cathedral and walking northwest along Pašićeva, you come to the entrance of the grounds of the Church of St Nicholas located in a quiet, shady corner between Pašićeva and Đurejakšića streets. The small **St Nicholas Church** (Nikolejevska Crkva) is the oldest Orthodox church in Novi Sad, mentioned in official records from 1739 as the endowment of the Bogadanović family, wealthy merchants in the city at that time. The church, unusually, has a small gold-plated onion dome in the style of a Russian Orthodox church.

There are many more churches dotted around Novi Sad, which is to be expected given the multi-ethnic make-up of the city. Scattered around the city centre are the places of worship of a broad range of denominations: as well as Orthodox and Roman Catholic there are Greek-Catholic, Reformist, Pentecostal, Adventist, Slovak-evangelistic, Baptist and Methodist. There is also a synagogue – before World War II Novi Sad had a sizeable Jewish population. The **synagogue** is on Jevrejska ('Jew Street') at number 9, with other important buildings previously owned by the Jewish community flanking it on both sides. The whole complex, all constructed using the same light-yellowish brick, was built in 1909, designed by the architect Lipot Baumhorn (1860–1932).

Museums and galleries
The city has a number of excellent galleries and museums.

Museum of Vojvodina Dunavska 35–7; ☎ 525 059, 420 566;
e museumv@eunet.yu
This is a large, rambling museum housed in two buildings next door to each other opposite Dunavska Park. The museum at number 35 deals with the archaeology, early history and ethnology of the province. At number 37 next door, the focus is on more recent history – from the first half of the 20th century up until the end of World War II. The museum's greatest treasure is undoubtedly that of a beautifully preserved Roman helmet fashioned from pure gold. *Open Tue–Fri 09.00–19.00, weekends 09.00–14.00; closed Mon.*

Novi Sad

Gallery of Matica Srpska Trg Galerija 1; ↘ 421 455; e galmats@eunet.yu.
This collection was founded by Matica Srpska in Budapest in 1826 and opened to the public in 1847. In 1864 the gallery was transferred to Novi Sad and it was placed in its current building in 1958. The gallery, one of the best collections of paintings in the country, represents Serbian artists working in Vojvodina from the 17th to the 20th centuries. *Open Tue, Wed, Thu, Sat 10.00–18.00, Fri 12.00–20.00; closed Sun and Mon. Entrance 50din.*

Pavle Beljanski Memorial Gallery Trg Galerija 2; ↘ 528 185; e szpb@eunet.yu.
This gallery, first opened to the public in 1961, is composed entirely of the work of Serbian artists from the first half of the 20th century. The collection of paintings, sculpture and tapestries was bequeathed to the city by Pavle Beljanski, a prominent Novi Sad lawyer and diplomat. *Open Wed, Fri, Sat, Sun 10.00–18.00, Thu 13.00–21.00, closed Mon and Tue.*

Collection of Rajko Mamuzić Vase Stajić 1; ↘ 520 467
This collection represents the work of post-World War II Serbian/Yugoslav painters. It was presented to the city of Novi Sad as a gift in 1972. *Open Wed–Sun 09.00–17.00, closed Mon and Tue.*

Institute for the Protection of Nature in Serbia Radnička 20a; ↘ 421 143, 421 144; e zzpsns@eunet.yu
The Institute has a collection of over 60,000 items from various fields of study:

geology, palaeontology, botany, ornithology etc. Among an extensive display of animal skeletons, stuffed birds, dioramas and fossils the most impressive item is the skull and tusks of a woolly mammoth from the Pleistocene period. *Open daily 08.00–19.00.*

The Museum of Foreign Art 29 Dunavska; ☎ 451 239
The work on show here is the legacy of Dr Branko Ilić and includes artworks from the Renaissance right up to the 20th century. Most of the collection comes from the central European region. *Open Tue–Sun 10.00–16.00; closed Mon.*

Petrovaradin Fortress
This impressive fortress has often been referred to as the 'Gibraltar of the Danube'. Petrovaradin started life as a Roman fortress and various additions were made through the medieval period. That which exists today, however, dates almost entirely from the early 18th century, when the fortress was comprehensively enlarged and fortified by the Austrians after their successful defeat of the Turkish army in 1692. Although the Turks returned for a final battle in 1717, the fortress was already a white elephant by the time the fortifications were complete. There are 18km of galleries in all, at four different levels beneath the fortress. Today, only 1km of the tunnel complex is open to the general public.

Above ground, many of the original buildings have been converted for alternative usage: the **City Museum** (see below) is housed in buildings that originally served as

Novi Sad

a barracks and an arsenal; the Historical Archive of Novi Sad is housed in another block of barracks, and the long terrace of barracks that look out over the Danube have been converted into the (currently closed) Hotel Varadin and a variety of art studios. Between the Hotel Varadin and the Historical Archive is a small street of craft shops. The seating area immediately below the clocktower – **Ludwig's Bastion** – and the terrace of the adjoining restaurant both offer excellent views over the Danube River and Novi Sad beyond. You may notice that the hands on the **clocktower** are the wrong way round, with the minute hand replacing the hour hand and vice versa. The reason for this is that it is said to make them easier to see at a distance.

The Novi Sad City Museum Petrovaradin Tvrđava 4; \ 433 145, 433 613; e muzgns@eunet.yu
The display here concerns the cultural history of the city, with a selection of fine and applied art from the mid 18th to the mid 20th centuries that includes paintings, religious icons, musical instruments and furniture. With some advance notice, the museum staff can organise tours of the fortress's underground galleries. Tours take place between 10.00 and 17.00, but not on Mondays. *Open daily 09.00–17.00.*

Language

12

The language spoken in Belgrade is Serbian, which is very close to the official languages of both Croatia and Bosnia and belongs to the group of South Slavonic languages along with Macedonian, Slovenian and Bulgarian. The break-up of Yugoslavia and the ensuing nationalism has meant that the languages spoken today in Croatia and Bosnia-Herzegovina have perhaps more differences with standard Serbian than they did during the years of the federation. Many linguists consider the languages of Bosnia and Croatia to be normal linguistic variations of the same common language (Serbo-Croat) rather than distinct languages, although there are many – mostly Croats and Bosnians – who would disagree with this. Nevertheless, Croatians, Bosnians and Serbs can still readily understand each other even though they may use some different words and expressions. Macedonian and Slovenian are languages that are further removed linguistically although, having received an educational grounding in Serbo-Croat from the old days of the federation, most Macedonians and Slovenes are able to make sense of Serbian.

Unfortunately, Serbian is not an easy language to master for the non-Slavic speaker as it is grammatically complex, having six cases to decline and three genders, which are distinct even in the plural (unlike Russian). There is no definite article in Serbian. Nouns may be masculine, feminine or neuter and are declined according to their function in a sentence. In their singular form, masculine nouns end with a consonant and generally end with an 'i' in the plural. Most feminine nouns end in '-a' in the singular and '-e' in the plural. Neuter nouns end in either '-e' or '-o' in the singular; generally, the plural form ends in '-a'.

The plus factor is that pronunciation is regular and predictable, having a perfectly phonetic script. It is written in both Roman and Cyrillic script, although use of the latter is perhaps slightly on the wane.

The good news is that many people in Belgrade can speak English, usually very well indeed. It is still a good idea to have a grasp of the basics, if only for politeness's sake. As anywhere else, people will be pleased and impressed if they can see that you have taken a little trouble to learn a little of their native tongue. If you leave Belgrade for the more remote Serbian hinterland you will find that a basic understanding of the language will come in very useful indeed.

PRONUNCIATION

In Serbian, almost every word is pronounced exactly as it is written. There are 30 letters in the Serbian alphabet, which is written in both Cyrillic and Latin forms. Stress is usually on the first syllable but in some cases, as in words that have a prefix, stress is on the middle syllable. Stress never falls on the last syllable of a word.

Roman   Cyrillic   Pronunciation

A a   A a   'a' as in ask

B b   Б б   'b' as in boy

C c	Ц ц	'c' like the 'ts' in flotsam
Č č	Ч ч	'ch' as in church
Ć ć	Ћ ћ	'tch' like the 't' in future
D d	Д д	'd' as in dog
Dž dž	Џ џ	'j' as in just
Đ đ	Ђ ђ	'dj' as in endure
E e	E e	'e' as in egg
F f	Ф ф	'f' as in father
G g	Г г	'g' as in girl
H h	X x	'h' as in hot; like the 'ch' in loch before another consonant
I i	И и	'i' as in machine
J j	J j	'y' as in young
K k	K k	'k' as in king
L l	Л л	'l' as in like
Lj lj	Љ љ	'ly' like the 'lli' in million
M m	M m	'm' as in man
N n	Н н	'n' as in nest
Nj nj	Њ њ	'nj' like the 'ny' in canyon
O o	O o	'o' between the 'o' in bone and the 'aw' in shawl
P p	П п	'p' as in perfect
R r	Р р	'r' as in rough
S s	C c	's' as in Serbia

Š š	**Ш ш**	'sh' as in lush
T t	**Т т**	't' as in test
U u	**У у**	'oo' as in boot
V v	**В в**	'v' as in victory
Z z	**З з**	'z' as in zebra
Ž ž	**Ж ж**	'zh' like the 's' in pleasure

WORDS AND PHRASES
Basics

Yes	*Da*	Thank you	*Hvala*
No	*Ne*	I don't understand	*Ne razumem*
Maybe	*Možda*	I don't speak	*Ne znam srpski*
Hello	*Zdravo*	Serbian	
Goodbye	*Doviđenja, čiao*	Sorry	*Pardon, Izvinite*
Good morning	*Dobro jutro*	No problem	*Nema problema*
Good day/	*Dobar dan*	Excuse me	*Izvinite*
afternoon		May I?	*Da li mogu?*
Good evening	*Dobro veče*	Please give me...	*Dajte mi...*
Good night	*Laku noć*	That's fine	*U redu je*
How are you?	*Kako ste?*	Good	*dobar*
Well, thank you	*Dobro, hvala*	Bad	*loš*
Please	*Molim*	Little	*malo*

Language

Today	danas	Mr	Gospodin
Yesterday	juče	Mrs	Gospoda
Tomorrow	sutra	Miss	Gospodica

Questions

Where is ...?	Gde je ...?	Do you speak English?	Govorite li engleski?
How?	Kako?	How much is it?	Koliko košta?
When?	Kada?	What time is it?	Koliko je sati?
Which?	Koji?	Where are you from?	Odakle ste?
Who?	Ko?		
Why?	Zašto?		
What's your name?	Kako se zovete?		

Introductions

My name is ...	Ja se zovem...
I am from ... England/America	Ja sam iz ... Engleske/Amerike
... Scotland/Wales/Ireland	... Škotske/Velsa/Irske
I am a foreigner	Ja sam stranac
Pleased to meet you	Drago mi je

Words and phrases

Signs

Entrance/exit	ulaz/izlaz	УЛАЗ/ИЗЛАЗ
Open/closed	otvoreno/zatvoreno	ОТВОРЕНО/ЗАТВОРЕНО
Information	informacije	ИНФОРМАЦИЈЕ
Prohibited	zabranjeno	ЗАБРАЊЕНО
Toilets	toalet	ТОАЛЕТ
Men	muški	МУШКИ
Women	ženski	ЖЕНСКИ
Danger	opasnost	ОПАСНОСТ
Arrival	dolazak	ДОЛАЗАК
Departure	polazak	ПОЛАЗАК
No smoking	zabranjeno pušenje	ЗАБРАЊЕНО ПУШЕЊЕ
No entry	ulaz zabranjen	УЛАЗ ЗАБРАЊЕН

Getting around

Where's the...	Gde je ...
bus station?	autobuska stanica?
railway station?	železnička stanica?
airport?	aerodrom?
How far is it to ...?	Koliko je daleko do ...?
What time's the next bus?	Kada polazi sledeći autobus?
What time does the ... leave/arrive?	Kada... polazi/dolazi?

I want to go to ...		Želim da odem u ...	
I would like a ...		Želim ...	
I want to get off!		Želim da siđem!	
How do I get to ...?		Kako mogu da dođem do ...?	
Is it near/far?		To je blizu/dalek?	
bus	autobus	straight on	pravo
train	voz	ahead/behind	napred/iza
tram	tramvaj	up/down	gore/dole
aeroplane	avion	under/over	ispod/iznad
boat	brod	north/south	sever/jug
car/taxi	auto/taksi	east/west	istok/zapad
one-way ticket	karta u jednom pravcu	here/there	ovde/tamo
		garage	garaža
return ticket	povratna karta	petrol (gas) station	benzinska stanica
two tickets	dve karte	road/street	put/ulica
1st class	prva klasa	bridge/river	most/reka
2nd class	druga klasa	waterfall	vodopad
left	levo	hill/mountain/peak	brdo/planina/vrh
right	desno	village/town	selo/grad

Words and phrases

Shopping

bank	*banka*	money	*novac*
bookshop	*knjižara*	newspaper	*novine*
chemist	*apoteka*	post office	*pošta*
(pharmacy)		postage stamp	*poštanska marka*
discount	*popust*	postcard	*dospisnica*
exchange office	*menjačnica*	shop	*radnja*
market	*pijaca*	souvenir	*uspomena*

Health

accident	*nesreća*	eye	*oko*
allergy	*alergija*	fever	*groznica*
ambulance	*ambulanta*	head	*glava*
anaemia	*anemija*	headache	*glavobolja*
back	*leđa*	heart	*srce*
chest	*grudi*	hospital	*bolnica*
cold	*nazeb*	indigestion	*loše varenje*
cough	*kašalj*	infection	*infekcija*
dentist	*zubar*	medicine	*lek*
doctor	*lekar*	pain	*bol*
ear	*uvo*	stomach ache	*bolovi u stomaku*
emergency	*nužda*		

Language

Numbers

0	*nula*	13	*trinaest*
1	*jedan*	14	*četrnaest*
2	*dva*	15	*petnaest*
3	*tri*	16	*šesnaest*
4	*četiri*	17	*sedamnaest*
5	*pet*	18	*osamnaest*
6	*šest*	19	*devetnaest*
7	*sedam*	20	*dvadeset*
8	*osam*	21	*dvadeset i jedan*
9	*devet*	100	*sto*
10	*deset*	200	*dvesta* or *dve stotine*
11	*jedanaest*	one thousand	*hiljada*
12	*dvanaest*	one million	*milion*

Time

afternoon	*popodine*	month	*mesec*
autumn	*jesen*	morning	*jutro*
day	*dan*	night	*noć*
evening	*veče*	now	*sada*
hour	*sat*	spring	*proleće*
minute	*minut*	summer	*leto*

Words and phrases

today	*danas*	winter	*zima*
tomorrow	*sutra*	year	*godina*
week	*nedelja, sedmica*	yesterday	*juče*

Monday	*ponedeljak*	Friday	*petak*
Tuesday	*utorak*	Saturday	*subota*
Wednesday	*sreda*	Sunday	*nedelja*
Thursday	*četvrtak*		

January	*januar*	July	*jul*
February	*februar*	August	*avgust*
March	*mart*	September	*septembar*
April	*april*	October	*oktobar*
May	*maj*	November	*novembar*
June	*jun*	December	*decembar*

Food and drink

apple	*jabuka*	beer	*pivo*
baked	*pečeno*	bill	*račun*
bean	*pasulj*	brandy	*rakija*
beef	*govedina*	bread	*hleb*
beefsteak	*biftek*	breakfast	*doručak*

Language

butter	*puter*	grilled	*sa roštilja*
cabbage	*kupus*	ham	*šunka*
cake	*kolač, torta*	homemade	*domaće*
carrot	*šargarepa*	honey	*med*
cheese	*sir*	ice cream	*sladoled*
chicken	*piletina*	juice	*sok*
chicken soup	*pileća supa*	knife	*nož*
chips	*pomfrit*	lamb	*jagnje*
coffee	*kafa*	lunch	*ručak*
(Turkish coffee)	*turska kafa*	meat	*meso*
(black/white)	*crna/bela*	milk	*mleko*
(cappuccino)	*kapučino*	mushrooms	*pečurke*
cognac	*konjak*	onion	*luk*
cup	*šoljica*	orange	*pomorandža*
dinner	*večera*	pancake	*palačinka*
drink (noun)	*piće*	pasta	*testenine*
eggs	*jaja*	peach	*breskva*
fish	*riba*	pear	*kruška*
fish soup	*riblja čorba*	pepper	*biber*
fork	*viljuška*	plate	*tanjir*
garlic	*beli luk*	plum	*šljiva*
glass	*staklo*	plum brandy	*šljivovica*

pork	svinjetina	sugar	šećer
potato	krompir	tavern	konoba
restaurant	restoran	tea	čaj
rice	pirinač	tomato	paradajz
roasted meat	pečeno meso	veal	teletina
roast pork	svinjsko pečenje	veal soup	teleća čorba
roast chicken	pečena piletina	vegetables	povrće
salad	salata	water	voda
salt	so	(mineral water)	mineralna voda
sausage	kobasica	wine	vino
soup	supa, čorba	(white/red)	belo/crno
spoon	kašika	yoghurt	jogurt
strawberry	jagoda		

Language

Further information

13

MAGAZINES
Entertainment

BelGuest is a quarterly magazine with listings and articles about the city in English and Serbian.

Yellow Cab (www.yellowcab.co.yu) is a free monthly magazine that is partly in English but mostly in Serbian, which has very useful listings of forthcoming cultural events, restaurants, galleries and concerts.

BOOKS
History and culture

Benson, Leslie *Yugoslavia: A Concise History* Palgrave Macmillan, 2004. The most up-to-date book about the history of the federation that is currently available.

Cohen, Lenard J *Serpent in the Bosom: the Rise and Fall of Slobodan Milošević* Basic Books, 2002. Not that Leonard Cohen! The title says it all really – a very readable study of the man. The book has been revised with new material on Milošević's indictment at the International Tribunal at The Hague.

Collin, Matthew *This is Serbia Calling: Rock 'n' Roll Radio and Belgrade's Underground Resistance* Serpent's Tail, 2001. A fascinating account of the history of radio (and now television) station B92 and its role in Milošević's downfall.

Drakulić, Slavenka *They Would Never Hurt a Fly* Abacus, 2004. An emotional account of the war trials tribunal in The Hague and an examination of how ordinary people can do dreadful things in times of war. Perhaps rather biased against the Serbs while more forgiving of the Croats (the author is a Croat) but fascinating reading nevertheless.

Glenny, Misha *The Balkans, Nationalism, War and the Great Powers* Granta, 1999, and *The Fall of Yugoslavia* Penguin, 1996. Two books by Misha Glenny, a BBC correspondent and renowned expert on Balkan history and politics.

Judah, Tim *The Serbs: History, Myth and the Destruction of Yugoslavia* Yale Nota Bene, 2000. An in-depth history of the Serbs from the Battle of Kosovo to the break-up of Yugoslavia.

Lazić, Mladen (editor) *Protest in Belgrade: Winter of Discontent* Central European University Press, 1999. This is a hard-to-find study of the widespread protests in the city during the winter of 1996–97 seen from a sociological perspective.

Lebor, Adam *Milošević: A Biography* Bloomsbury, 2002. A balanced biography that gives a three-dimensional account of Milošević's complex, but deeply unpleasant, character.

Levinson, Florence Hamlish *Belgrade: Among the Serbs* Ivan R Dee Inc, 1994. This book helps redress the customary anti-Serb stance of the Western media. The author questions the way Serbs have been demonised through various conversations with intellectuals in the capital.

Little, Allan and Silber, Laura *The Death of Yugoslavia* Penguin, 1996. This is the book of the highly lauded BBC television series on Yugoslavia's break-up.

Lomas, Robert *The Man Who Invented the Twentieth Century: Nikola Tesla, Forgotten Genius of Electricity* Headline, 2000. A biography of Nikola Tesla, the highly eccentric scientific genius who never quite achieved the recognition he deserved.

Macdonald, David Bruce *Balkan Holocausts?: Serbian and Croatian Victim Centred Propaganda and the War in Yugoslavia (New Approaches to Conflict Management)* Manchester University Press, 2003. Despite the long, off-putting title this is a fascinating account of how both Serbs and Croats have exploited holocaust imagery to help claim historical victimisation and the way propaganda was used as a weapon in Yugoslavia's secessionist wars.

Parenti, Michael *To Kill a Nation* Verso Books, 2001. This book painstakingly examines the details hidden from us during the wars in Yugoslavia showing that, in his opinion at least, the Croatian and Bosnian leaders were just as manipulative and bloodthirsty as the Serbs and even more nationalist. Very critical of US and NATO policy, it could be argued that the book goes too far in invoking conspiracy theories that the West was engaged in a premeditated dismantling of Serbia as a nation.

Pavlowitch, Stevan *Tito: Yugoslavia's Great Dictator – A Reassessment* C Hurst & Co, 1993. This is probably the most recent of the biographies about the Yugoslav leader.

Stephen, Chris *Judgement Day: The Trial of Slobodan Milošević* Atlantic Books, 2004. Of interest to those following the slow turn of events at The Hague.

Tesanović, Jasmina *The Diary of a Political Idiot* Midnight Editions, 2002. A first-hand account of life in Belgrade in 1999 by a dissident journalist who was against the war in Kosovo.

Thomas, Robert *Serbia under Milošević: Politics in the 1990s* C Hurst & Co, 2001. A rather scholarly account of how Milošević was able to exploit national and constitutional tensions to maintain his power base.

Books

Architecture

Blagojević, Ljiljana *Modernism in Serbia: The Elusive Margins of Belgrade Architecture, 1919–1941*
MIT Press, 2003. An illustrated account of the city's modernist architecture movement
between the wars.

Language

Davidović, Mladen (Editor) *Serbian–English, English–Serbian Concise Dictionary* Hippocrene
Books, 1997. A good, up-to-date dictionary but the Serbian component uses Cyrillic
only.

Norris, David and Ribnikar, Vladislava *Serbian (Teach Yourself Languages series)* Teach Yourself
Books, 2003. An excellent book if you are keen to learn the language.

Guidebooks

Ćorović, Ljubica *Belgrade Tourist Guide* Kreativni centar, Belgrade, 2003. This is an extremely
detailed guide to Belgrade's sights and monuments, organised by way of walking tours
through the city. Apart from public transport routes, it contains little practical advice. It
is available in English translation at some Belgrade bookshops.

Cuddon, J A *The Companion Guide to Jugoslavia* Prentice-Hall, 1984 (Out of print). Very
out of date now but still an interesting and opinionated guide to the former
Yugoslavia.

Mitchell, Laurence *Serbia: The Bradt Travel Guide* Bradt, 2005. What you need if you are
considering a trip beyond the capital to see what the rest of the country has to offer.

Travel writing

Murphy, Dervla *Through the Embers of Chaos, Balkan Journeys* John Murray, 2003. This is a
superb and moving account of this stoic Irishwoman's journey through a deeply troubled
political landscape in 1999 and 2000. Even more remarkable is that she travelled by
bicycle at the age of 70. Full of perceptive insights and informed political analysis.

West, Rebecca *Black Lamb and Grey Falcon, a Journey through Yugoslavia* Canongate, 2001. A
classic, this weighty tome with nearly 1,200 pages chronicles the pre-war Balkan
peregrinations of this socialist aristocrat and her husband. Highly opinionated, her prose,
which can meander as much as her journeys do, infuriates and charms in equal measure.
Not a light read in any sense of the word but recommended.

Serbian literature

Selenić, Slobodan *Fathers and Forefathers* Harvill Press, 2003 and *Premeditated Murder* Harvill
Press, 1996. Two novels set in Belgrade, that span the period from World War II to the
present day.

WEB RESOURCES

Below are a few of the most useful websites devoted to Belgrade and Serbia.

www.b92.net/english Daily English-language news on Serbia
www.beograd.org.yu/english Information on Belgrade
www.serbia-tourism.org National Tourist Office of Serbia website
www.belgradetourism.org.yu The website of the Tourist Organisation of Belgrade

WIN £100 CASH!

READER QUESTIONNAIRE

Send in your completed questionnaire for the chance to win
£100 cash in our regular draw
All respondents may order a Bradt guide at half the UK retail price – please
complete the order form overleaf.

Have you used any other Bradt guides? If so, which titles? . . . .
. . . .
. . . .

What other publishers' travel guides do you use regularly? . . . .
. . . .
. . . .

Where did you buy this guidebook? . . . .

What was the main purpose of your trip to Belgrade (or for what other reason did
you read our guide)? eg: holiday/business/charity etc. . . . .
. . . .

What other destinations would you like to see covered by a Bradt guide?
. . . .

What other destinations would you like to see covered by a Bradt guide?

. . . .

Would you like to receive our catalogue/newsletters?

YES / NO (If yes, please complete details on reverse)

If yes – by post or email?. . . . .

Age (circle relevant category) 16–25   26–45   46–60   60+

Male/Female (delete as appropriate)

Home country . . . .

Please send us any comments about our guide to Belgrade or other Bradt Travel Guides. . . . .

. . . .

. . . .

. . . .

Bradt Travel Guides

23 High Street, Chalfont St Peter, Bucks SL9 9QE, UK
Telephone: +44 1753 893444 Fax: +44 1753 892333
Email: info@bradtguides.com
www.bradtguides.com

CLAIM YOUR HALF-PRICE BRADT GUIDE!

To order your half-price copy of a Bradt guide, and to enter our £100 prize draw, fill in the form below, complete the questionnaire on pages 292–3, and send it to us by post, fax or email. Details of some Bradt city guides can be found on pages VIII–IX; the full range of titles and prices is on our website (www.bradtguides.com).

Title	Retail price	Half price
....	....	....
Post & packing (£1/book UK; £2/book Europe; £3/book rest of world)		....
	Total	....

Name ....
....
Address...
....
Tel........................ Email ....

❑ I enclose a cheque for £........ made payable to Bradt Travel Guides Ltd
❑ I would like to pay by VISA or MasterCard
    Number......................... Expiry date ....
❑ Please add my name to your catalogue mailing list.

Serbia
The Bradt Travel Guide

'...a good introduction to the country.'
The Independent

A perfect complement to Bradt's *Belgrade* guide for those keen to discover what lies beyond the capital. A prime destination for winter sports, mountain resorts as well as a range of health spas in spectacular settings, Serbia deserves to be explored.

'I'm from Belgrade. I wanted to thank you for the beautiful *Serbia* guide. I've bought it and it's fantastic, something that Serbia needed. We really needed this.'
Reader comment

Bradt Travel Guides Ltd
+44 (0)1753 893444   www.bradtguides.com

Index

index

index

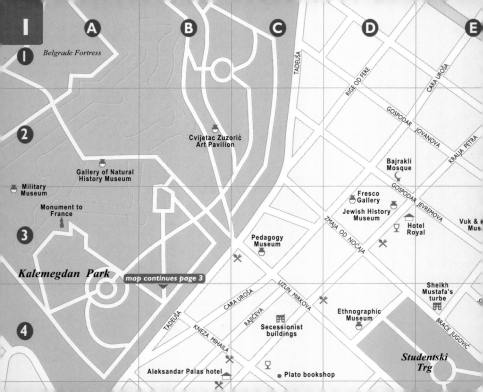

I A B C D **E**

1 *Belgrade Fortress*

2
Cvijetac Zuzorić
Art Pavilion

Gallery of Natural
History Museum

Military
Museum

Monument to
France

3

Kalemegdan Park

map continues page 3

Pedagogy
Museum

TADEUŠA

RIGE OD FERE

CARA UROŠA

GOSPODAR JOVANOVA

KRALJA PETRA

Bajrakli
Mosque

Fresco
Gallery

Jewish History
Museum

GOSPODAR JEVREMOVA

Hotel
Royal

Vuk &
Mus

ZMAJA OD NOĆAJA

Sheikh
Mustafa's
turbe

Ethnographic
Museum

4

TADEUŠA

KNEZA MIHAILA

CARA UROŠA

RAJIĆEVA

UZUN MIRKOVA

BRAĆE JUGOVIĆ

Secessionist
buildings

*Studentski
Trg*

Aleksandar Palas hotel

Plato bookshop

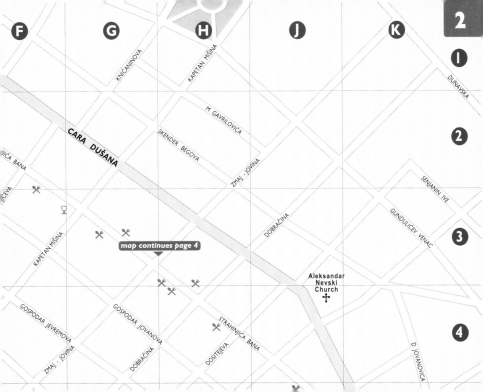

map continues page 4

Aleksandar
Nevski
Church

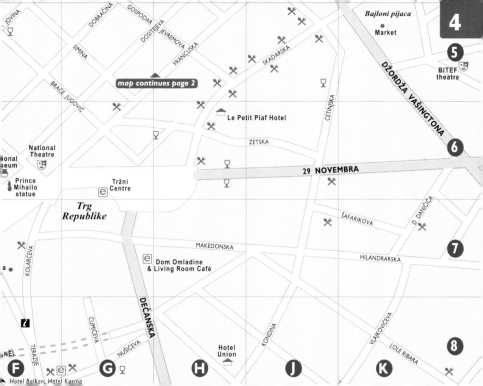

4

Bajloni pijaca
● Market

5
BITEF theatre

DŽORDŽA VAŠINGTONA

6

DOBRAČINA
GOSPODAR
DOSITEJEVA
JEVREMOVA
FRANCUSKA
SIMINA

SKADARSKA

BRACE JUGOVIĆ

map continues page 2

🍴 Le Petit Piaf Hotel

CETINJSKA

ZETSKA

National Theatre

ional seum

29 NOVEMBRA

Prince Mihailo statue

Tržni Centre

Trg Republike

ŠAFARIKOVA

D DANIČIĆA

7

MAKEDONSKA

KOLARČEVA

HILANDRARSKA

🅴 Dom Omladine & Living Room Café

a ●

DEĆANSKA

ĆUMIĆEVA

KONDINA

VLAJKOVIĆEVA

LOLE RIBARA

8

i

NEL

TERAZIJE

NUŠIĆEVA

Hotel Union

F 🍴🅴🍴 **G** 🍷 **H** **J** **K** 🍴

▲ Hotel Balkan, Hotel Kasina

Prince Mihailo equestrian statue

Karađorđe statue and
St Sava's Church

Rooftops of Zemun with River Danube

Evening sunset glow at Kalemegdan terrace

19th-century Balkan-style *konak* in Kalemegdan Park

Kalemegdan Park

Sunset over the Danube